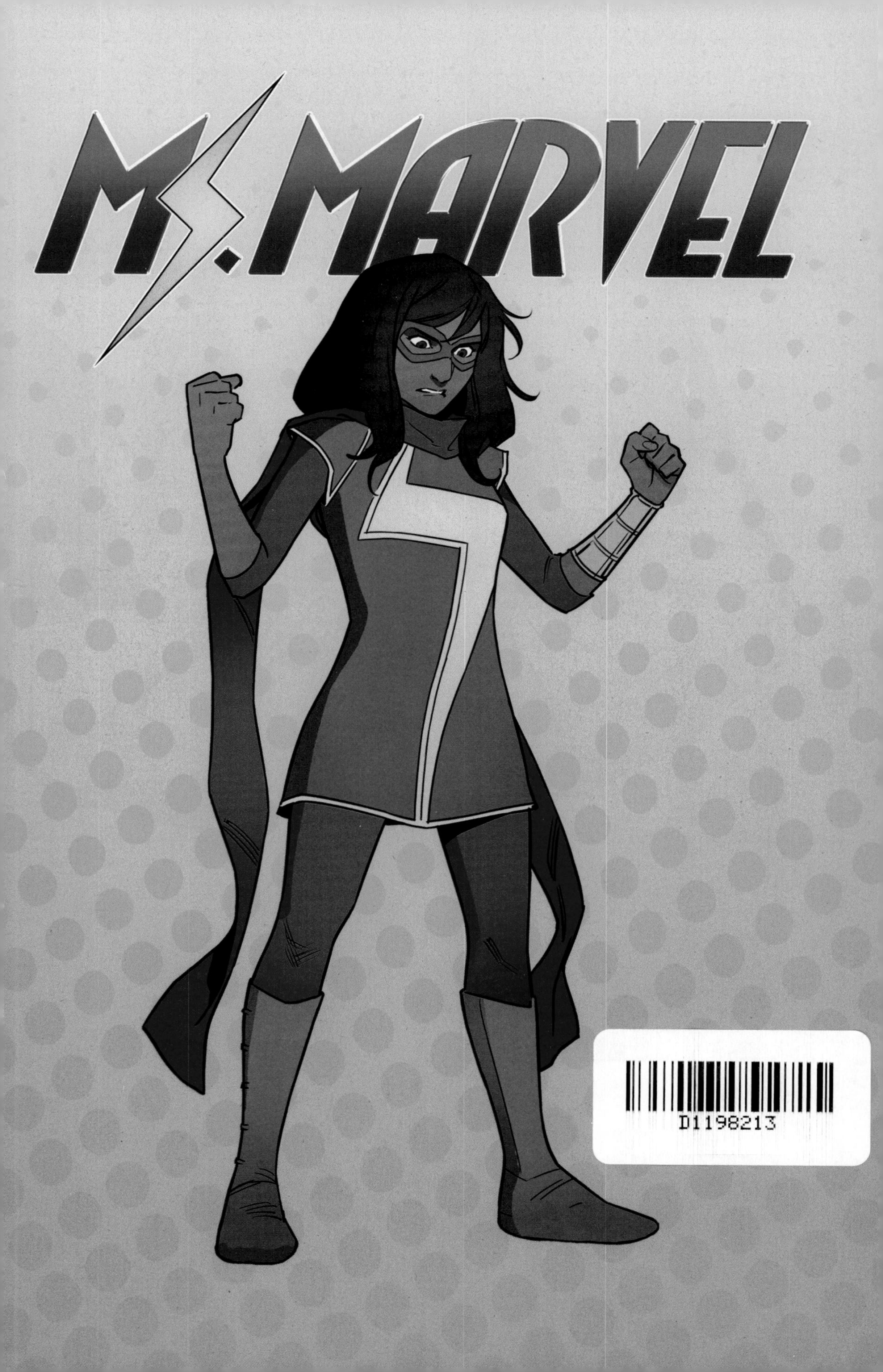
MS. MARVEL

WHEN A STRANGE TERRIGEN MIST DESCENDED UPON JERSEY CITY, KAMALA KHAN WAS IMBUED WITH POLYMORPH POWERS. USING HER NEW ABILITIES TO FIGHT EVIL AND PROTECT HER CITY, SHE BECAME…

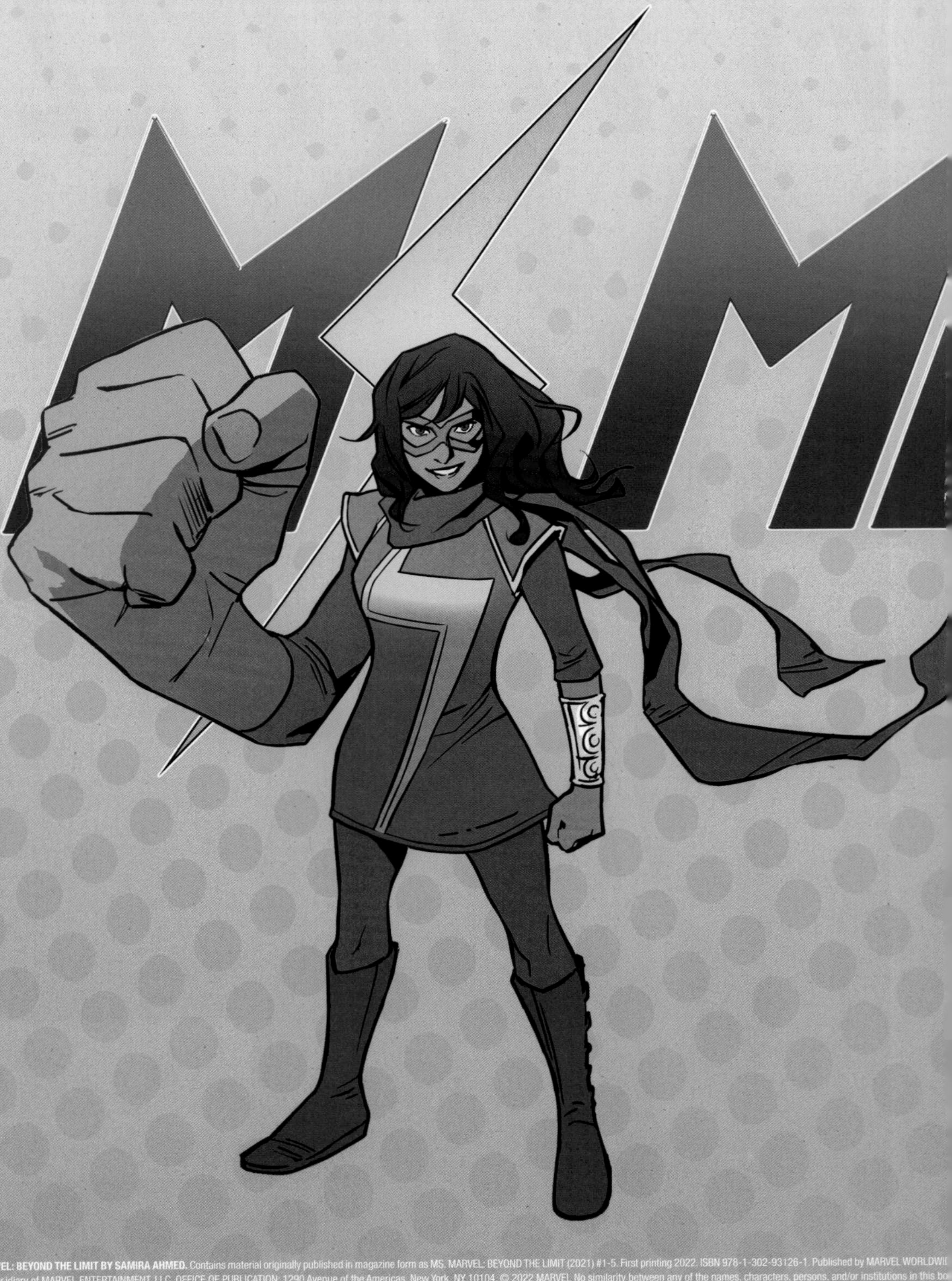

MS. MARVEL: BEYOND THE LIMIT BY SAMIRA AHMED. Contains material originally published in magazine form as MS. MARVEL: BEYOND THE LIMIT (2021) #1-5. First printing 2022. ISBN 978-1-302-93126-1. Published by MARVEL WORLDWI INC., a subsidiary of MARVEL ENTERTAINMENT, LLC. OFFICE OF PUBLICATION: 1290 Avenue of the Americas, New York, NY 10104. © 2022 MARVEL No similarity between any of the names, characters, persons, and/or institutions in this bo with those of any living or dead person or institution is intended, and any such similarity which may exist is purely coincidental. **Printed in Canada.** KEVIN FEIGE, Chief Creative Officer; DAN BUCKLEY, President, Marvel Entertainment; J QUESADA, EVP & Creative Director; DAVID BOGART, Associate Publisher & SVP of Talent Affairs; TOM BREVOORT, VP, Executive Editor; NICK LOWE, Executive Editor, VP of Content, Digital Publishing; DAVID GABRIEL, VP of Print & Digital Publishi MARK ANNUNZIATO, VP of Planning & Forecasting; JEFF YOUNGQUIST, VP of Production & Special Projects; ALEX MORALES, Director of Publishing Operations; DAN EDINGTON, Director of Editorial Operations; RICKEY PURDIN, Director of Tal Relations; JENNIFER GRÜNWALD, Director of Production & Special Projects; SUSAN CRESPI, Production Manager; STAN LEE, Chairman Emeritus. For information regarding advertising in Marvel Comics or on Marvel.com, please contact Vit DeBel Custom Solutions & Integrated Advertising Manager, at vdebellis@marvel.com. For Marvel subscription inquiries, please call 888-511-5480. **Manufactured between 4/15/2022 and 5/17/2022 by SOLISCO PRINTERS, SCOTT, QC, CANAD**

10 9 8 7 6 5 4 3 2 1

ARVEL
BEYOND THE LIMIT

SAMIRA AHMED
WRITER

ANDRÉS GENOLET
ARTIST

TRÍONA FARRELL
COLOR ARTIST

ZÉ CARLOS
#5 EPILOGUE ARTIST

VC's **JOE CARAMAGNA**
LETTERER

MASHAL AHMED
COVER ARTIST

CAITLIN O'CONNELL
ASSOCIATE EDITOR

LAUREN BISOM
EDITOR

COLLECTION EDITOR DANIEL KIRCHHOFFER
ASSISTANT MANAGING EDITOR MAIA LOY
ASSOCIATE MANAGER, TALENT RELATIONS LISA MONTALBANO
DIRECTOR, PRODUCTION & SPECIAL PROJECTS JENNIFER GRÜNWALD
VP PRODUCTION & SPECIAL PROJECTS JEFF YOUNGQUIST

BOOK DESIGNERS SARAH SPADACCINI & STACIE ZUCKER
SENIOR DESIGNER JAY BOWEN
SVP PRINT, SALES & MARKETING DAVID GABRIEL
EDITOR IN CHIEF C.B. CEBULSKI

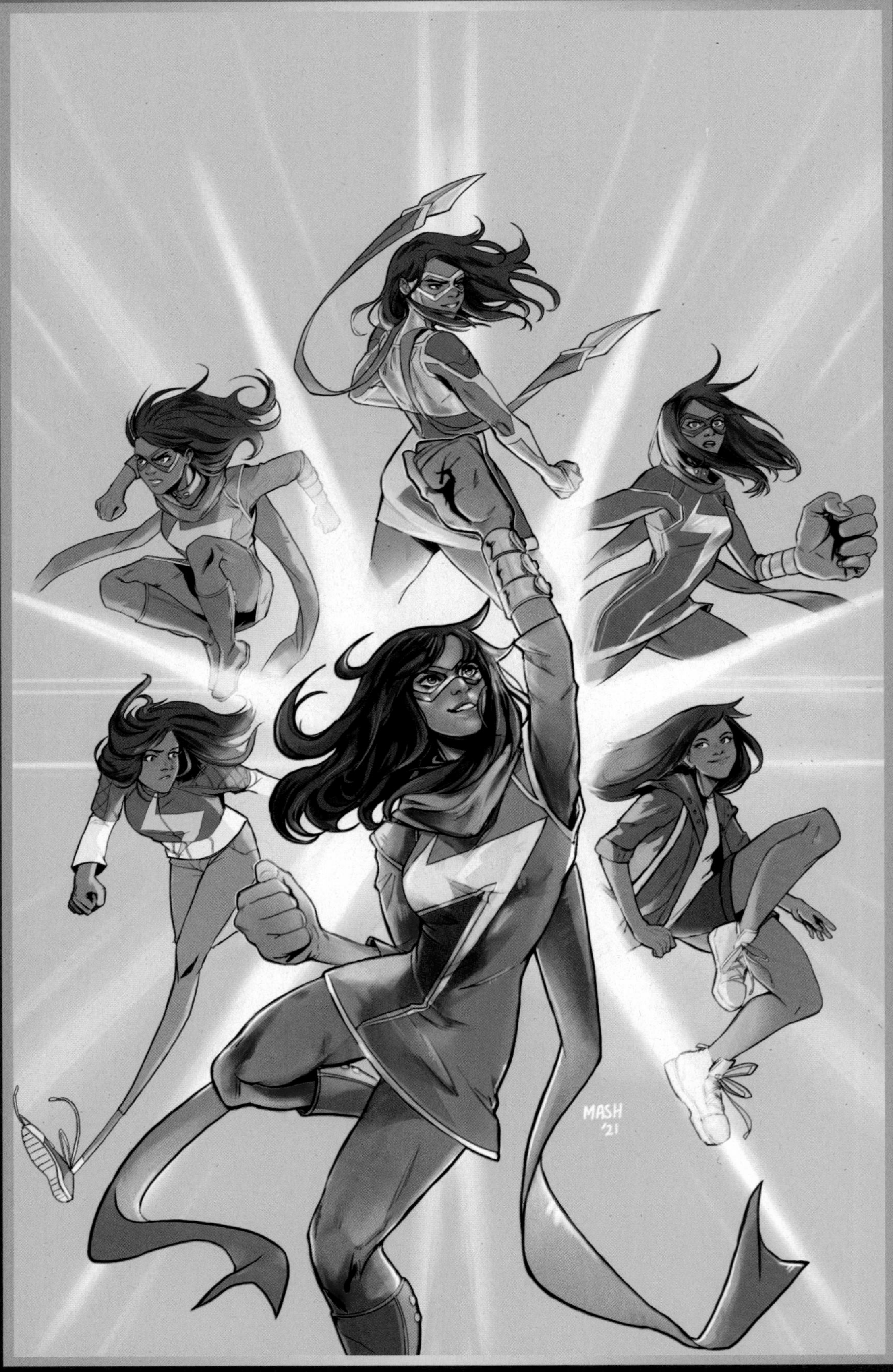
MASH
'21

1

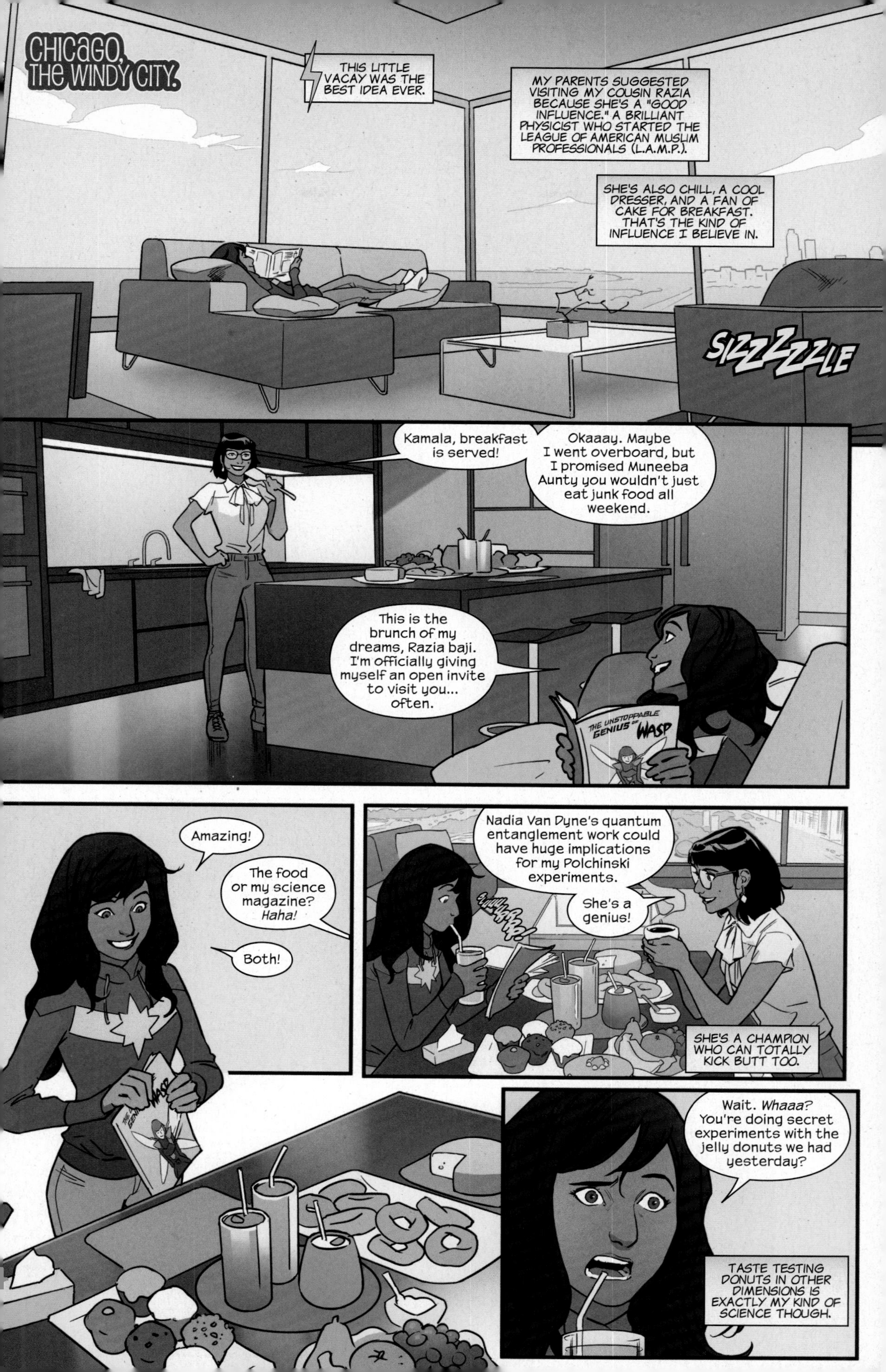

CHICAGO, THE WINDY CITY.
THIS LITTLE VACAY WAS THE BEST IDEA EVER.
MY PARENTS SUGGESTED VISITING MY COUSIN RAZIA BECAUSE SHE'S A "GOOD INFLUENCE." A BRILLIANT PHYSICIST WHO STARTED THE LEAGUE OF AMERICAN MUSLIM PROFESSIONALS (L.A.M.P.).
SHE'S ALSO CHILL, A COOL DRESSER, AND A FAN OF CAKE FOR BREAKFAST. THAT'S THE KIND OF INFLUENCE I BELIEVE IN.
SIZZZZZZLE
Kamala, breakfast is served!
Okaaay. Maybe I went overboard, but I promised Muneeba Aunty you wouldn't just eat junk food all weekend.
This is the brunch of my dreams, Razia baji. I'm officially giving myself an open invite to visit you... often.
THE UNSTOPPABLE GENIUS OF WASP
Amazing!
The food or my science magazine? Haha!
Both!
Nadia Van Dyne's quantum entanglement work could have huge implications for my Polchinski experiments.
She's a genius!
SHE'S A CHAMPION WHO CAN TOTALLY KICK BUTT TOO.
Wait. Whaaa? You're doing secret experiments with the jelly donuts we had yesterday?
TASTE TESTING DONUTS IN OTHER DIMENSIONS IS EXACTLY MY KIND OF SCIENCE THOUGH.

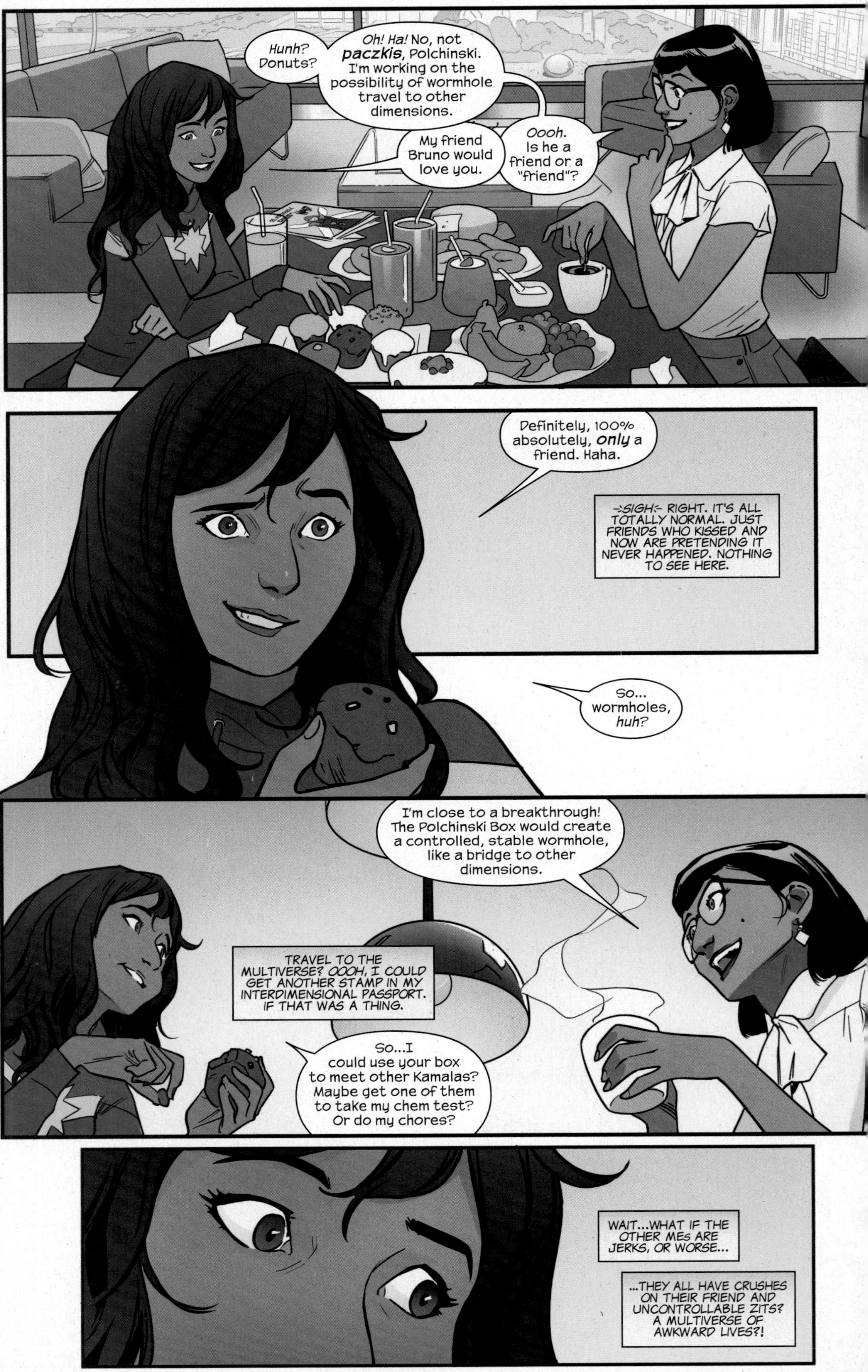
Hunh? Donuts?
Oh! Ha! No, not paczkis, Polchinski. I'm working on the possibility of wormhole travel to other dimensions.
My friend Bruno would love you.
Oooh. Is he a friend or a "friend"?
Definitely, 100% absolutely, only a friend. Haha.
-SIGH- RIGHT. IT'S ALL TOTALLY NORMAL. JUST FRIENDS WHO KISSED AND NOW ARE PRETENDING IT NEVER HAPPENED. NOTHING TO SEE HERE.
So... wormholes, huh?
I'm close to a breakthrough! The Polchinski Box would create a controlled, stable wormhole, like a bridge to other dimensions.
TRAVEL TO THE MULTIVERSE? OOOH, I COULD GET ANOTHER STAMP IN MY INTERDIMENSIONAL PASSPORT. IF THAT WAS A THING.
So...I could use your box to meet other Kamalas? Maybe get one of them to take my chem test? Or do my chores?
WAIT...WHAT IF THE OTHER MES ARE JERKS, OR WORSE...
...THEY ALL HAVE CRUSHES ON THEIR FRIEND AND UNCONTROLLABLE ZITS? A MULTIVERSE OF AWKWARD LIVES?!

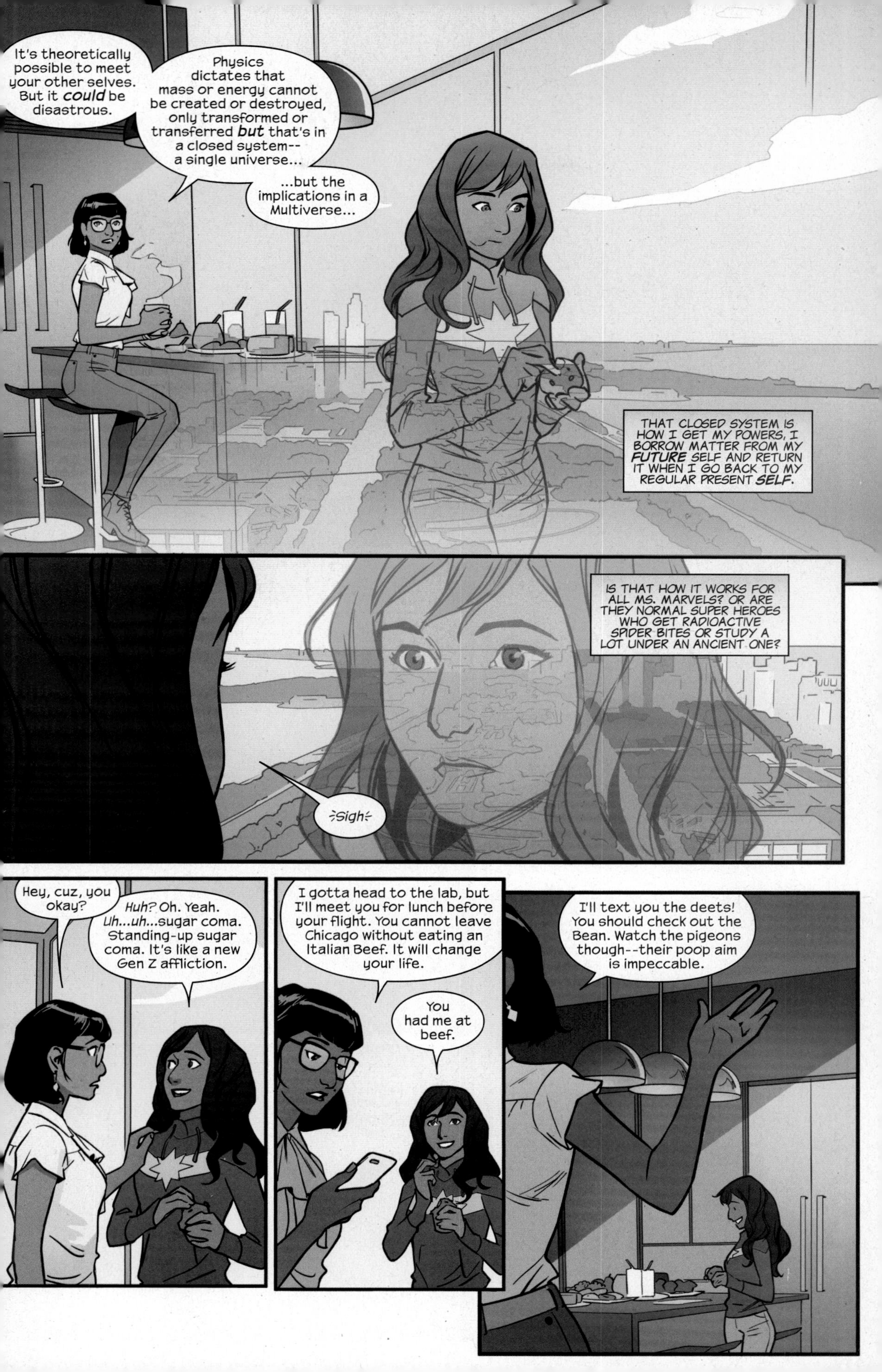
It's theoretically possible to meet your other selves. But it *could* be disastrous.
Physics dictates that mass or energy cannot be created or destroyed, only transformed or transferred *but* that's in a closed system--a single universe...
...but the implications in a Multiverse...
THAT CLOSED SYSTEM IS HOW I GET MY POWERS, I BORROW MATTER FROM MY *FUTURE* SELF AND RETURN IT WHEN I GO BACK TO MY REGULAR PRESENT *SELF*.
IS THAT HOW IT WORKS FOR ALL MS. MARVELS? OR ARE THEY NORMAL SUPER HEROES WHO GET RADIOACTIVE SPIDER BITES OR STUDY A LOT UNDER AN ANCIENT ONE?
Sigh
Hey, cuz, you okay?
Huh? Oh. Yeah. *Uh...uh...*sugar coma. Standing-up sugar coma. It's like a new Gen Z affliction.
I gotta head to the lab, but I'll meet you for lunch before your flight. You cannot leave Chicago without eating an Italian Beef. It will change your life.
You had me at beef.
I'll text you the deets! You should check out the Bean. Watch the pigeons though--their poop aim is impeccable.

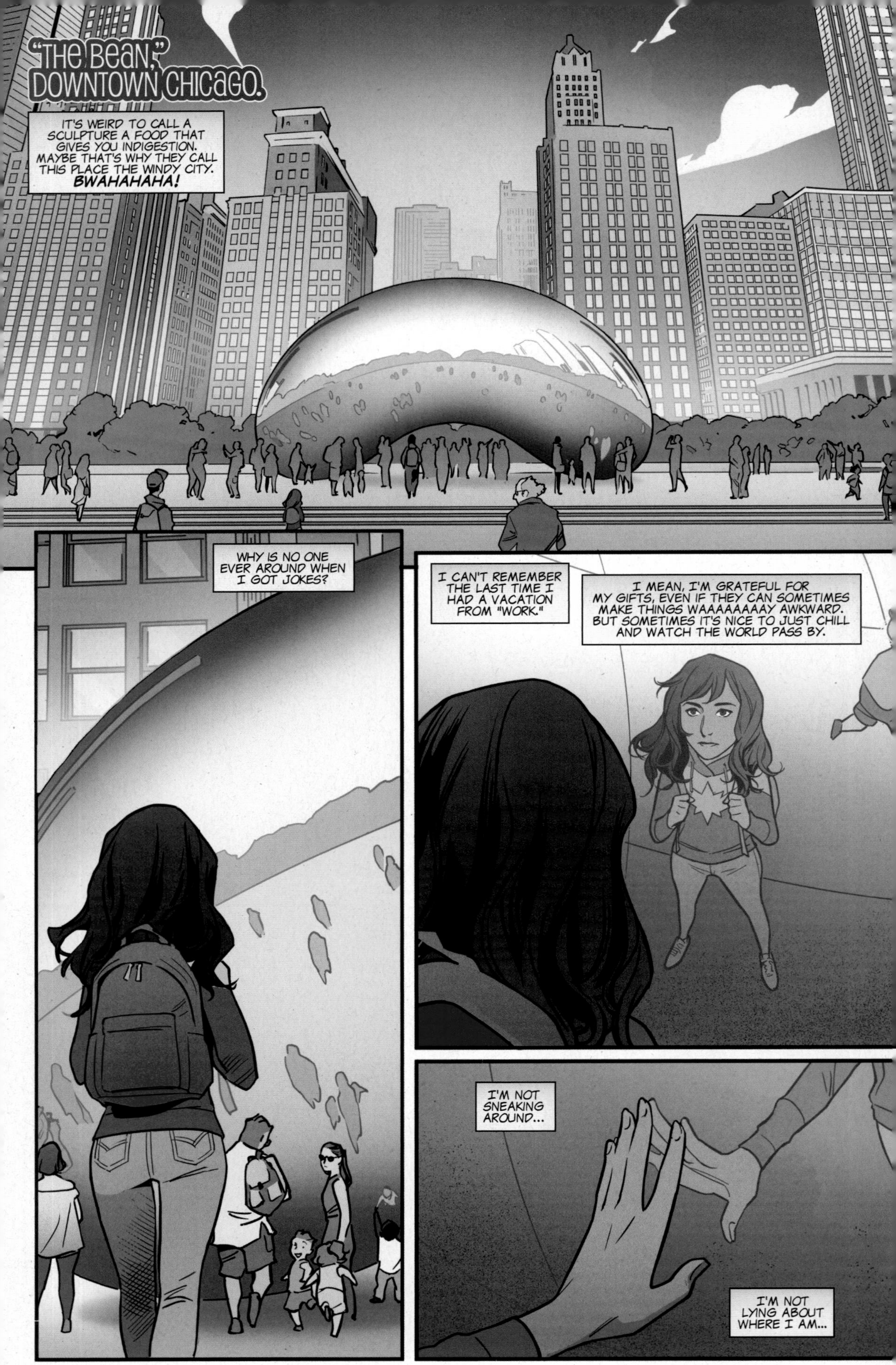
"THE BEAN," DOWNTOWN CHICAGO.
IT'S WEIRD TO CALL A SCULPTURE A FOOD THAT GIVES YOU INDIGESTION. MAYBE THAT'S WHY THEY CALL THIS PLACE THE WINDY CITY. BWAHAHAHA!
WHY IS NO ONE EVER AROUND WHEN I GOT JOKES?
I CAN'T REMEMBER THE LAST TIME I HAD A VACATION FROM "WORK."
I MEAN, I'M GRATEFUL FOR MY GIFTS, EVEN IF THEY CAN SOMETIMES MAKE THINGS WAAAAAAAAY AWKWARD. BUT SOMETIMES IT'S NICE TO JUST CHILL AND WATCH THE WORLD PASS BY.
I'M NOT SNEAKING AROUND...
I'M NOT LYING ABOUT WHERE I AM...

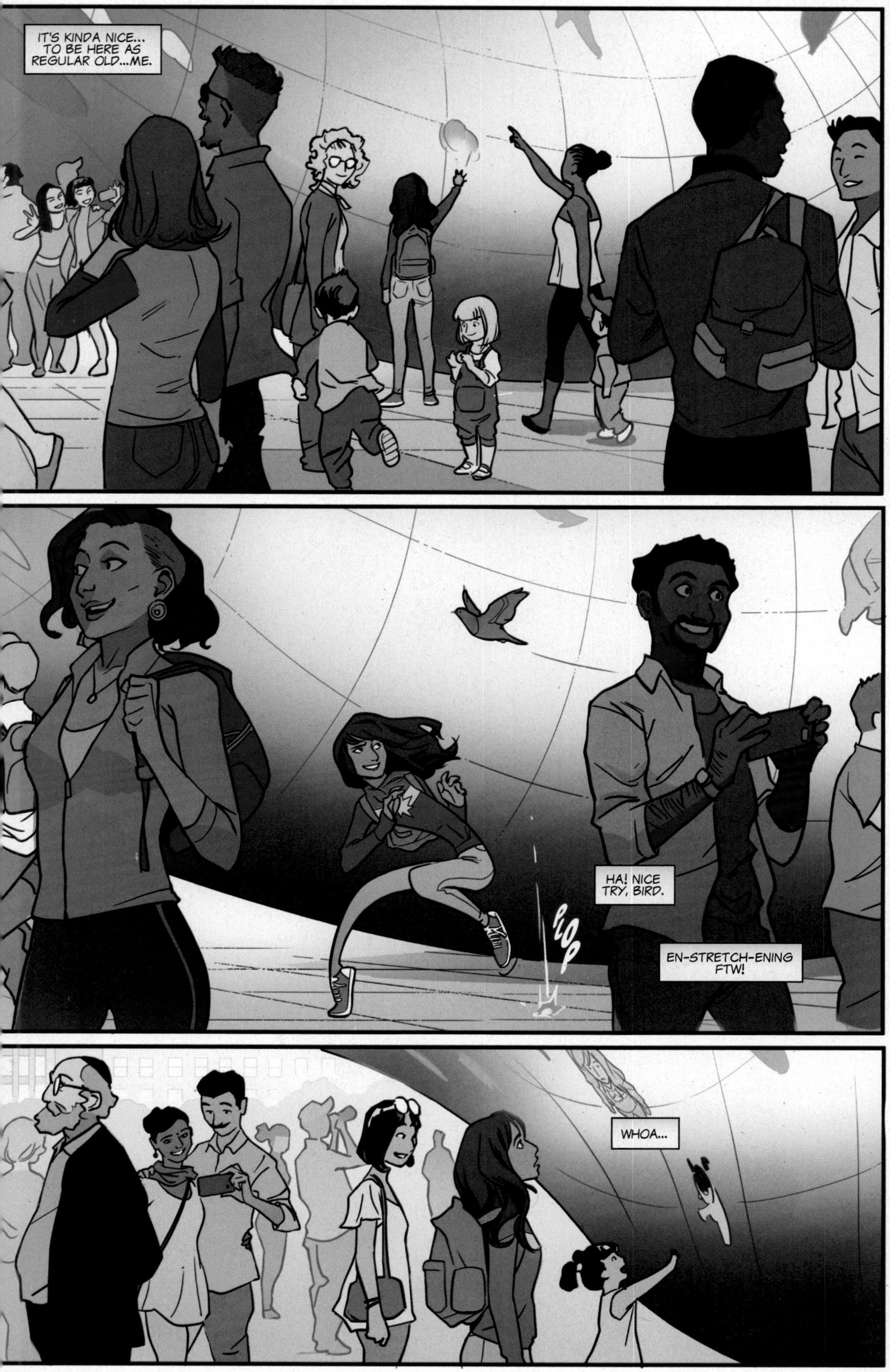
IT'S KINDA NICE... TO BE HERE AS REGULAR OLD...ME.
HA! NICE TRY, BIRD.
PLOP
EN-STRETCH-ENING FTW!
WHOA...

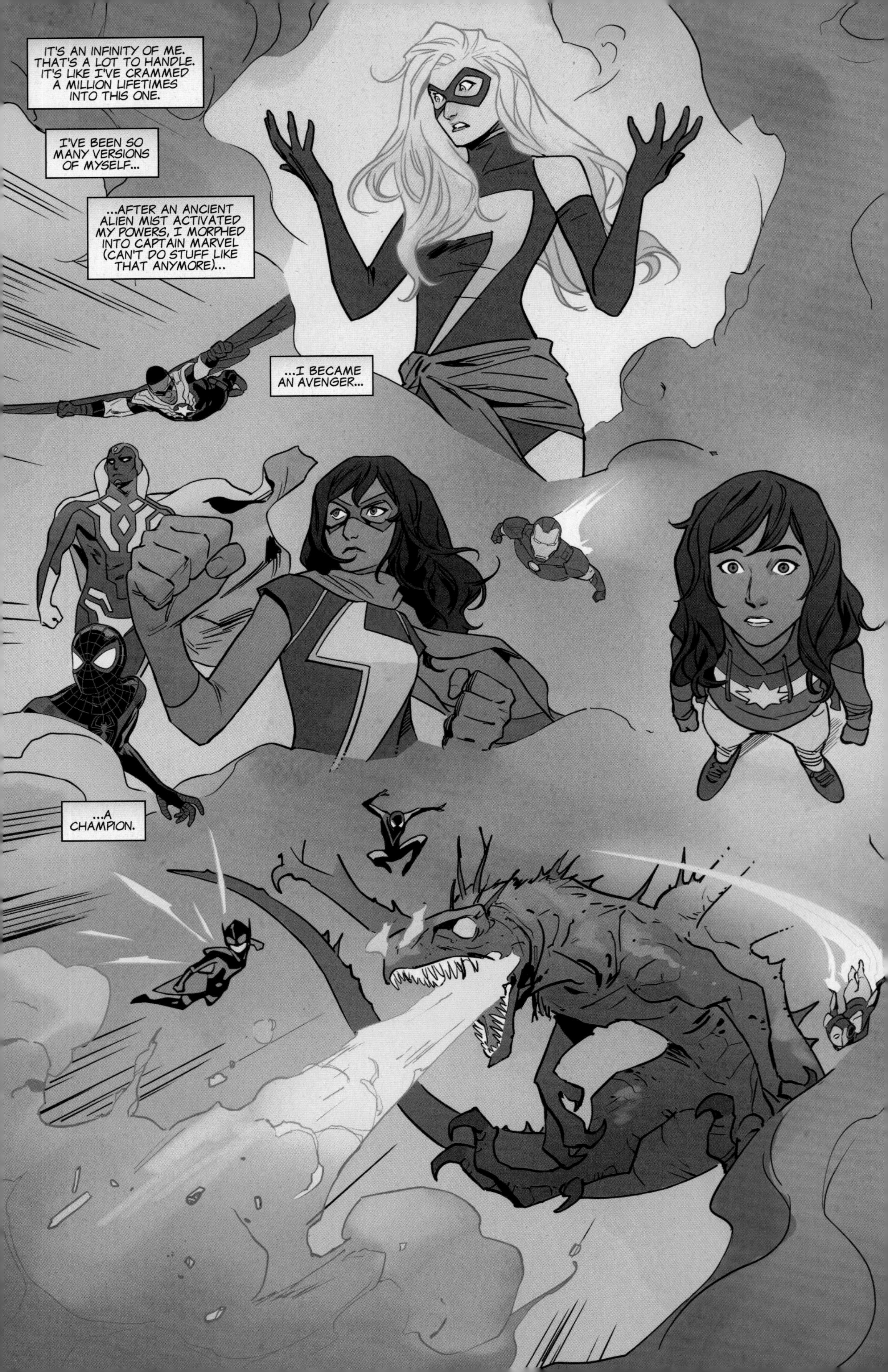
IT'S AN INFINITY OF ME. THAT'S A LOT TO HANDLE. IT'S LIKE I'VE CRAMMED A MILLION LIFETIMES INTO THIS ONE.
I'VE BEEN SO MANY VERSIONS OF MYSELF...
...AFTER AN ANCIENT ALIEN MIST ACTIVATED MY POWERS, I MORPHED INTO CAPTAIN MARVEL (CAN'T DO STUFF LIKE THAT ANYMORE)...
...I BECAME AN AVENGER...
...A CHAMPION.

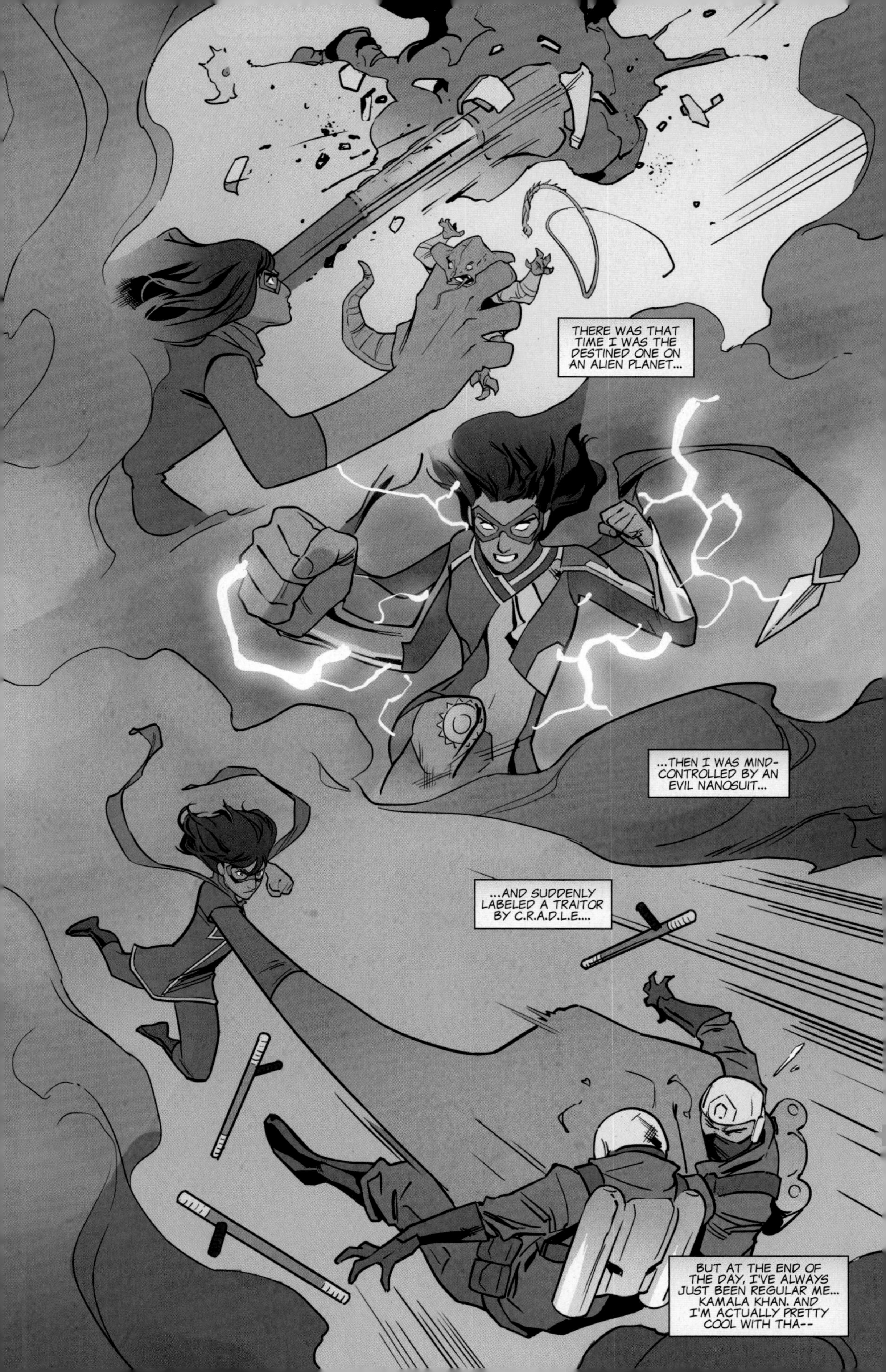
THERE WAS THAT TIME I WAS THE DESTINED ONE ON AN ALIEN PLANET...
...THEN I WAS MIND-CONTROLLED BY AN EVIL NANOSUIT...
...AND SUDDENLY LABELED A TRAITOR BY C.R.A.D.L.E....
BUT AT THE END OF THE DAY, I'VE ALWAYS JUST BEEN REGULAR ME... KAMALA KHAN. AND I'M ACTUALLY PRETTY COOL WITH THA--

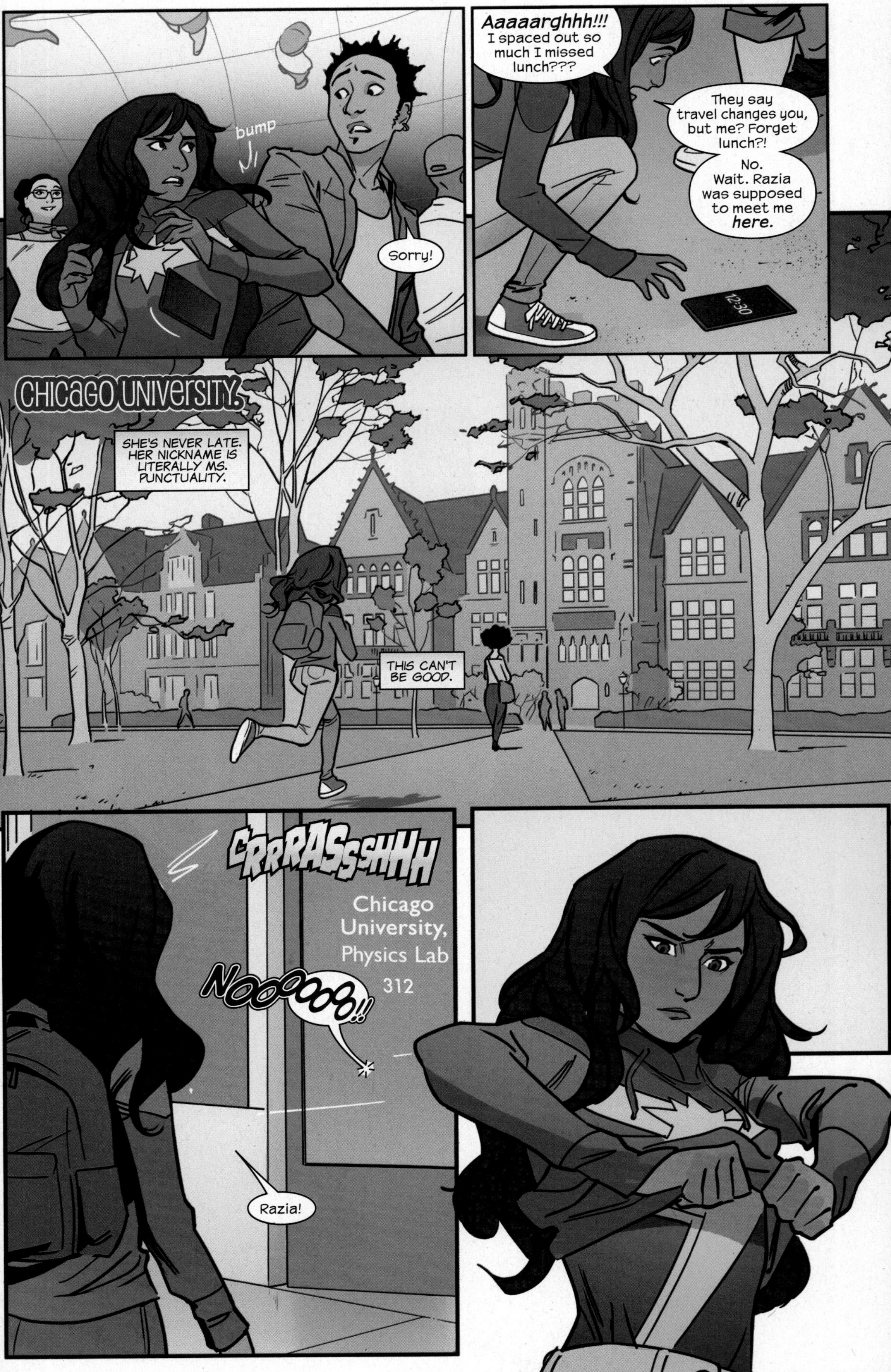
bump
Sorry!
Aaaaarghhh!!! I spaced out so much I missed lunch???
They say travel changes you, but me? Forget lunch?!
No. Wait. Razia was supposed to meet me here.
12:30
CHICAGO UNIVERSITY.
SHE'S NEVER LATE. HER NICKNAME IS LITERALLY MS. PUNCTUALITY.
THIS CAN'T BE GOOD.
CRRRASSSHHH
Chicago University, Physics Lab 312
NOOOOOO!!
Razia!

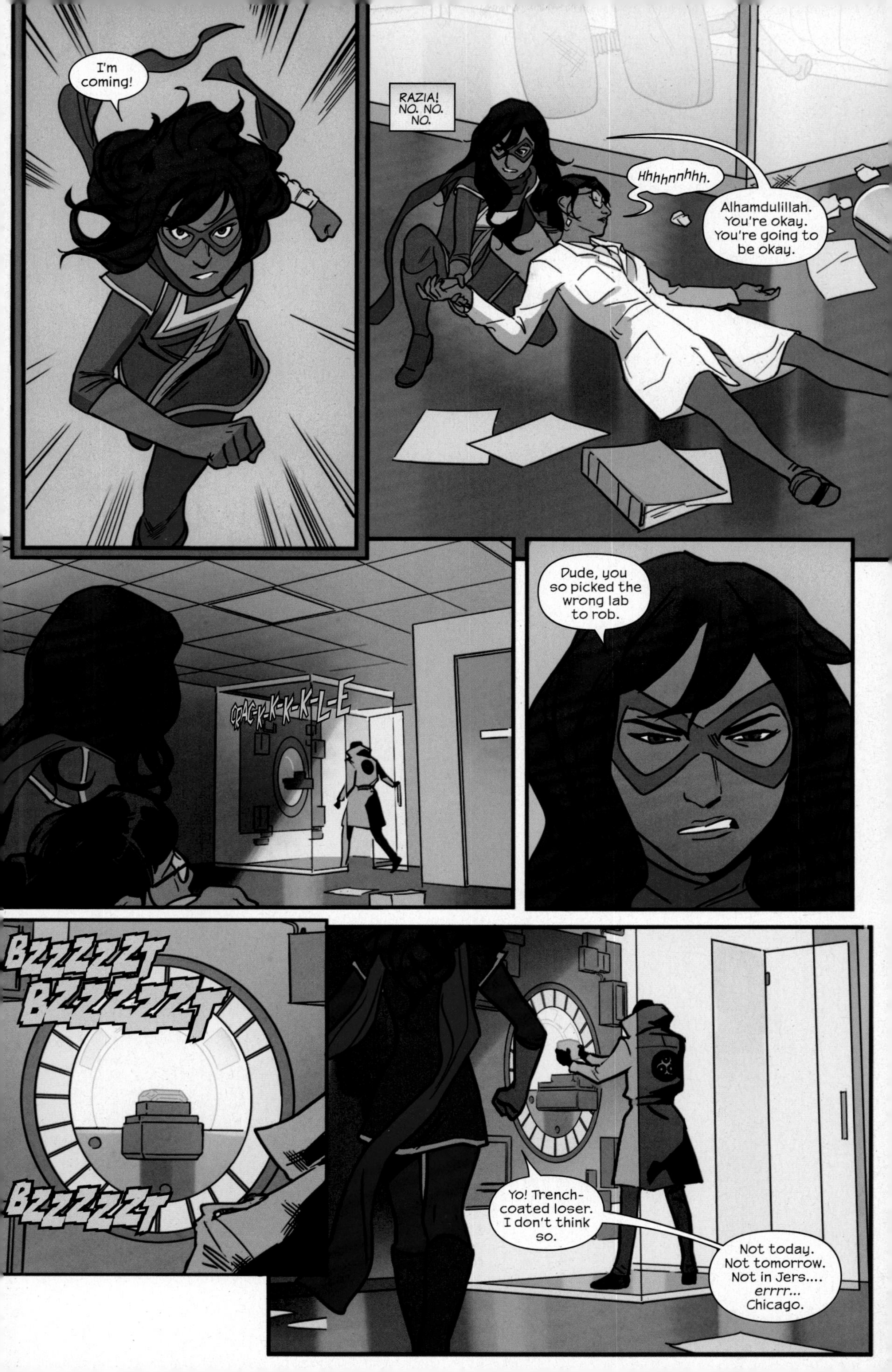
I'm coming!
RAZIA! NO. NO. NO.
Hhhhnnhhh.
Alhamdulillah. You're okay. You're going to be okay.
CRAC-K-K-K-K-L-E
Dude, you so picked the wrong lab to rob.
BZZZZZZT
BZZZZZZT
BZZZZZZT
Yo! Trench-coated loser. I don't think so.
Not today. Not tomorrow. Not in Jers.... errrr... Chicago.

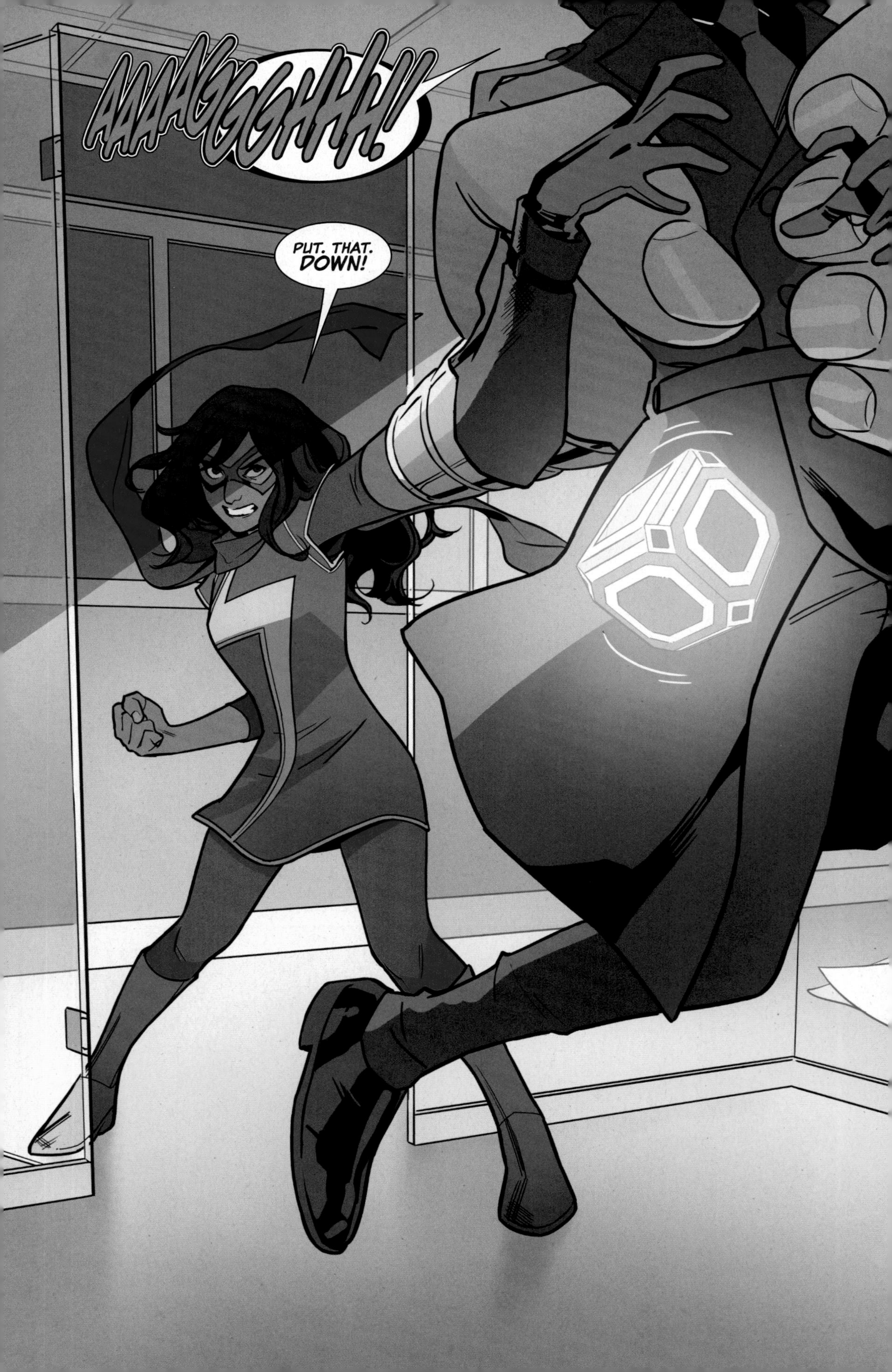
AAAAGGGHHH!!
PUT. THAT. DOWN!

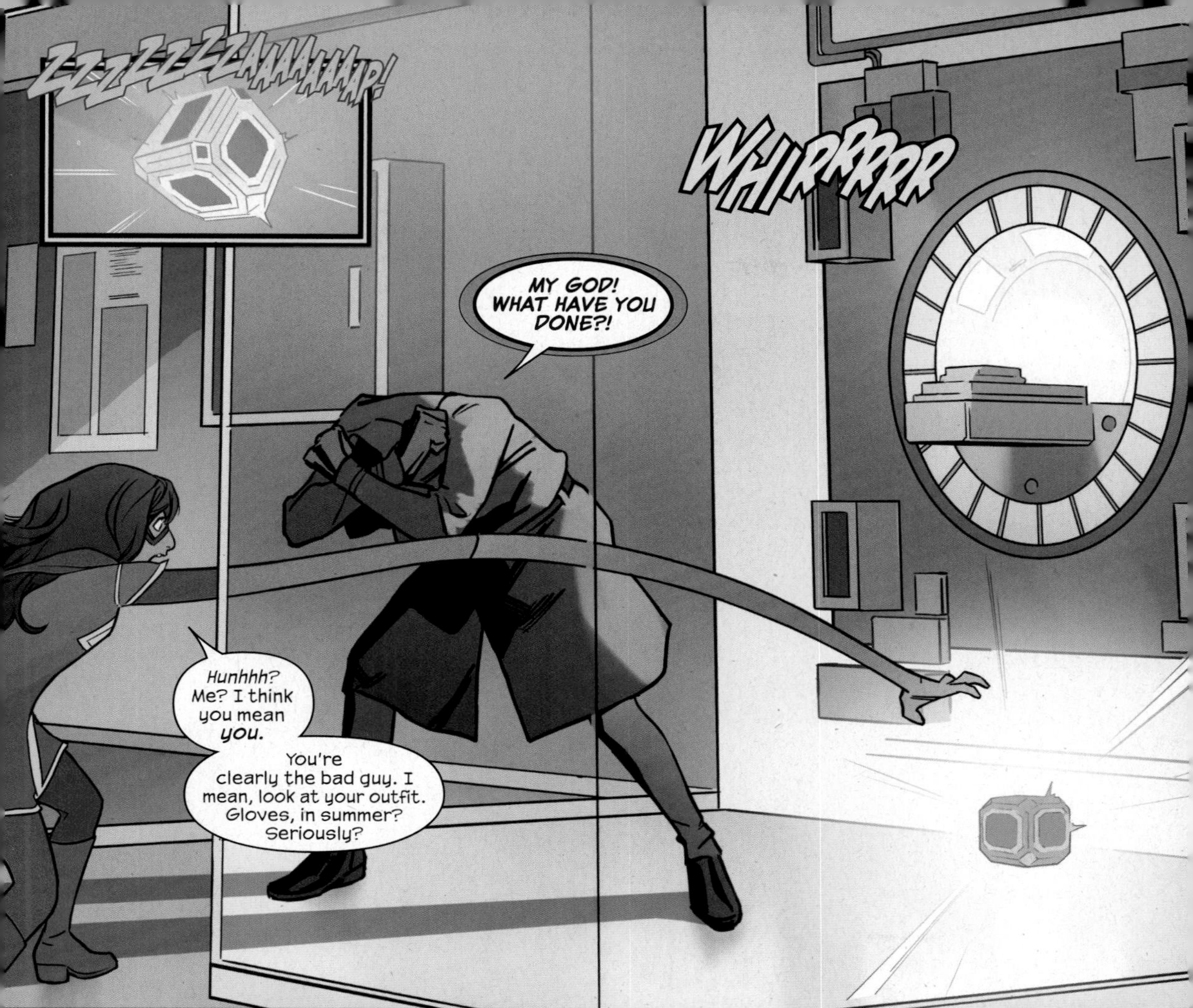
ZZZZZZZZAAAAAAAP!
WHIRRRRR
MY GOD! WHAT HAVE YOU DONE?!
Hunhhh? Me? I think you mean *you.*
You're clearly the bad guy. I mean, look at your outfit. Gloves, in summer? Seriously?

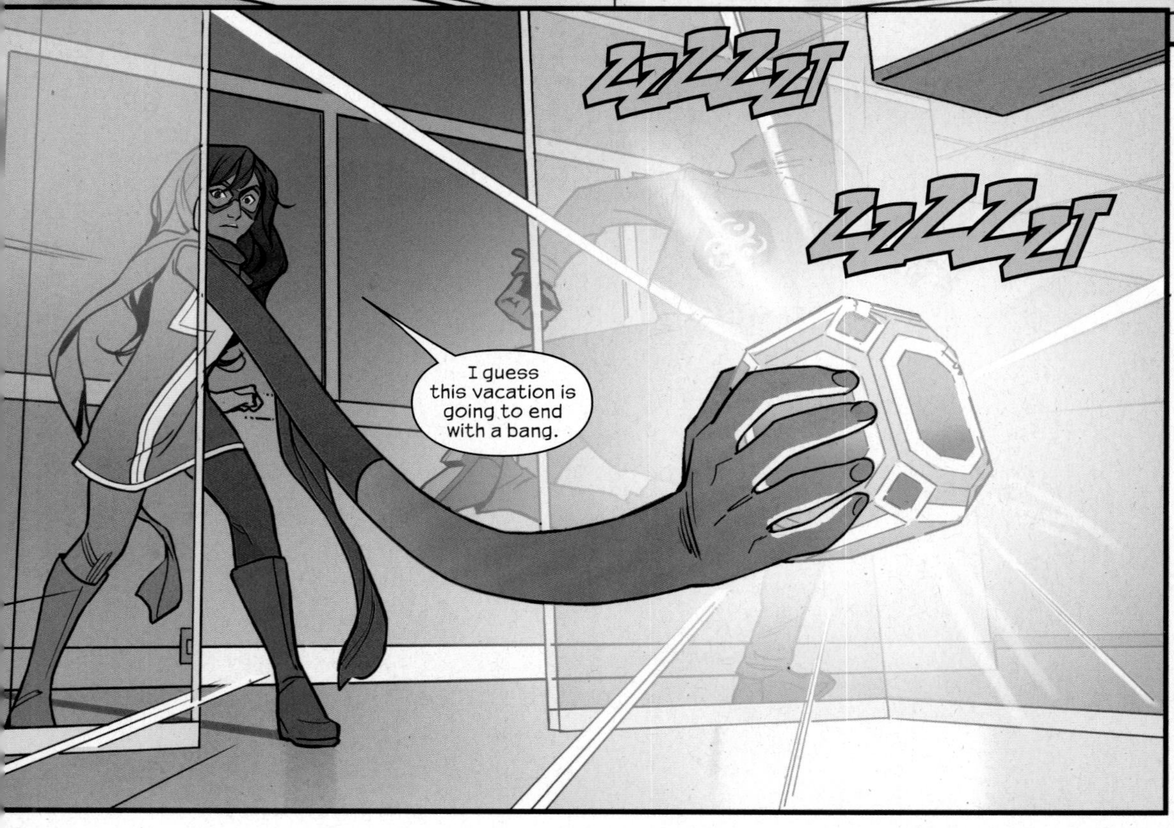
ZZZZZZT
ZZZZZZT
I guess this vacation is going to end with a bang.

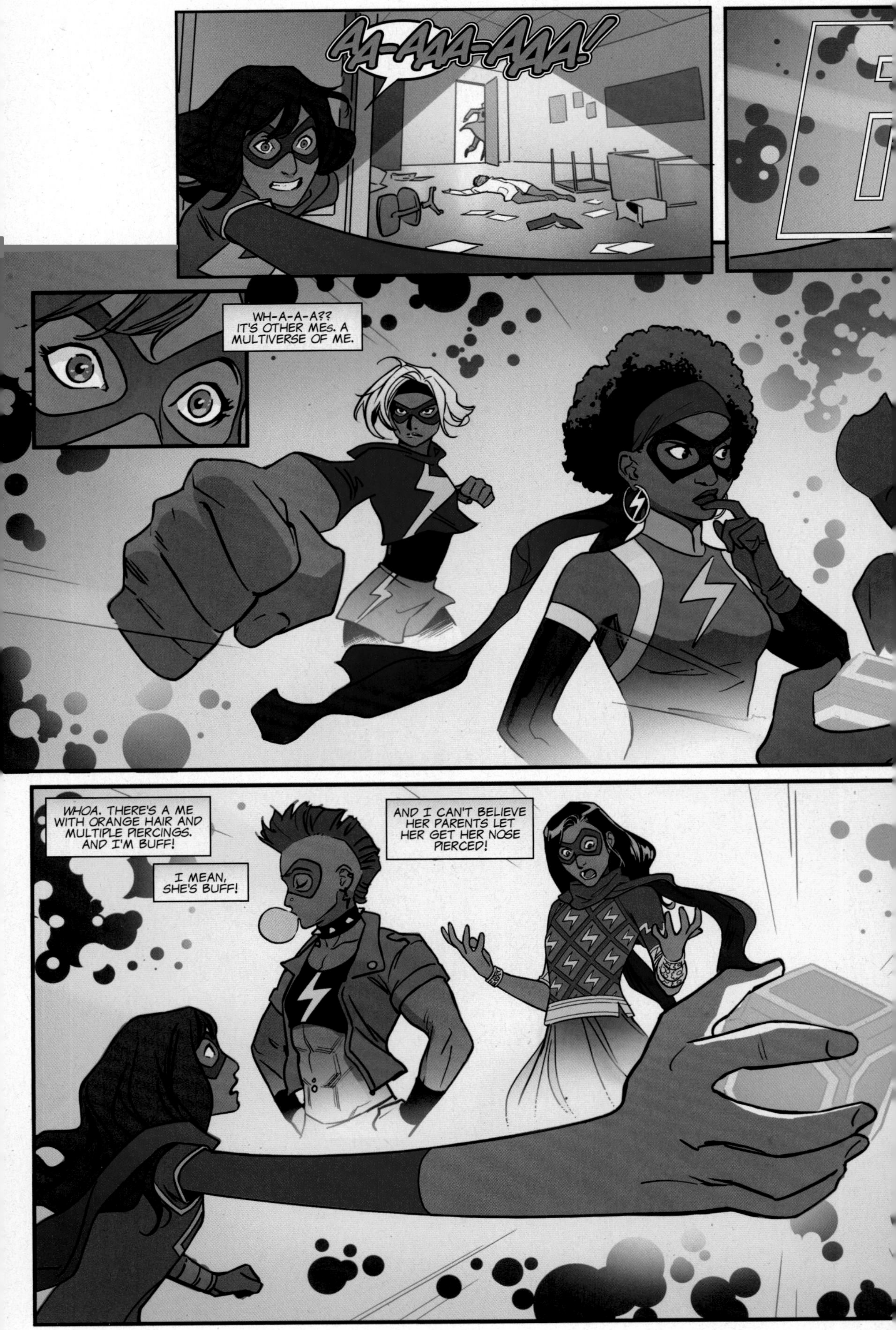
AA-AAA-AAA!
WH-A-A-A?? IT'S OTHER MEs. A MULTIVERSE OF ME.
WHOA. THERE'S A ME WITH ORANGE HAIR AND MULTIPLE PIERCINGS. AND I'M BUFF!
I MEAN, SHE'S BUFF!
AND I CAN'T BELIEVE HER PARENTS LET HER GET HER NOSE PIERCED!

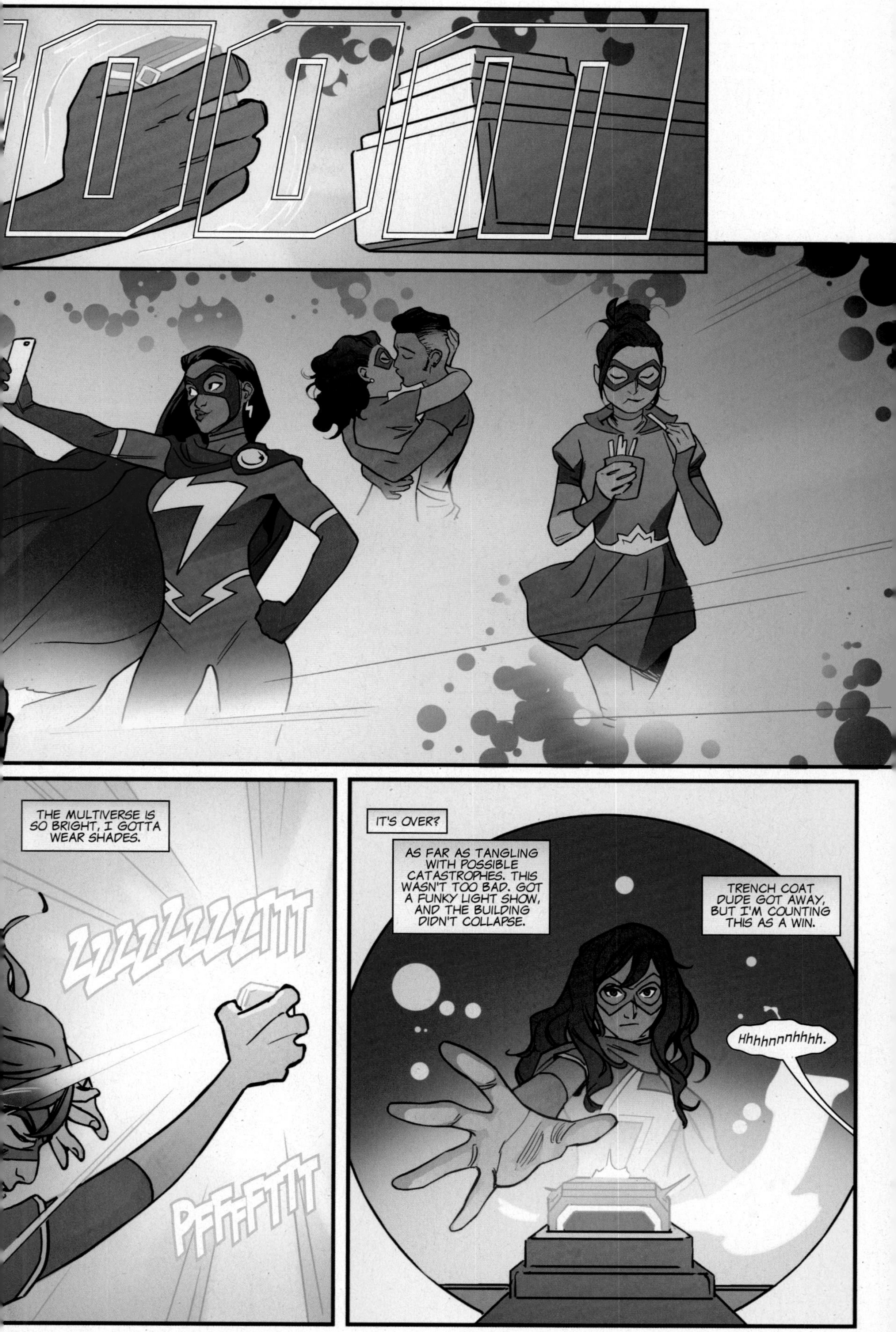
THE MULTIVERSE IS SO BRIGHT, I GOTTA WEAR SHADES.
ZZZZZZZZTTT
PFFFFTTT
IT'S OVER?
AS FAR AS TANGLING WITH POSSIBLE CATASTROPHES. THIS WASN'T TOO BAD. GOT A FUNKY LIGHT SHOW, AND THE BUILDING DIDN'T COLLAPSE.
TRENCH COAT DUDE GOT AWAY, BUT I'M COUNTING THIS AS A WIN.
Hhhhnnnhhhh.

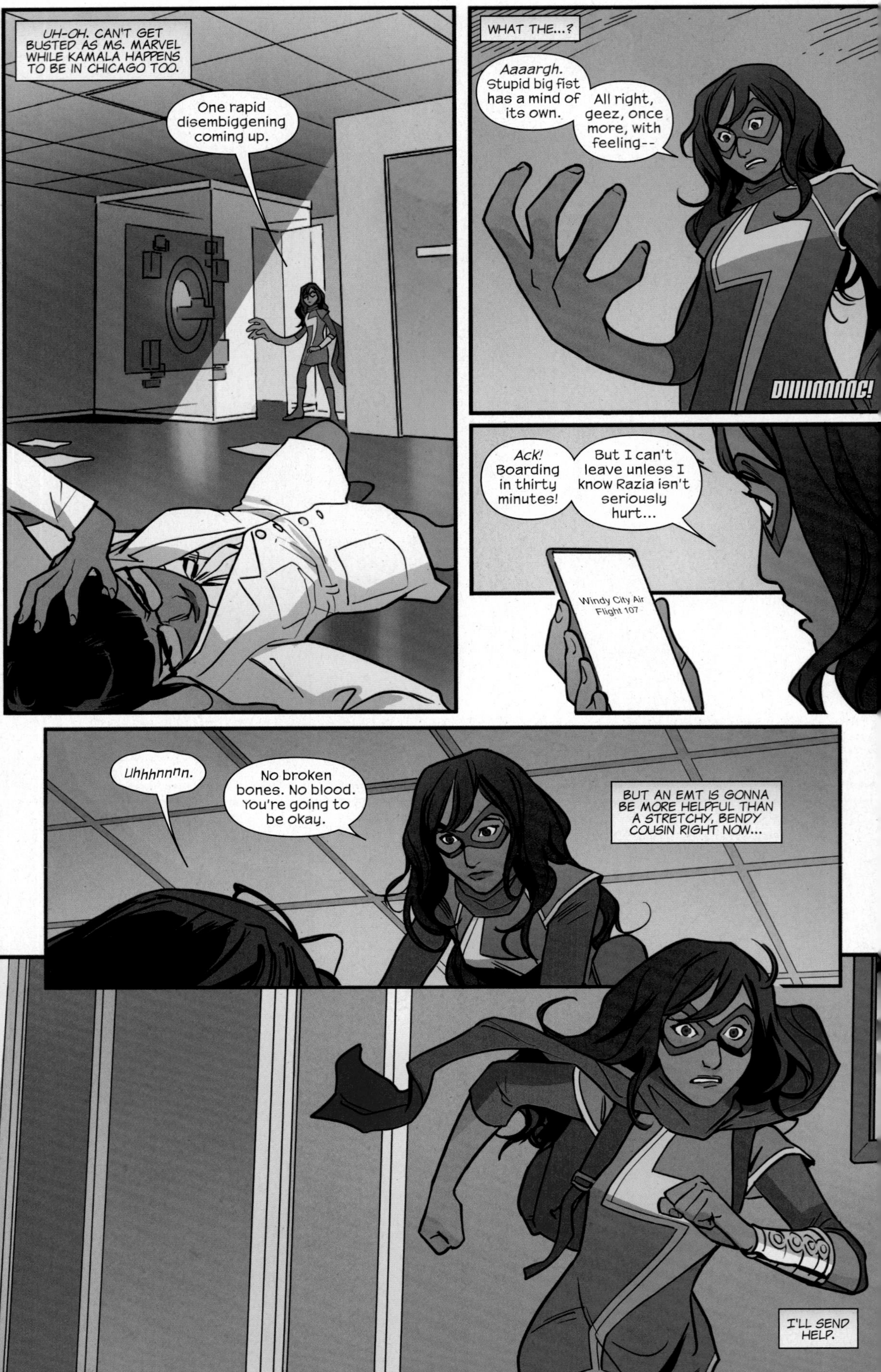
UH-OH. CAN'T GET BUSTED AS MS. MARVEL WHILE KAMALA HAPPENS TO BE IN CHICAGO TOO.
One rapid disembiggening coming up.
WHAT THE...?
Aaaargh. Stupid big fist has a mind of its own.
All right, geez, once more, with feeling--
DIIIIINNNNG!
Ack! Boarding in thirty minutes!
But I can't leave unless I know Razia isn't seriously hurt...
Windy City Air Flight 107
Uhhhnnnn.
No broken bones. No blood. You're going to be okay.
BUT AN EMT IS GONNA BE MORE HELPFUL THAN A STRETCHY, BENDY COUSIN RIGHT NOW...
I'LL SEND HELP.

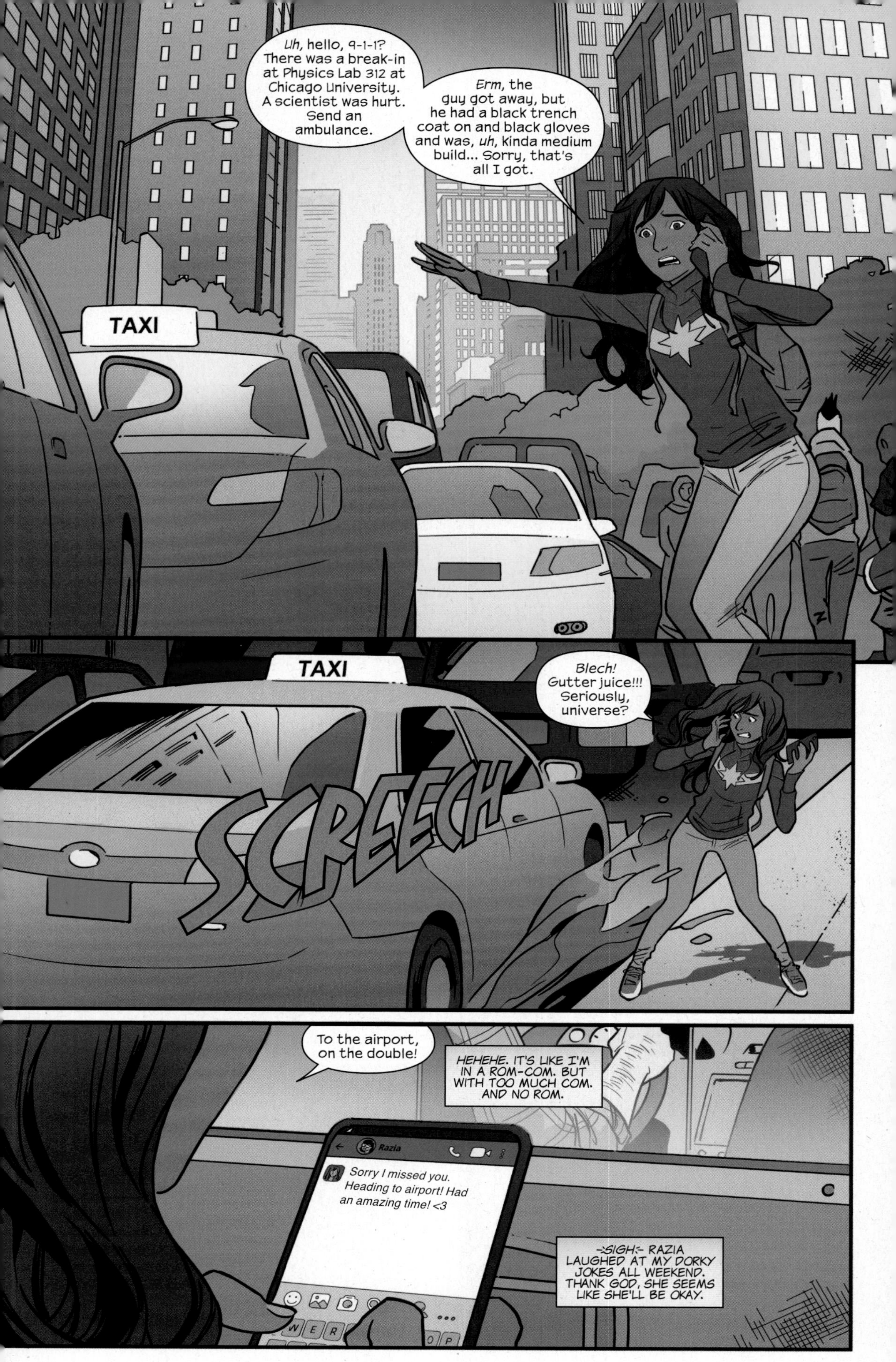
Uh, hello, 9-1-1? There was a break-in at Physics Lab 312 at Chicago University. A scientist was hurt. Send an ambulance.
Erm, the guy got away, but he had a black trench coat on and black gloves and was, uh, kinda medium build... Sorry, that's all I got.
TAXI
TAXI
Blech! Gutter juice!!! Seriously, universe?
SCREECH
To the airport, on the double!
HEHEHE. IT'S LIKE I'M IN A ROM-COM. BUT WITH TOO MUCH COM. AND NO ROM.
Razia
Sorry I missed you. Heading to airport! Had an amazing time! <3
-SIGH- RAZIA LAUGHED AT MY DORKY JOKES ALL WEEKEND. THANK GOD, SHE SEEMS LIKE SHE'LL BE OKAY.

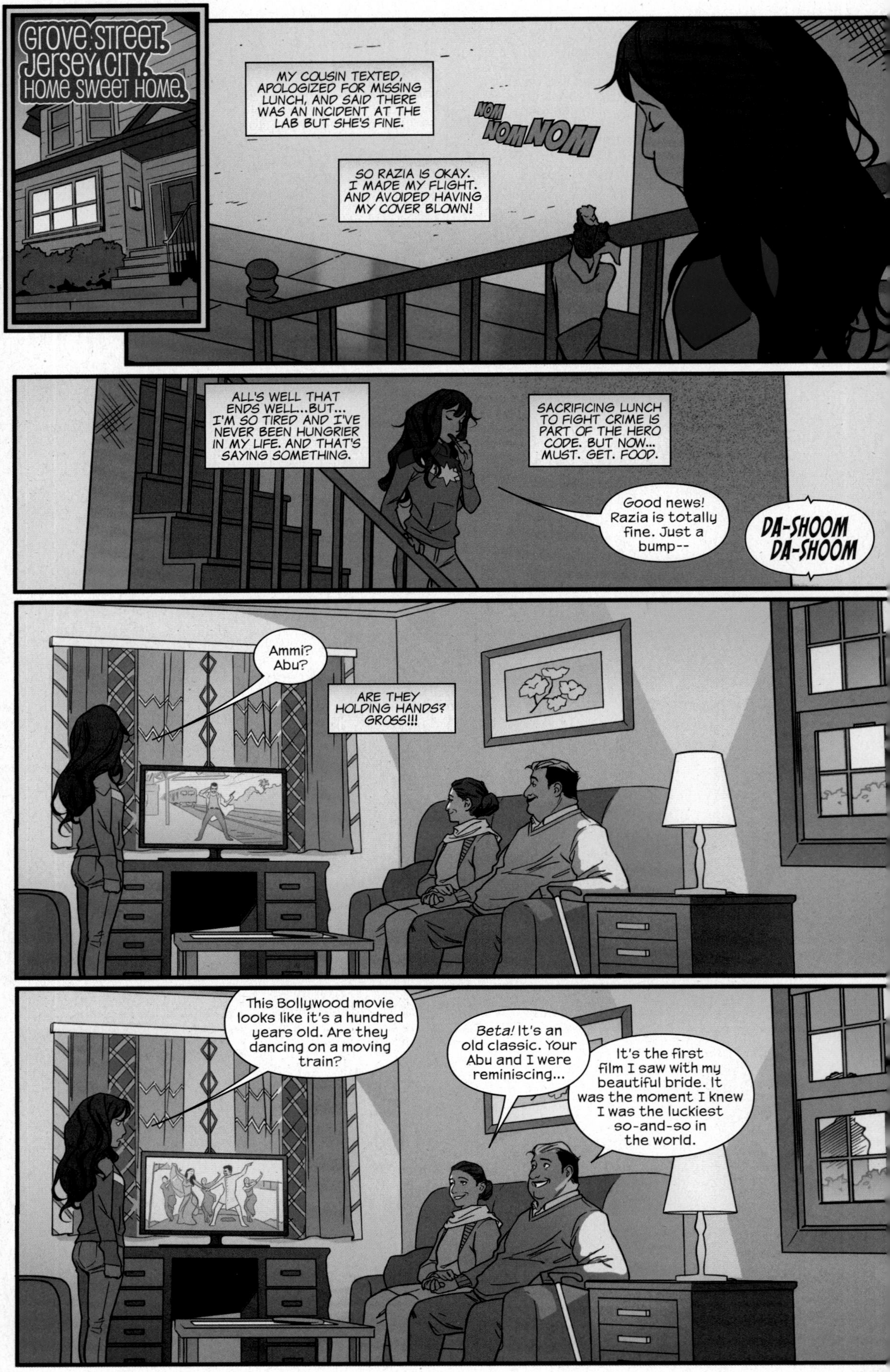

Grove Street. Jersey City. Home sweet home.
MY COUSIN TEXTED, APOLOGIZED FOR MISSING LUNCH, AND SAID THERE WAS AN INCIDENT AT THE LAB BUT SHE'S FINE.
NOM NOM NOM
SO RAZIA IS OKAY. I MADE MY FLIGHT. AND AVOIDED HAVING MY COVER BLOWN!
ALL'S WELL THAT ENDS WELL...BUT... I'M SO TIRED AND I'VE NEVER BEEN HUNGRIER IN MY LIFE. AND THAT'S SAYING SOMETHING.
SACRIFICING LUNCH TO FIGHT CRIME IS PART OF THE HERO CODE. BUT NOW... MUST. GET. FOOD.
Good news! Razia is totally fine. Just a bump--
DA-SHOOM DA-SHOOM
Ammi? Abu?
ARE THEY HOLDING HANDS? GROSS!!!
This Bollywood movie looks like it's a hundred years old. Are they dancing on a moving train?
Beta! It's an old classic. Your Abu and I were reminiscing...
It's the first film I saw with my beautiful bride. It was the moment I knew I was the luckiest so-and-so in the world.

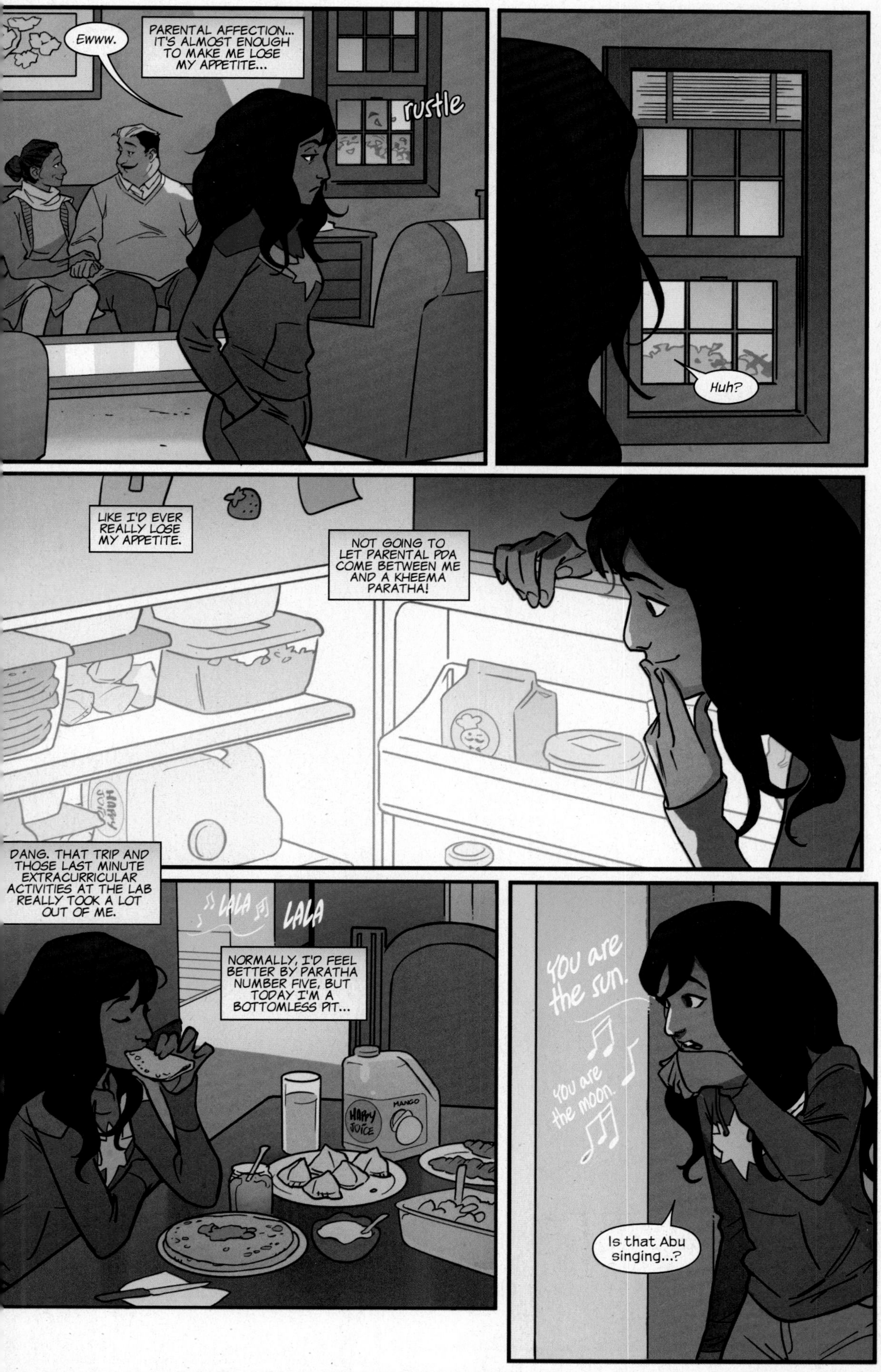
Ewww.
PARENTAL AFFECTION... IT'S ALMOST ENOUGH TO MAKE ME LOSE MY APPETITE...
rustle
Huh?
LIKE I'D EVER REALLY LOSE MY APPETITE.
NOT GOING TO LET PARENTAL PDA COME BETWEEN ME AND A KHEEMA PARATHA!
DANG. THAT TRIP AND THOSE LAST MINUTE EXTRACURRICULAR ACTIVITIES AT THE LAB REALLY TOOK A LOT OUT OF ME.
LALA
LALA
NORMALLY, I'D FEEL BETTER BY PARATHA NUMBER FIVE, BUT TODAY I'M A BOTTOMLESS PIT...
MANGO
You are the sun.
You are the moon.
Is that Abu singing...?

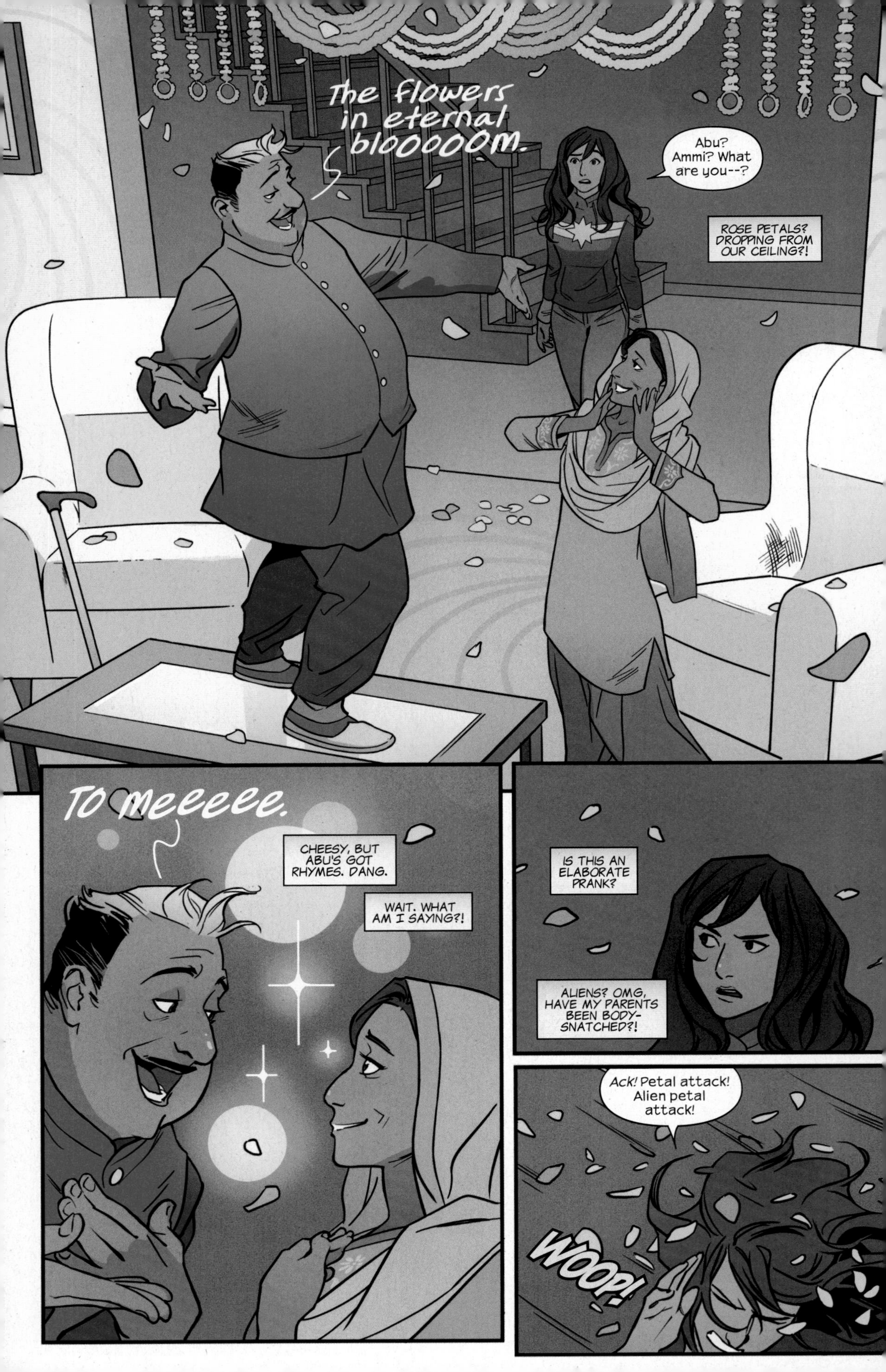

The flowers in eternal blooooom.
Abu? Ammi? What are you--?
ROSE PETALS? DROPPING FROM OUR CEILING?!
TO meeeee.
CHEESY, BUT ABU'S GOT RHYMES. DANG.
WAIT. WHAT AM I SAYING?!
IS THIS AN ELABORATE PRANK?
ALIENS? OMG, HAVE MY PARENTS BEEN BODY-SNATCHED?!
Ack! Petal attack! Alien petal attack!
WOOP!

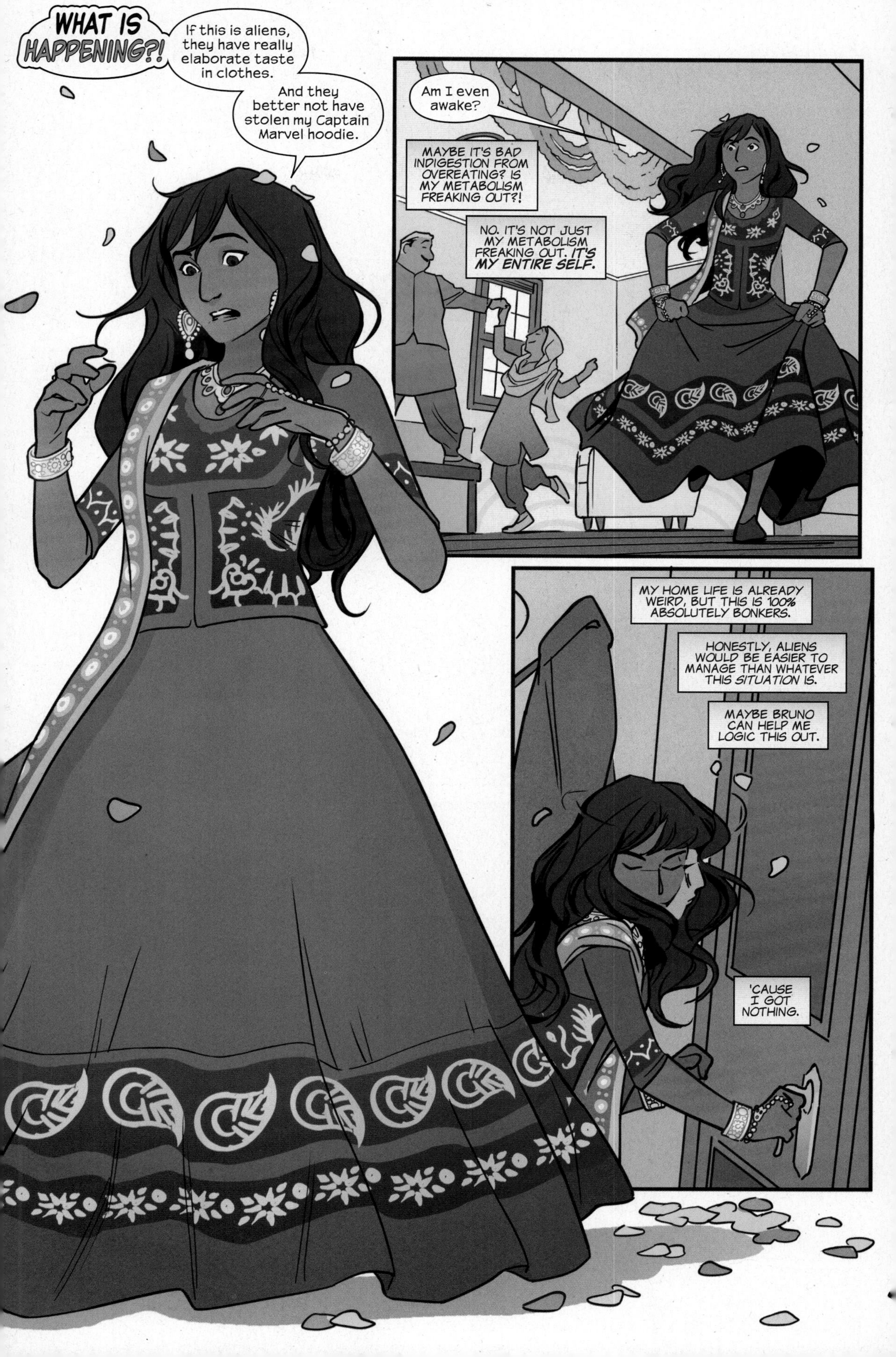
WHAT IS HAPPENING?!
If this is aliens, they have really elaborate taste in clothes.
And they better not have stolen my Captain Marvel hoodie.
Am I even awake?
MAYBE IT'S BAD INDIGESTION FROM OVEREATING? IS MY METABOLISM FREAKING OUT?!
NO. IT'S NOT JUST MY METABOLISM FREAKING OUT. IT'S MY ENTIRE SELF.
MY HOME LIFE IS ALREADY WEIRD, BUT THIS IS 100% ABSOLUTELY BONKERS.
HONESTLY, ALIENS WOULD BE EASIER TO MANAGE THAN WHATEVER THIS SITUATION IS.
MAYBE BRUNO CAN HELP ME LOGIC THIS OUT.
'CAUSE I GOT NOTHING.

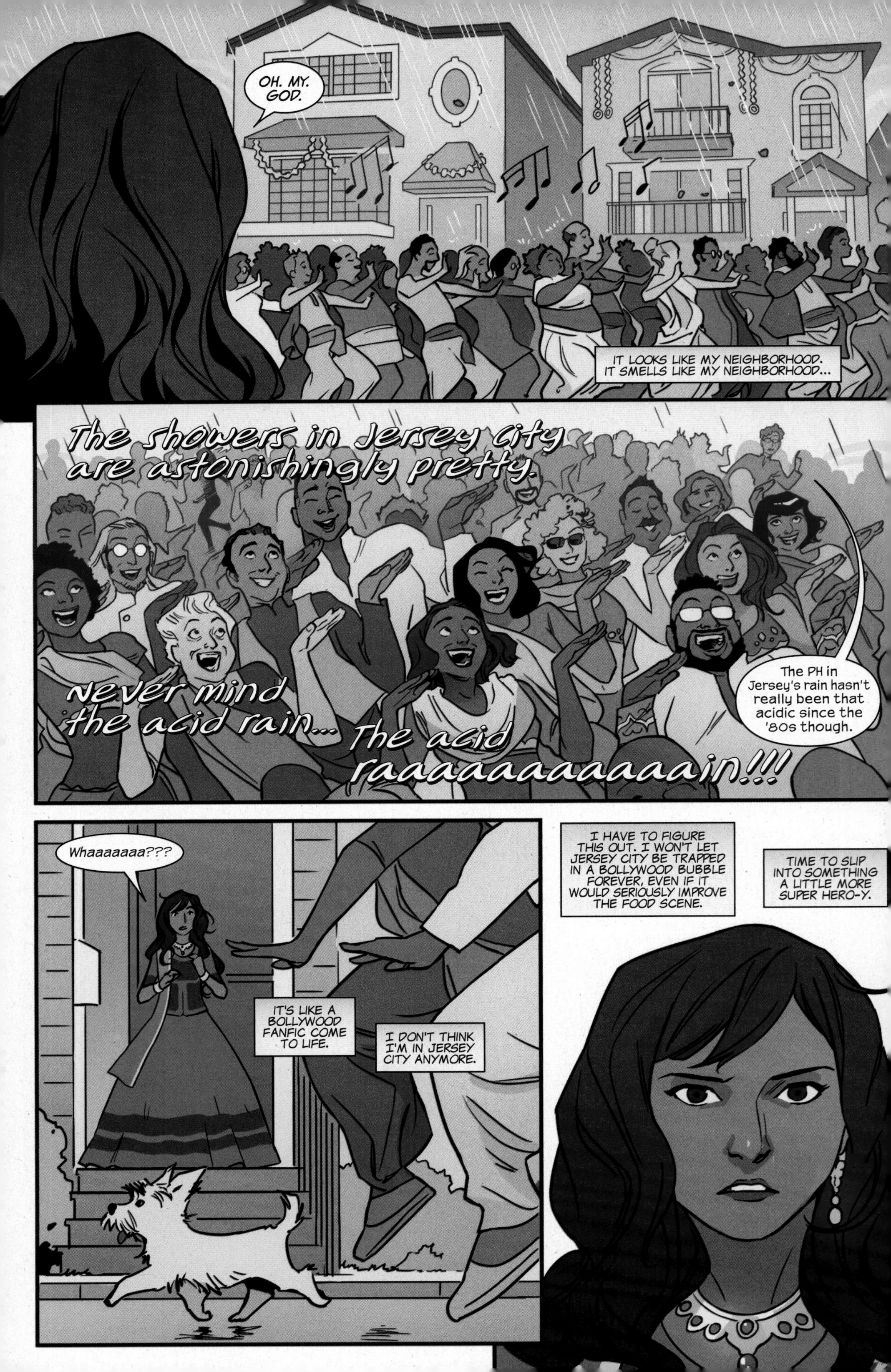
OH. MY. GOD.
IT LOOKS LIKE MY NEIGHBORHOOD. IT SMELLS LIKE MY NEIGHBORHOOD...
The showers in Jersey City are astonishingly pretty.
Never mind the acid rain...
The acid raaaaaaaaaaaaain!!!
The PH in Jersey's rain hasn't really been that acidic since the '80s though.
Whaaaaaaa???
IT'S LIKE A BOLLYWOOD FANFIC COME TO LIFE.
I DON'T THINK I'M IN JERSEY CITY ANYMORE.
I HAVE TO FIGURE THIS OUT. I WON'T LET JERSEY CITY BE TRAPPED IN A BOLLYWOOD BUBBLE FOREVER, EVEN IF IT WOULD SERIOUSLY IMPROVE THE FOOD SCENE.
TIME TO SLIP INTO SOMETHING A LITTLE MORE SUPER HERO-Y.

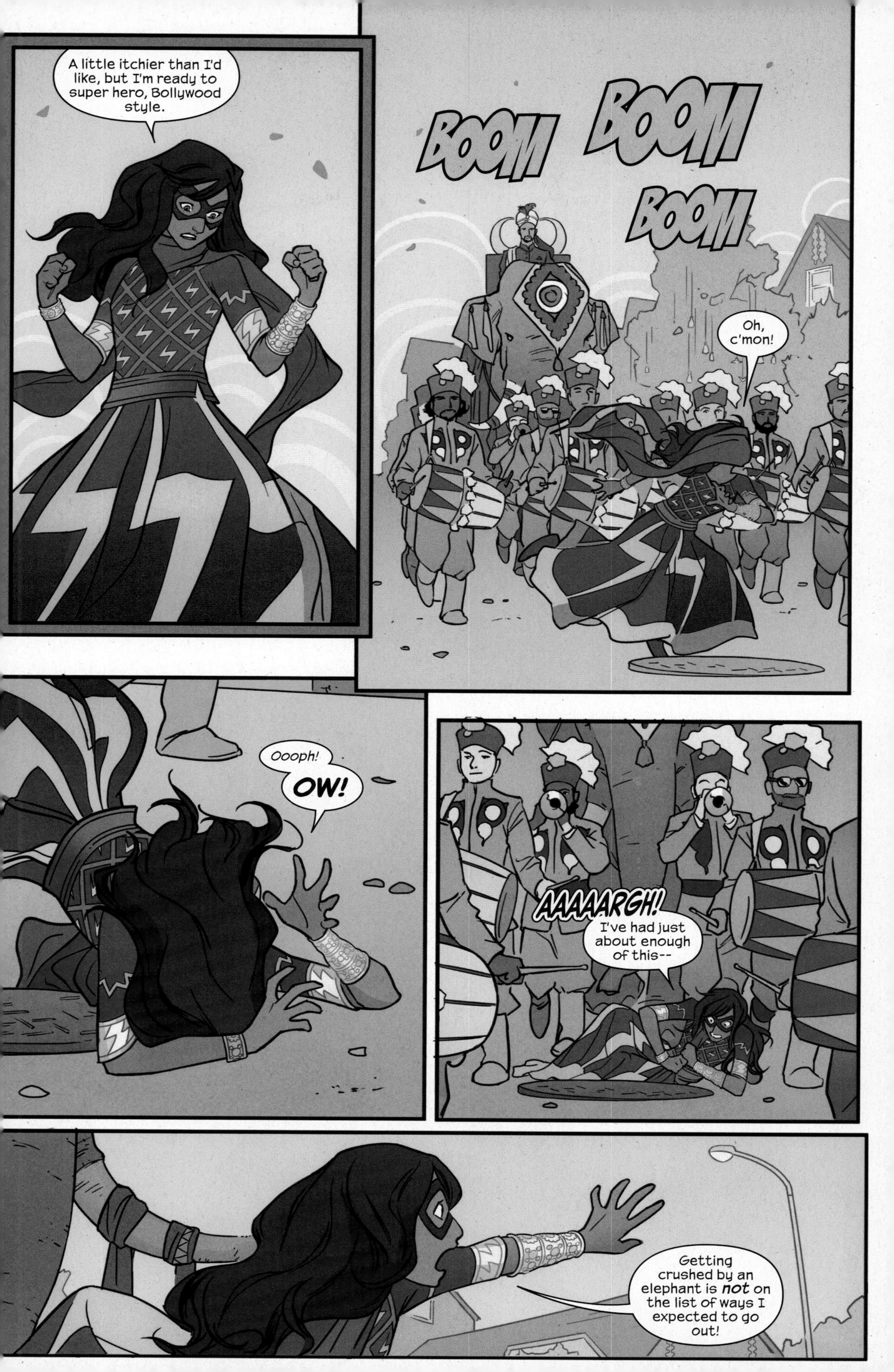
A little itchier than I'd like, but I'm ready to super hero, Bollywood style.
BOOM BOOM BOOM
Oh, c'mon!
Oooph!
OW!
AAAAARGH!
I've had just about enough of this--
Getting crushed by an elephant is *not* on the list of ways I expected to go out!

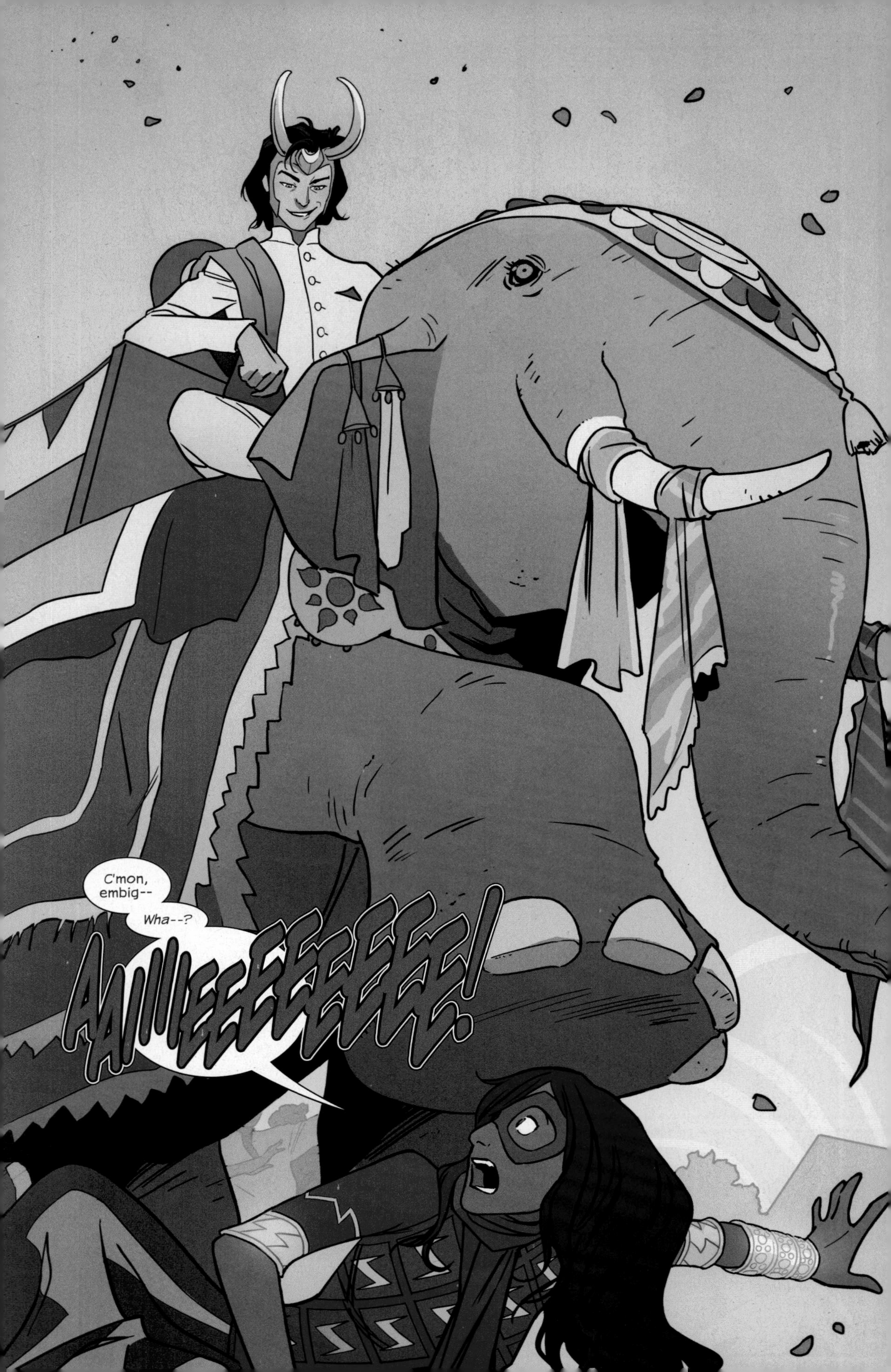
C'mon, embig--
Wha--?
AAIIIEEEEEEEEE!

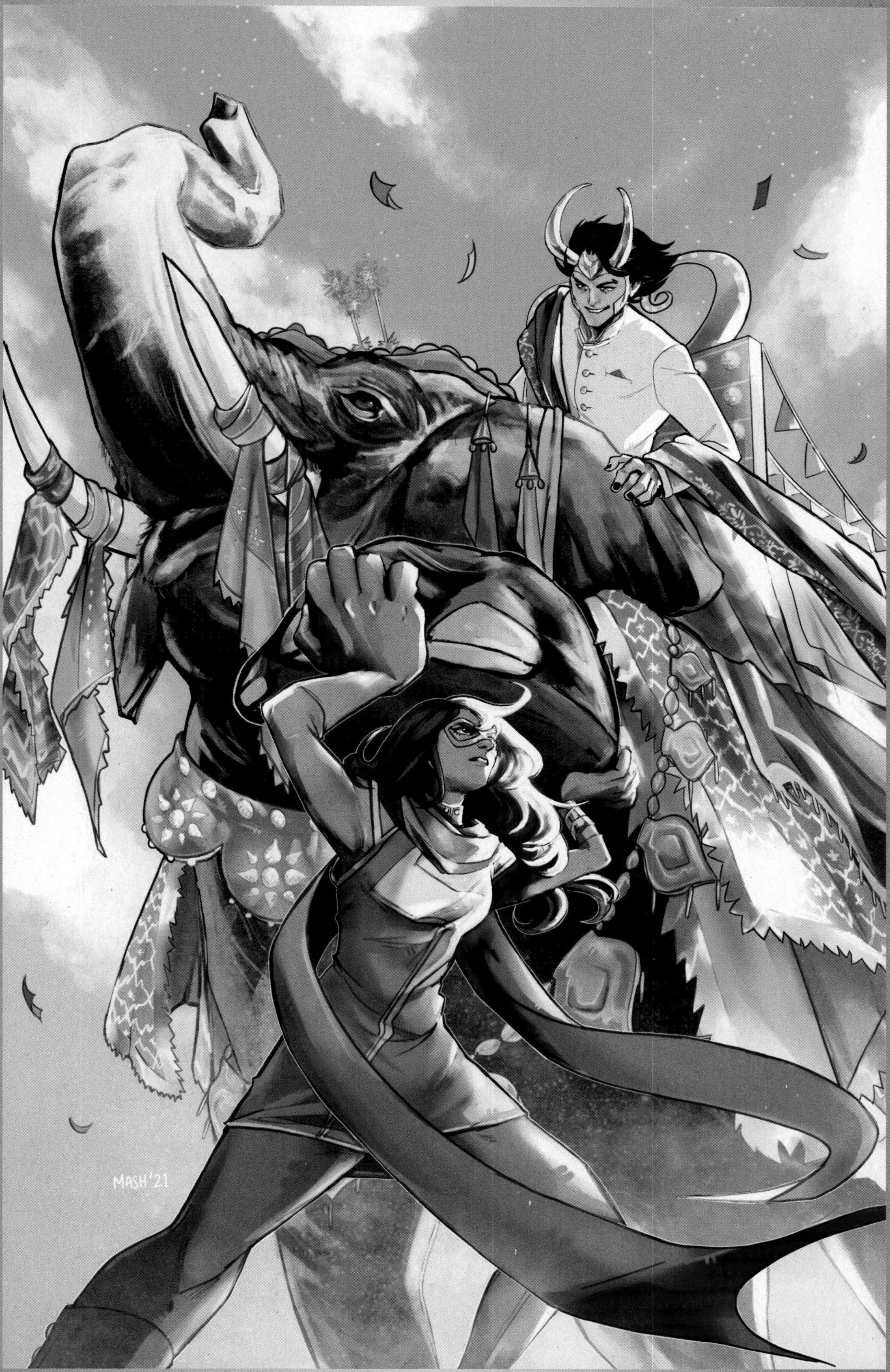
MASH'21

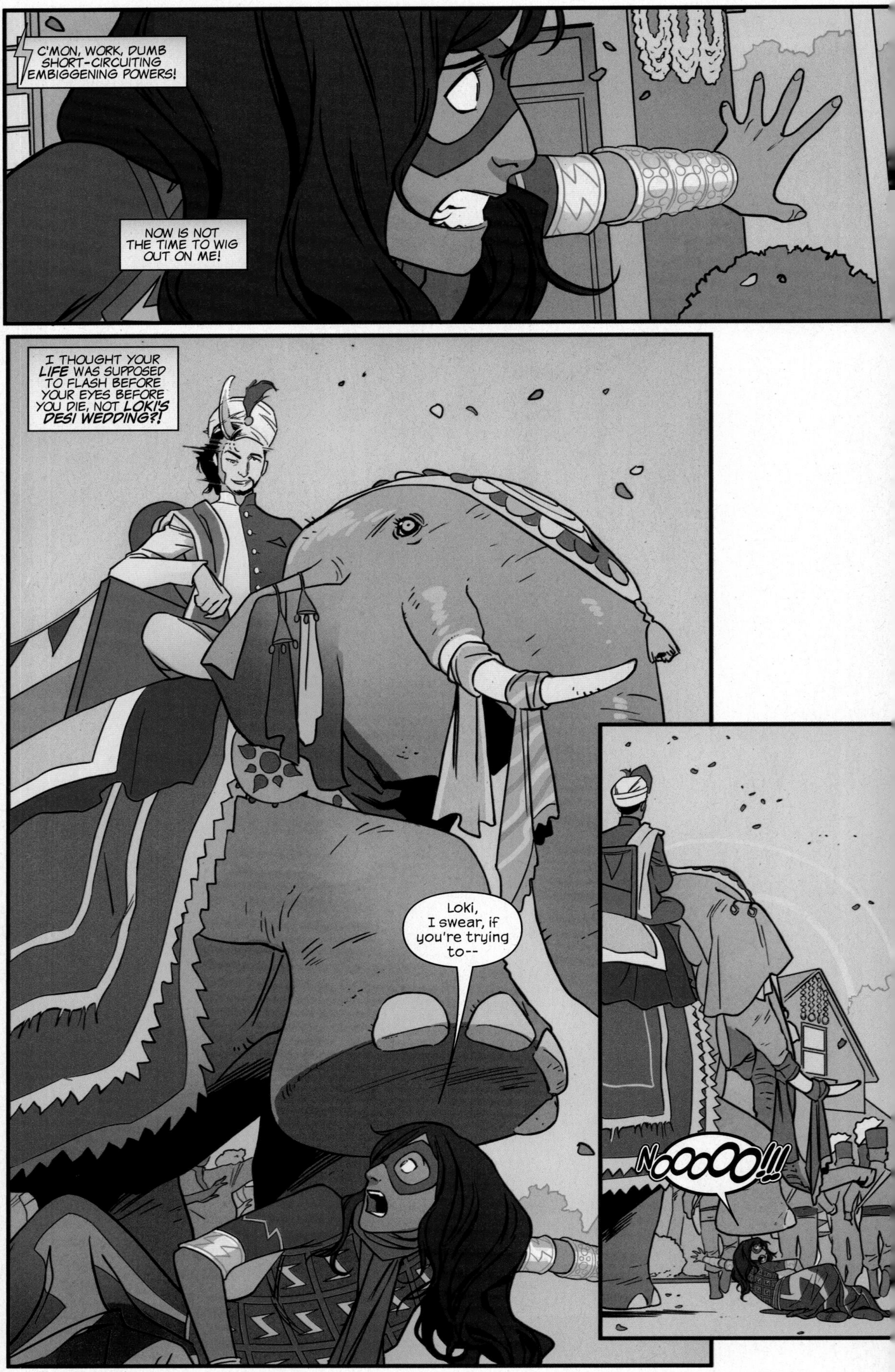
C'MON, WORK, DUMB SHORT-CIRCUITING EMBIGGENING POWERS!
NOW IS NOT THE TIME TO WIG OUT ON ME!
I THOUGHT YOUR LIFE WAS SUPPOSED TO FLASH BEFORE YOUR EYES BEFORE YOU DIE, NOT LOKI'S DESI WEDDING?!
Loki, I swear, if you're trying to--
NOOOOO!!!

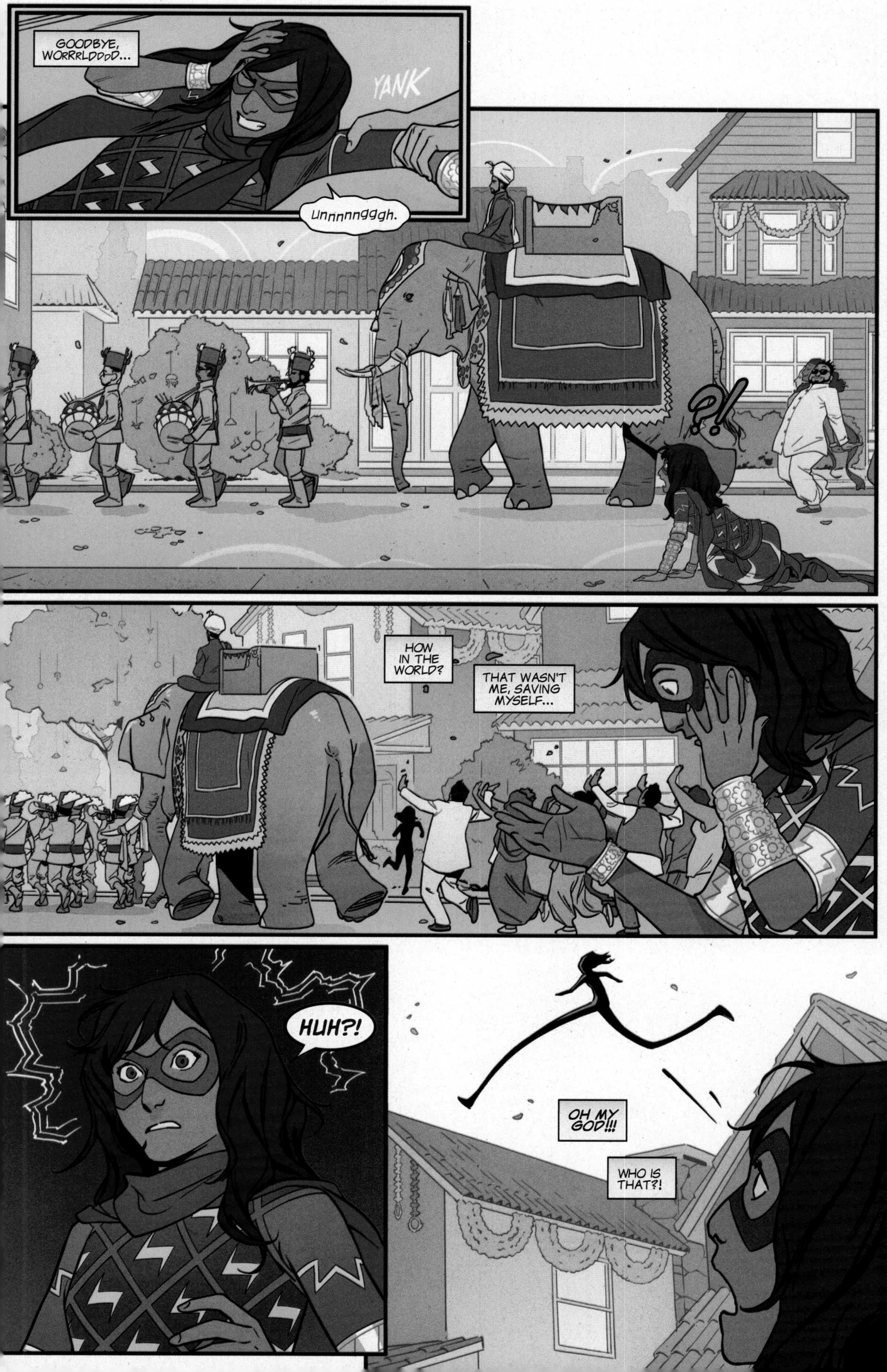
GOODBYE, WORRRLDDDD...
YANK
Unnnnnnggh.
?!
HOW IN THE WORLD?
THAT WASN'T ME, SAVING MYSELF...
HUH?!
OH MY GOD!!!
WHO IS THAT?!

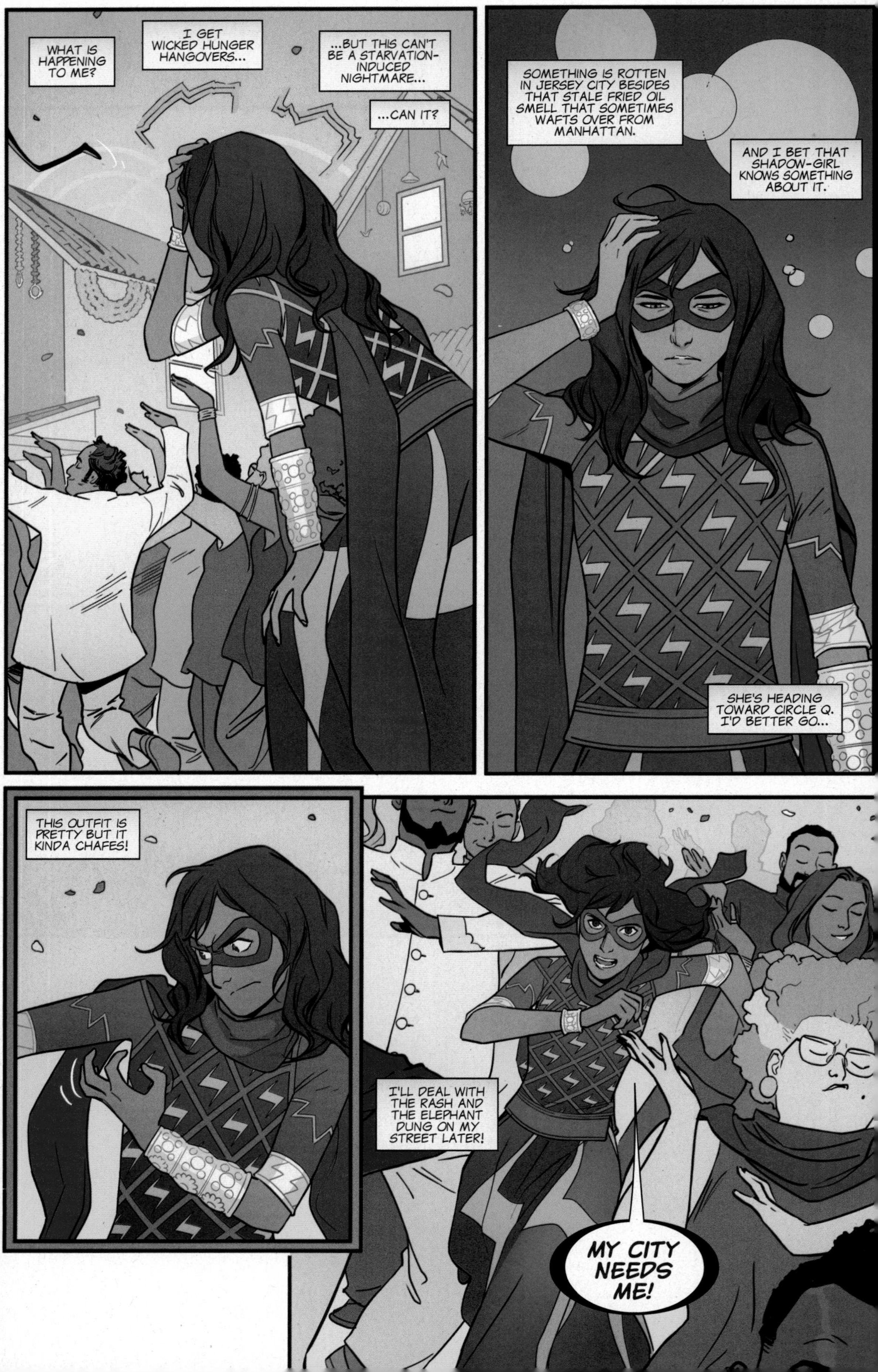
WHAT IS HAPPENING TO ME?
I GET WICKED HUNGER HANGOVERS...
...BUT THIS CAN'T BE A STARVATION-INDUCED NIGHTMARE...
...CAN IT?
SOMETHING IS ROTTEN IN JERSEY CITY BESIDES THAT STALE FRIED OIL SMELL THAT SOMETIMES WAFTS OVER FROM MANHATTAN.
AND I BET THAT SHADOW-GIRL KNOWS SOMETHING ABOUT IT.
SHE'S HEADING TOWARD CIRCLE Q. I'D BETTER GO...
THIS OUTFIT IS PRETTY BUT IT KINDA CHAFES!
I'LL DEAL WITH THE RASH AND THE ELEPHANT DUNG ON MY STREET LATER!
MY CITY NEEDS ME!

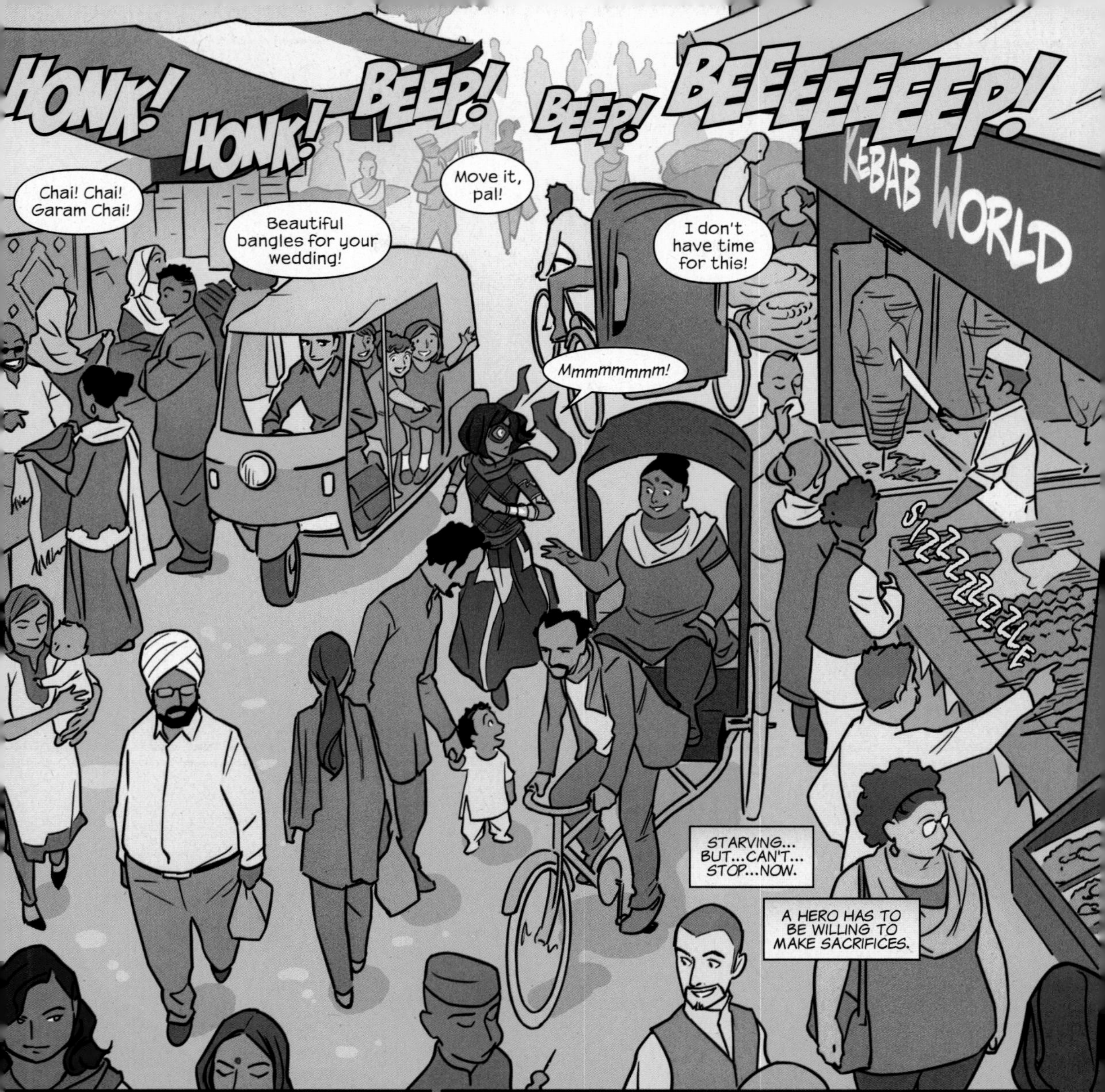
HONK! HONK! BEEP! BEEP! BEEEEEEEP!
KEBAB WORLD
Chai! Chai! Garam Chai!
Beautiful bangles for your wedding!
Move it, pal!
I don't have time for this!
Mmmmmmmm!
SIZZZZZZZLE
STARVING... BUT...CAN'T... STOP...NOW.
A HERO HAS TO BE WILLING TO MAKE SACRIFICES.

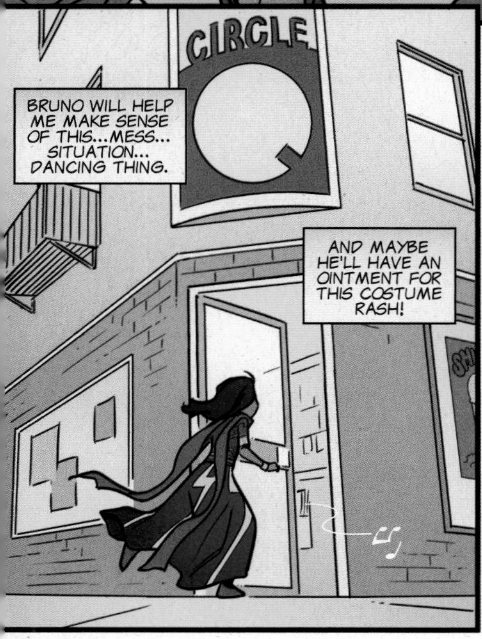
CIRCLE Q
BRUNO WILL HELP ME MAKE SENSE OF THIS...MESS... SITUATION... DANCING THING.
AND MAYBE HE'LL HAVE AN OINTMENT FOR THIS COSTUME RASH!

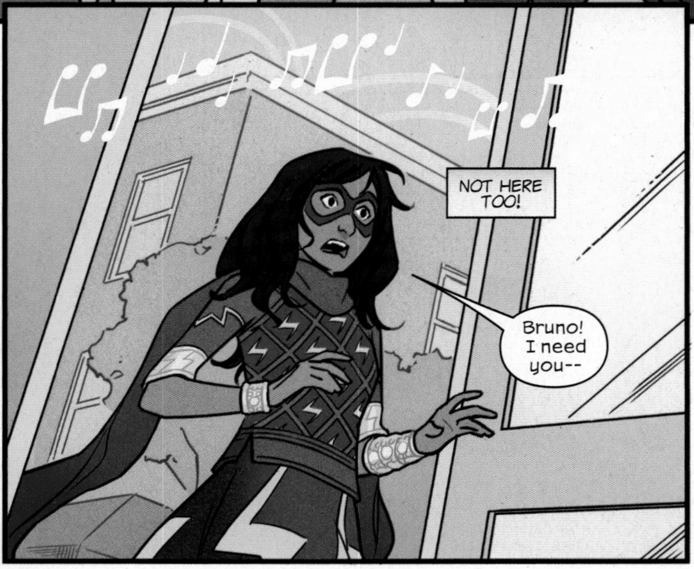
NOT HERE TOO!
Bruno! I need you--

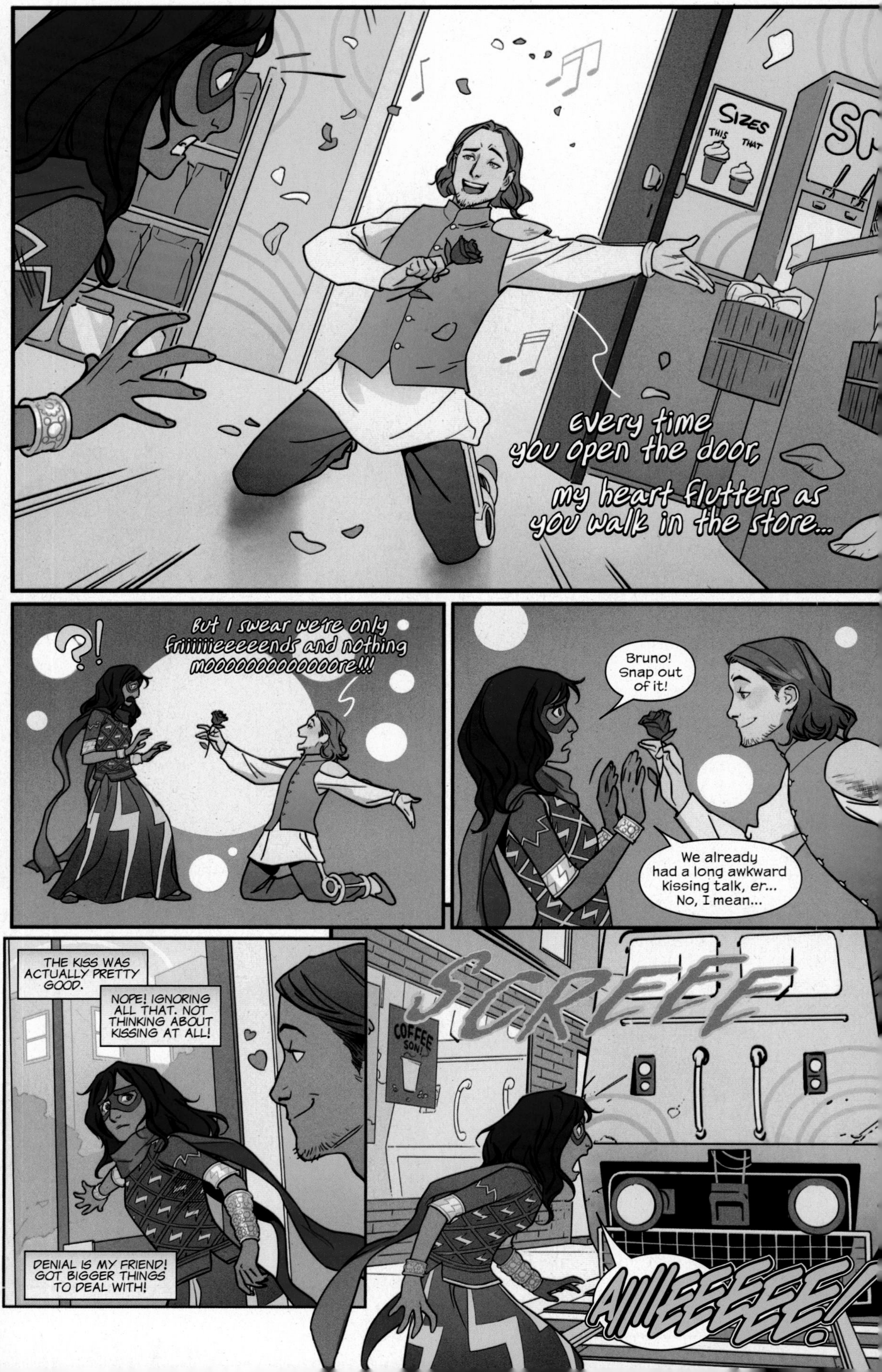
Sizes
This
That
Every time you open the door,
my heart flutters as you walk in the store...
?!
But I swear we're only friiiiiieeeeends and nothing moooooooooooooore!!!
Bruno! Snap out of it!
We already had a long awkward kissing talk, er... No, I mean...
THE KISS WAS ACTUALLY PRETTY GOOD.
NOPE! IGNORING ALL THAT. NOT THINKING ABOUT KISSING AT ALL!
DENIAL IS MY FRIEND! GOT BIGGER THINGS TO DEAL WITH!
Coffee
SCREEE
AIIIEEEEE!

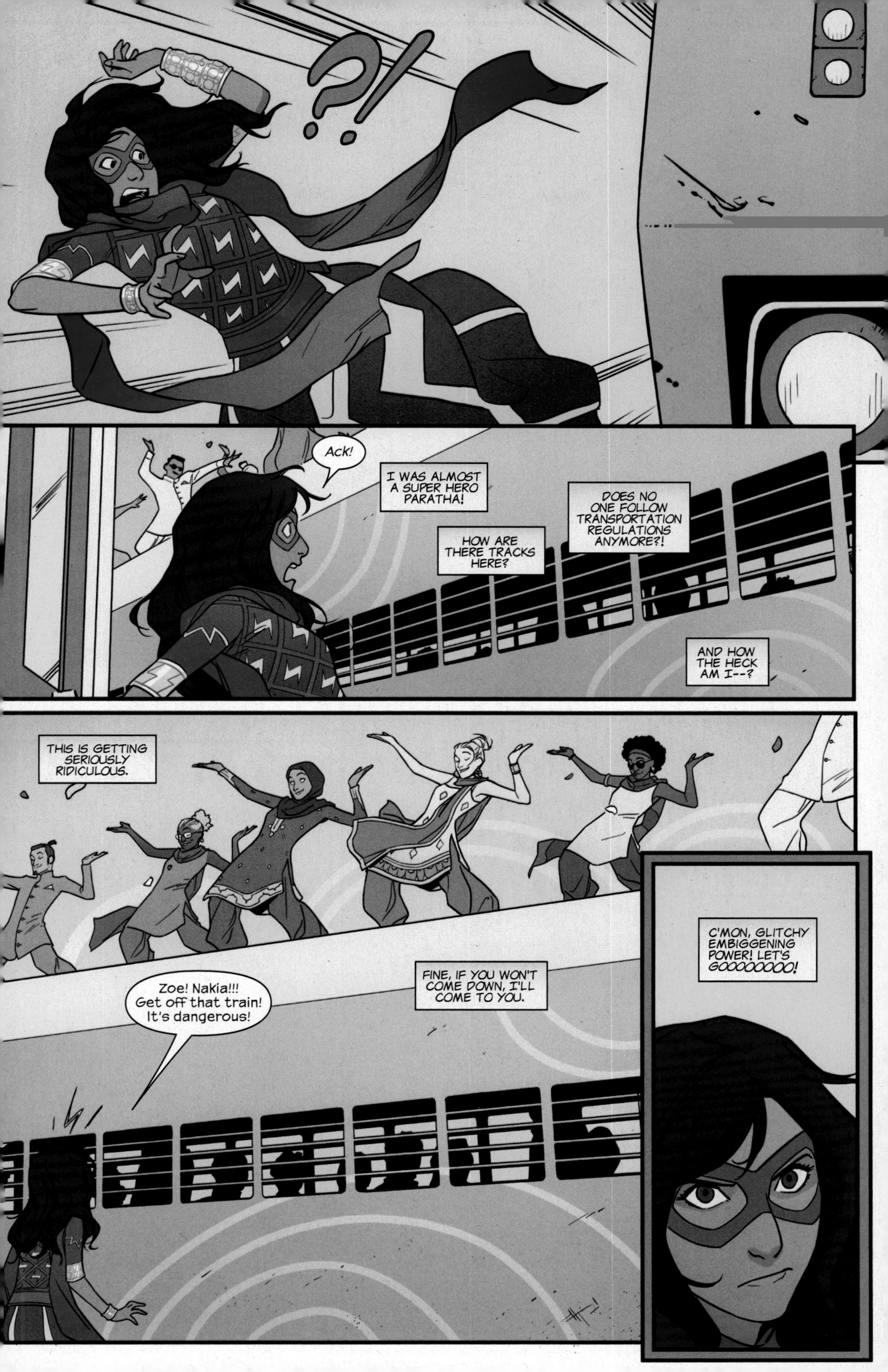
?!
Ack!
I WAS ALMOST A SUPER HERO PARATHA!
HOW ARE THERE TRACKS HERE?
DOES NO ONE FOLLOW TRANSPORTATION REGULATIONS ANYMORE?!
AND HOW THE HECK AM I--?
THIS IS GETTING SERIOUSLY RIDICULOUS.
Zoe! Nakia!!! Get off that train! It's dangerous!
FINE, IF YOU WON'T COME DOWN, I'LL COME TO YOU.
C'MON, GLITCHY EMBIGGENING POWER! LET'S GOOOOOOOO!

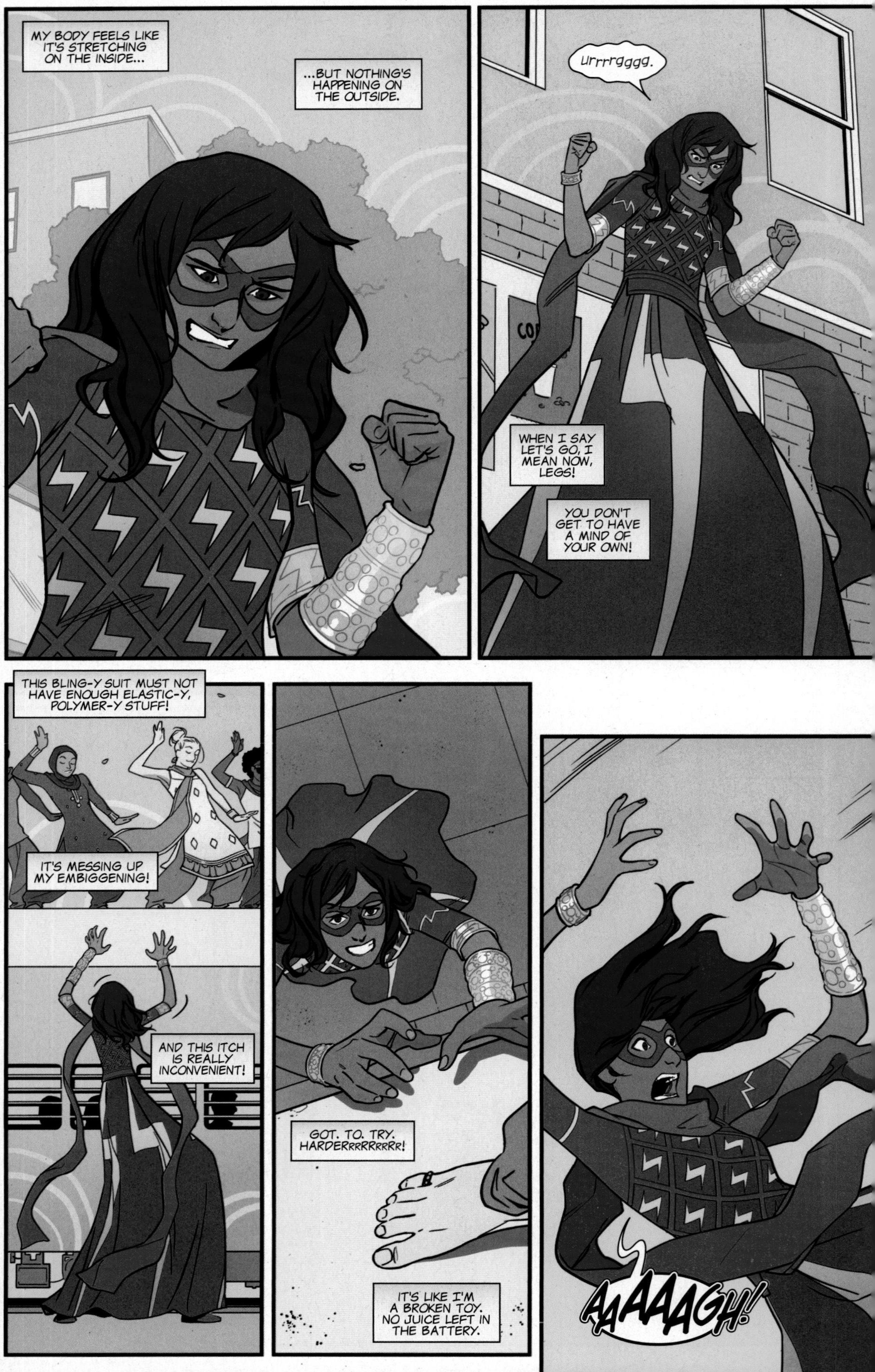
MY BODY FEELS LIKE IT'S STRETCHING ON THE INSIDE...
...BUT NOTHING'S HAPPENING ON THE OUTSIDE.
Urrrrgggg.
WHEN I SAY LET'S GO, I MEAN NOW, LEGS!
YOU DON'T GET TO HAVE A MIND OF YOUR OWN!
THIS BLING-Y SUIT MUST NOT HAVE ENOUGH ELASTIC-Y, POLYMER-Y STUFF!
IT'S MESSING UP MY EMBIGGENING!
AND THIS ITCH IS REALLY INCONVENIENT!
GOT. TO. TRY. HARDERRRRRRRR!
IT'S LIKE I'M A BROKEN TOY. NO JUICE LEFT IN THE BATTERY.
AAAAAGH!

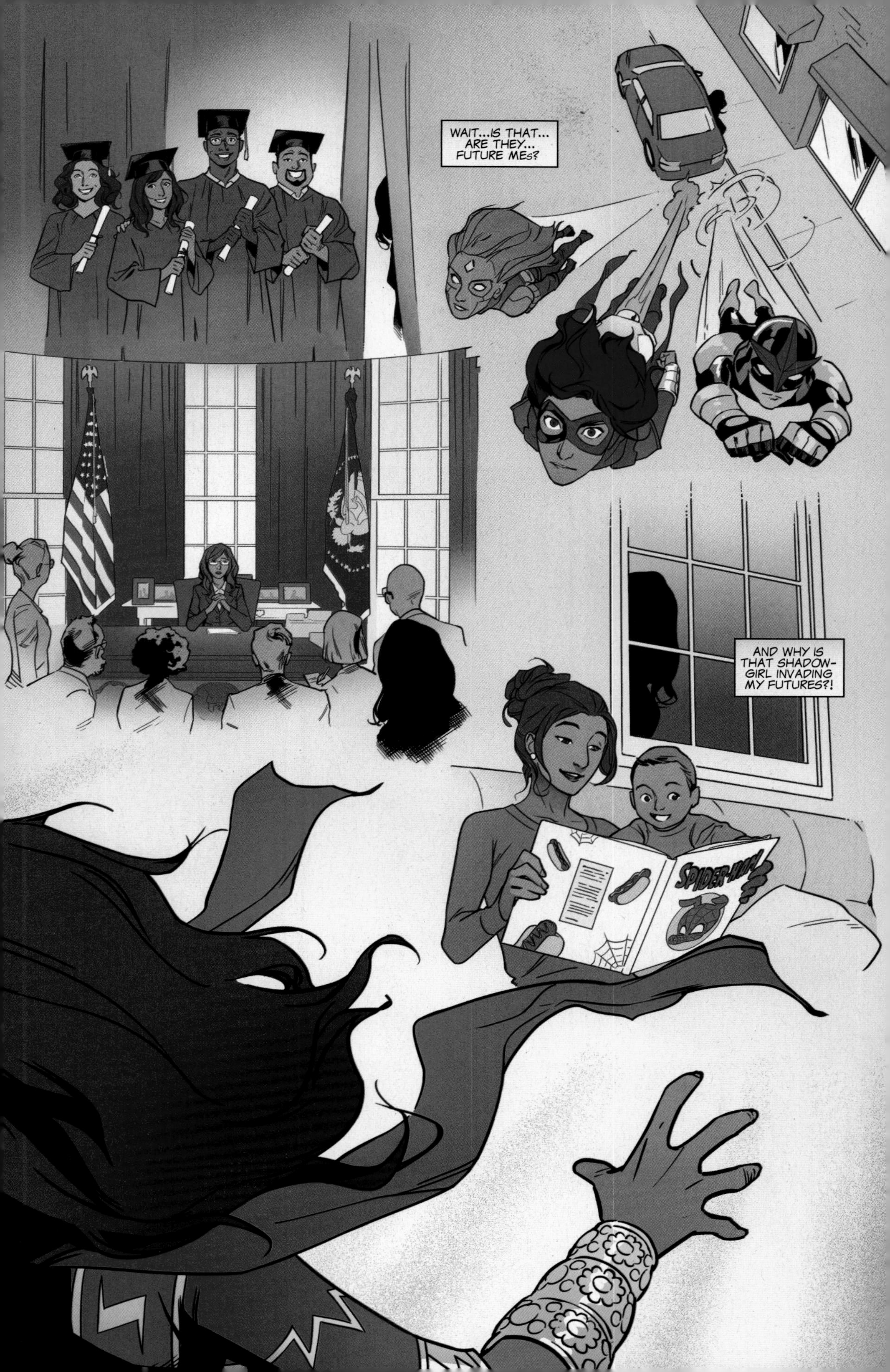
WAIT...IS THAT... ARE THEY... FUTURE MEs?
AND WHY IS THAT SHADOW-GIRL INVADING MY FUTURES?!
SPIDER-HAM

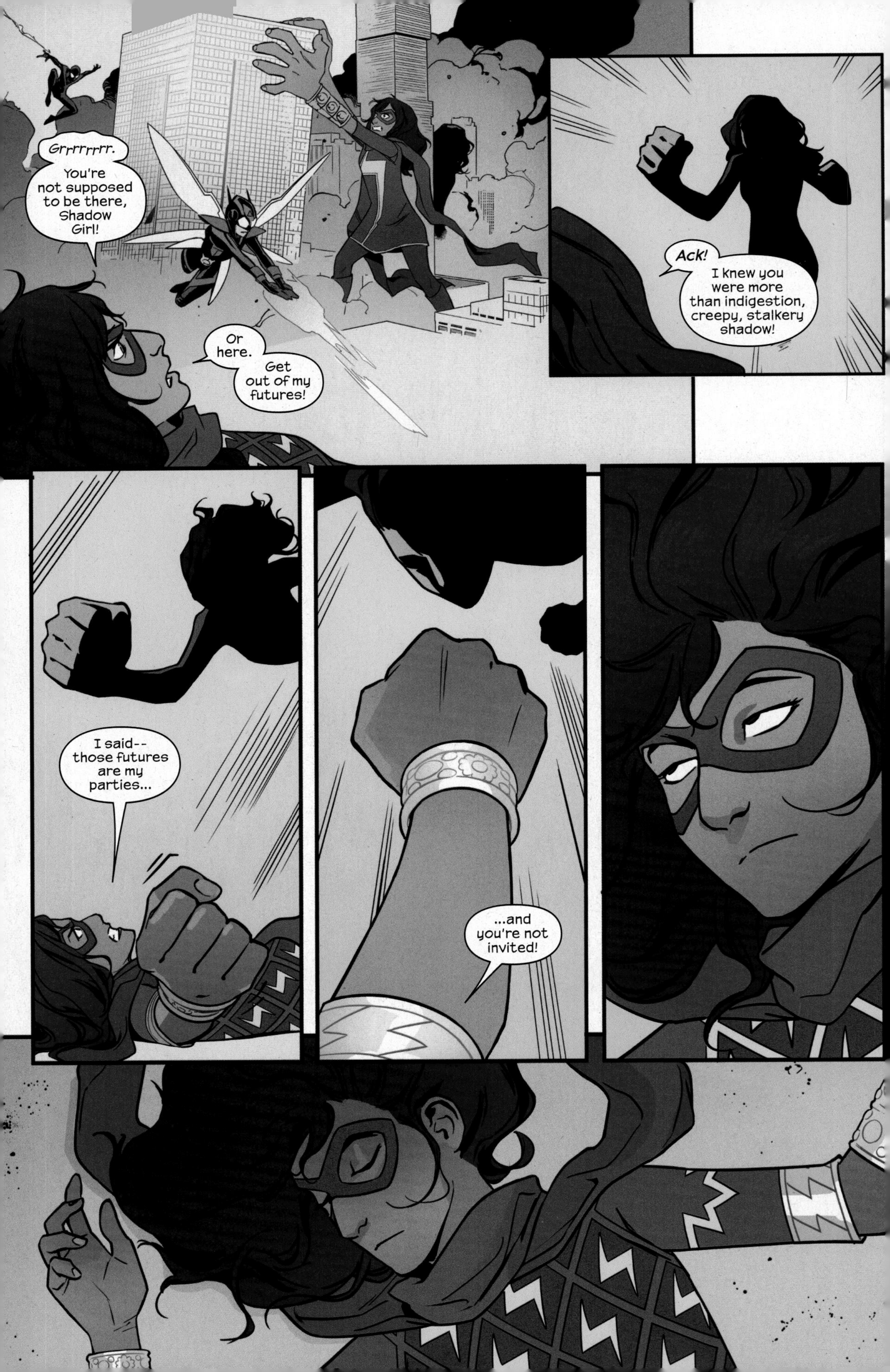
Grrrrrrrr. You're not supposed to be there, Shadow Girl!
Or here. Get out of my futures!
Ack! I knew you were more than indigestion, creepy, stalkery shadow!
I said-- those futures are my parties...
...and you're not invited!

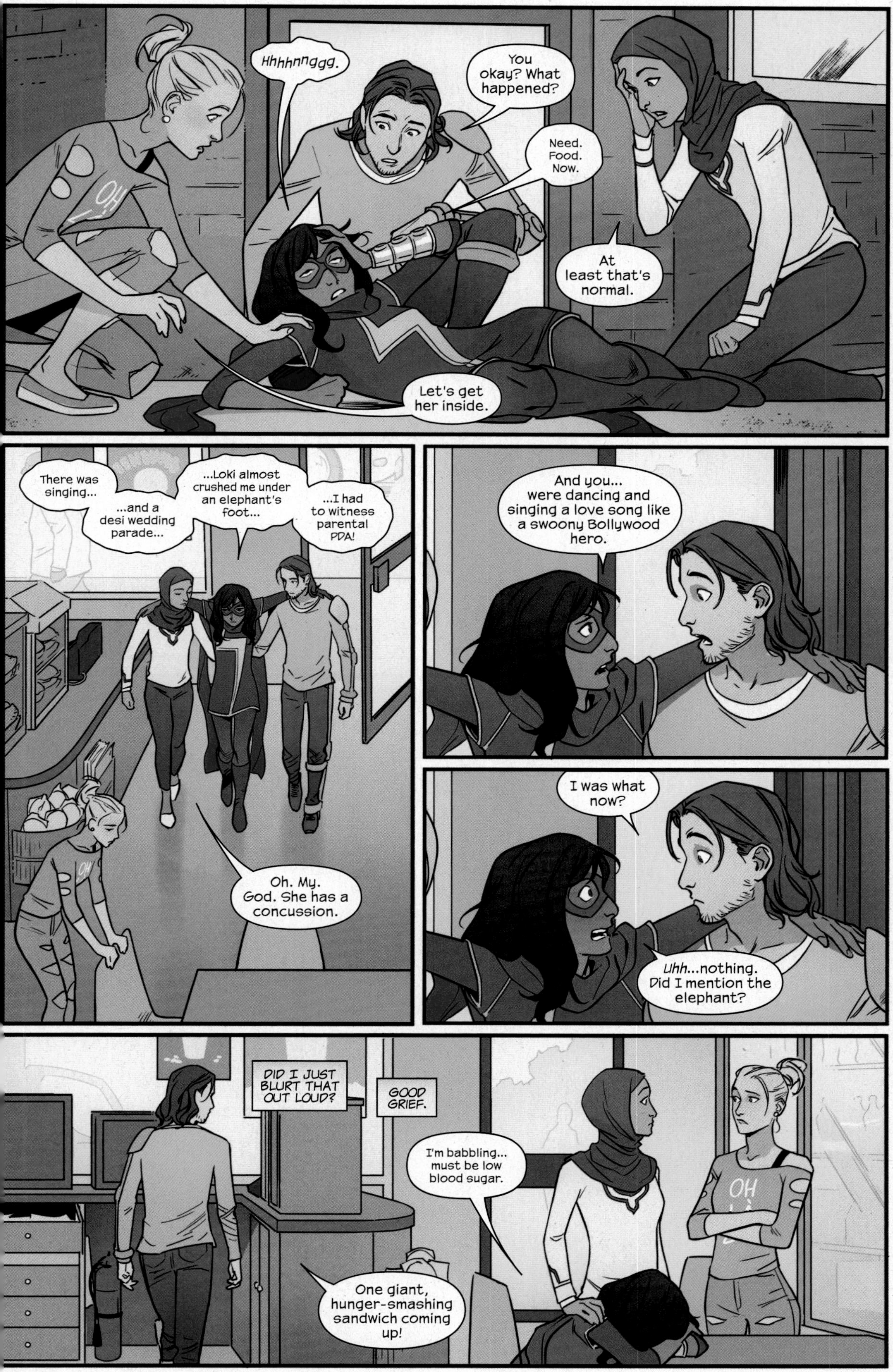
Hhhhhⁿⁿggg.
You okay? What happened?
Need. Food. Now.
At least that's normal.
Let's get her inside.
There was singing...
...and a desi wedding parade...
...Loki almost crushed me under an elephant's foot...
...I had to witness parental PDA!
Oh. My. God. She has a concussion.
And you... were dancing and singing a love song like a swoony Bollywood hero.
I was what now?
Uhh...nothing. Did I mention the elephant?
DID I JUST BLURT THAT OUT LOUD?
GOOD GRIEF.
I'm babbling... must be low blood sugar.
One giant, hunger-smashing sandwich coming up!
OH

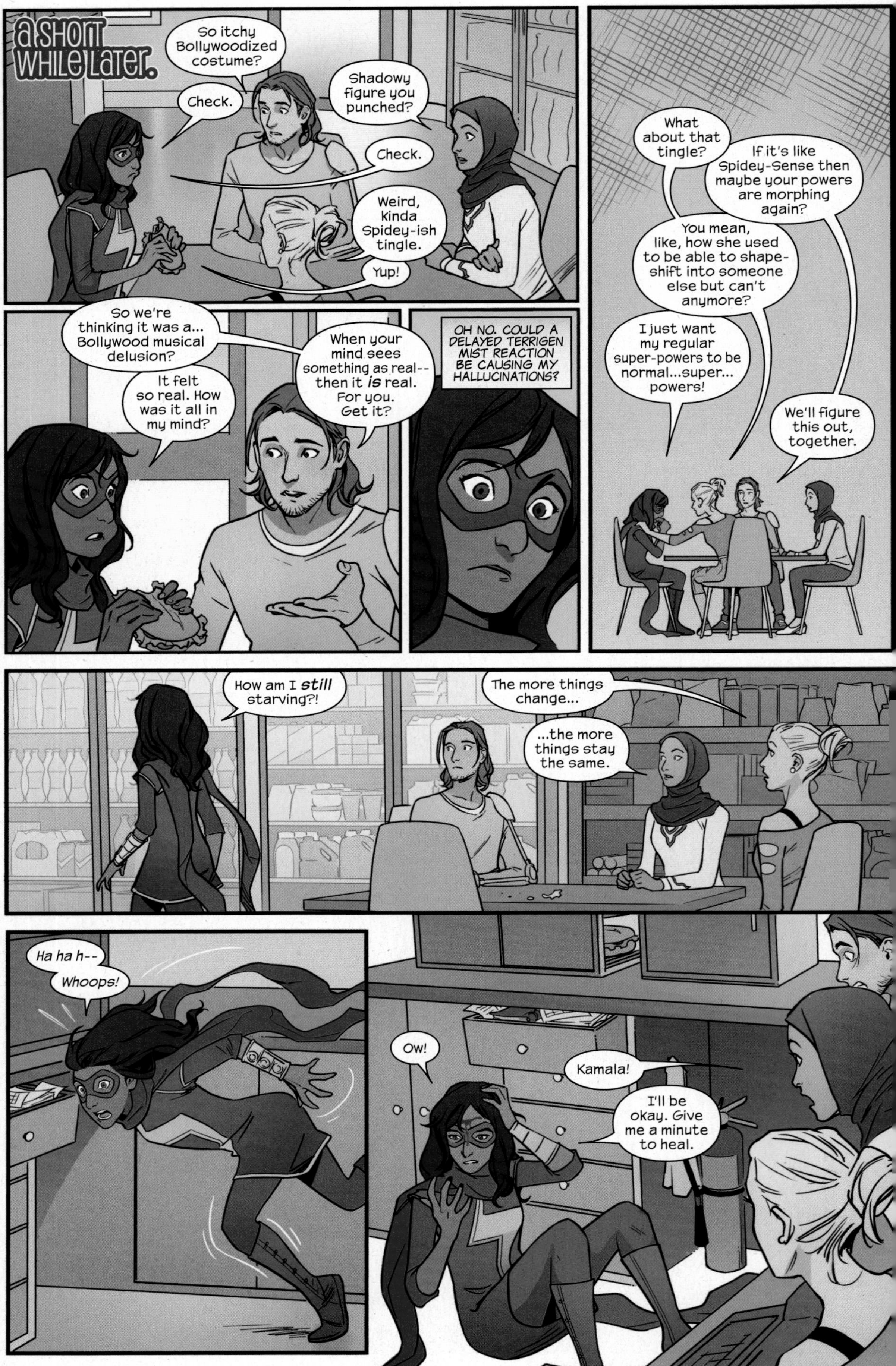
A SHORT WHILE LATER.
So itchy Bollywoodized costume?
Check.
Shadowy figure you punched?
Check.
Weird, kinda Spidey-ish tingle.
Yup!
So we're thinking it was a... Bollywood musical delusion?
It felt so real. How was it all in my mind?
When your mind sees something as real--then it *is* real. For you. Get it?
OH NO. COULD A DELAYED TERRIGEN MIST REACTION BE CAUSING MY HALLUCINATIONS?
What about that tingle?
If it's like Spidey-Sense then maybe your powers are morphing again?
You mean, like, how she used to be able to shape-shift into someone else but can't anymore?
I just want my regular super-powers to be normal...super... powers!
We'll figure this out, together.
How am I *still* starving?!
The more things change...
...the more things stay the same.
Ha ha h--
Whoops!
Ow!
Kamala!
I'll be okay. Give me a minute to heal.

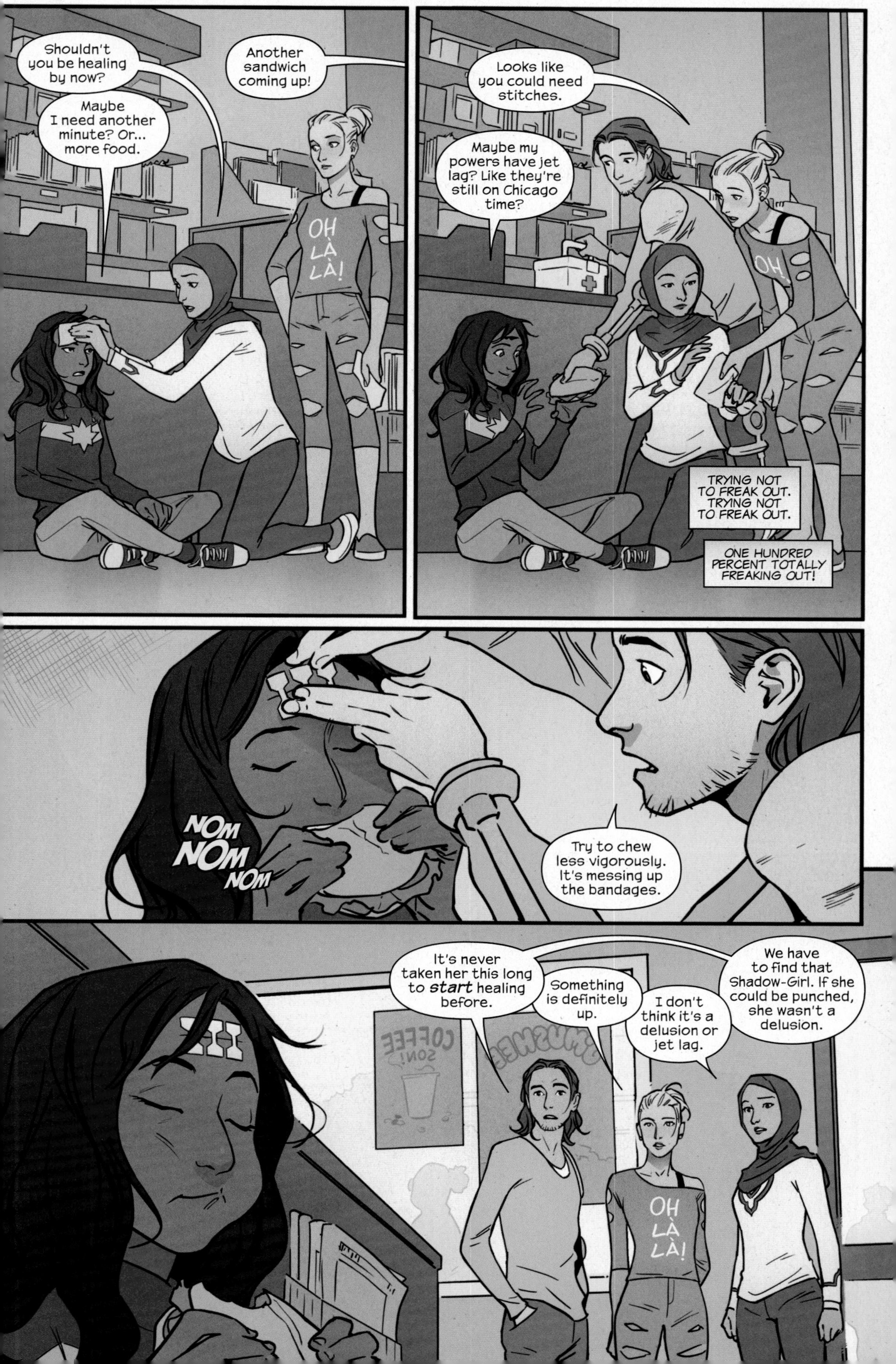

Shouldn't you be healing by now?
Maybe I need another minute? Or... more food.
Another sandwich coming up!
OH LÀ LÀ!
Looks like you could need stitches.
Maybe my powers have jet lag? Like they're still on Chicago time?
OH!
TRYING NOT TO FREAK OUT. TRYING NOT TO FREAK OUT.
ONE HUNDRED PERCENT TOTALLY FREAKING OUT!
NOM NOM NOM
Try to chew less vigorously. It's messing up the bandages.
It's never taken her this long to *start* healing before.
Something is definitely up.
I don't think it's a delusion or jet lag.
We have to find that Shadow-Girl. If she could be punched, she wasn't a delusion.
COFFEE SON!
OH LÀ LÀ!

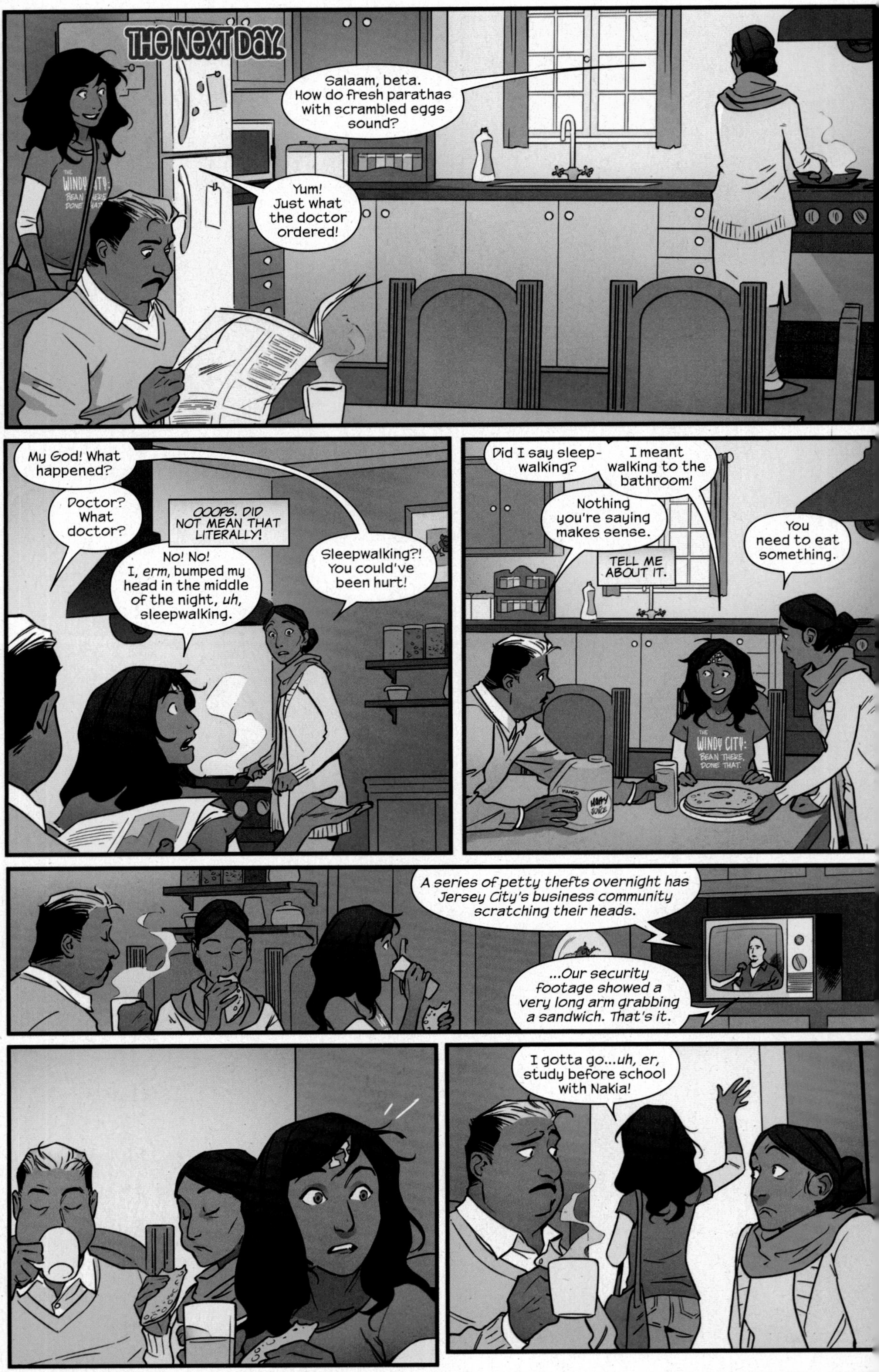
THE NEXT DAY.
Salaam, beta. How do fresh parathas with scrambled eggs sound?
Yum! Just what the doctor ordered!
My God! What happened?
Doctor? What doctor?
OOOPS. DID NOT MEAN THAT LITERALLY!
No! No! I, *erm*, bumped my head in the middle of the night, *uh*, sleepwalking.
Sleepwalking?! You could've been hurt!
Did I say sleep-walking?
I meant walking to the bathroom!
Nothing you're saying makes sense.
TELL ME ABOUT IT.
You need to eat something.
THE WINDY CITY: BEAN THERE, DONE THAT.
A series of petty thefts overnight has Jersey City's business community scratching their heads.
...Our security footage showed a very long arm grabbing a sandwich. That's it.
I gotta go...*uh, er*, study before school with Nakia!

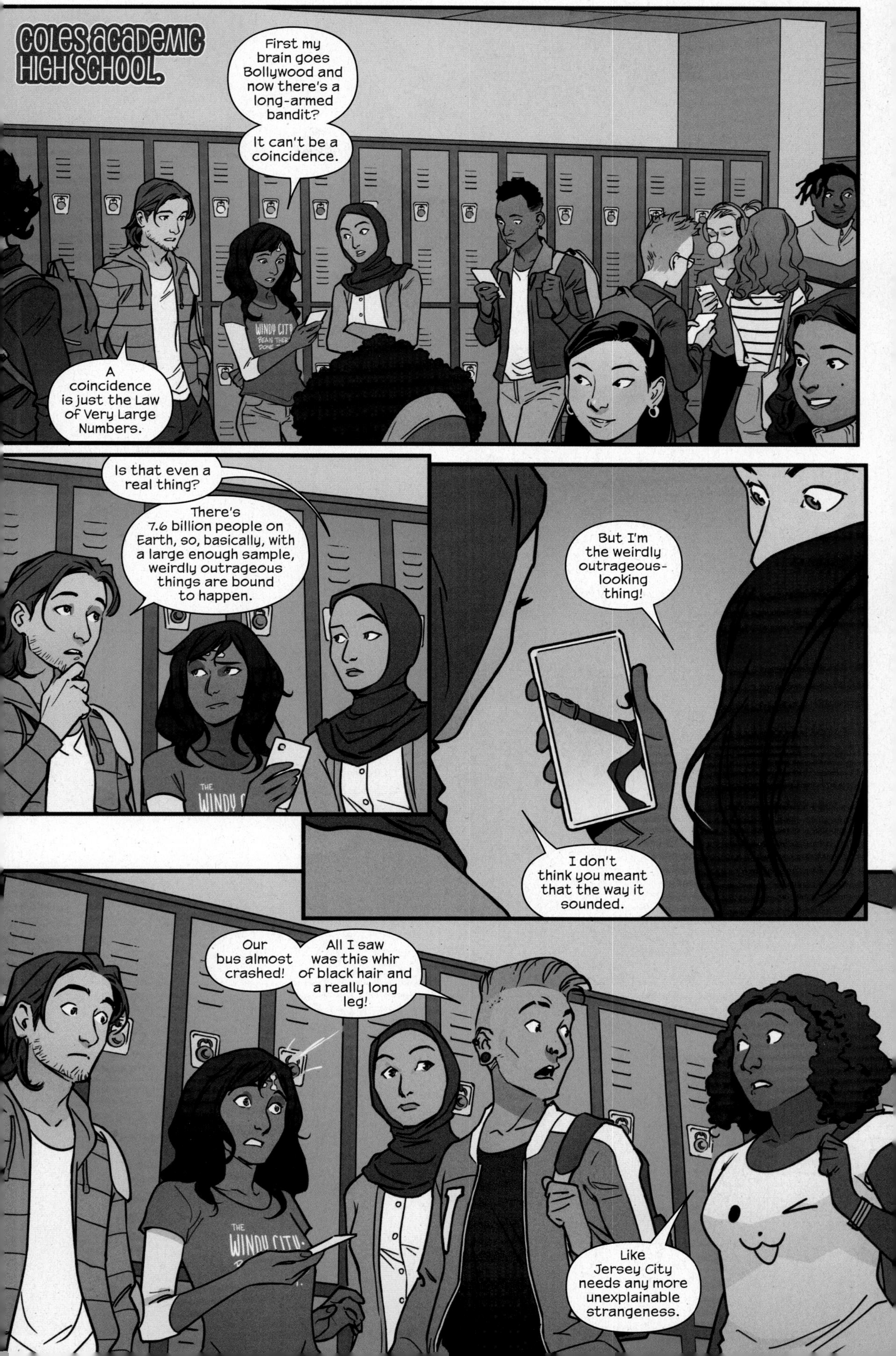
COLES ACADEMIC HIGH SCHOOL.
First my brain goes Bollywood and now there's a long-armed bandit?
It can't be a coincidence.
A coincidence is just the Law of Very Large Numbers.
WINDY CITY BEAN THERE DONE THAT
Is that even a real thing?
There's 7.6 billion people on Earth, so, basically, with a large enough sample, weirdly outrageous things are bound to happen.
But I'm the weirdly outrageous-looking thing!
I don't think you meant that the way it sounded.
Our bus almost crashed!
All I saw was this whir of black hair and a really long leg!
Like Jersey City needs any more unexplainable strangeness.

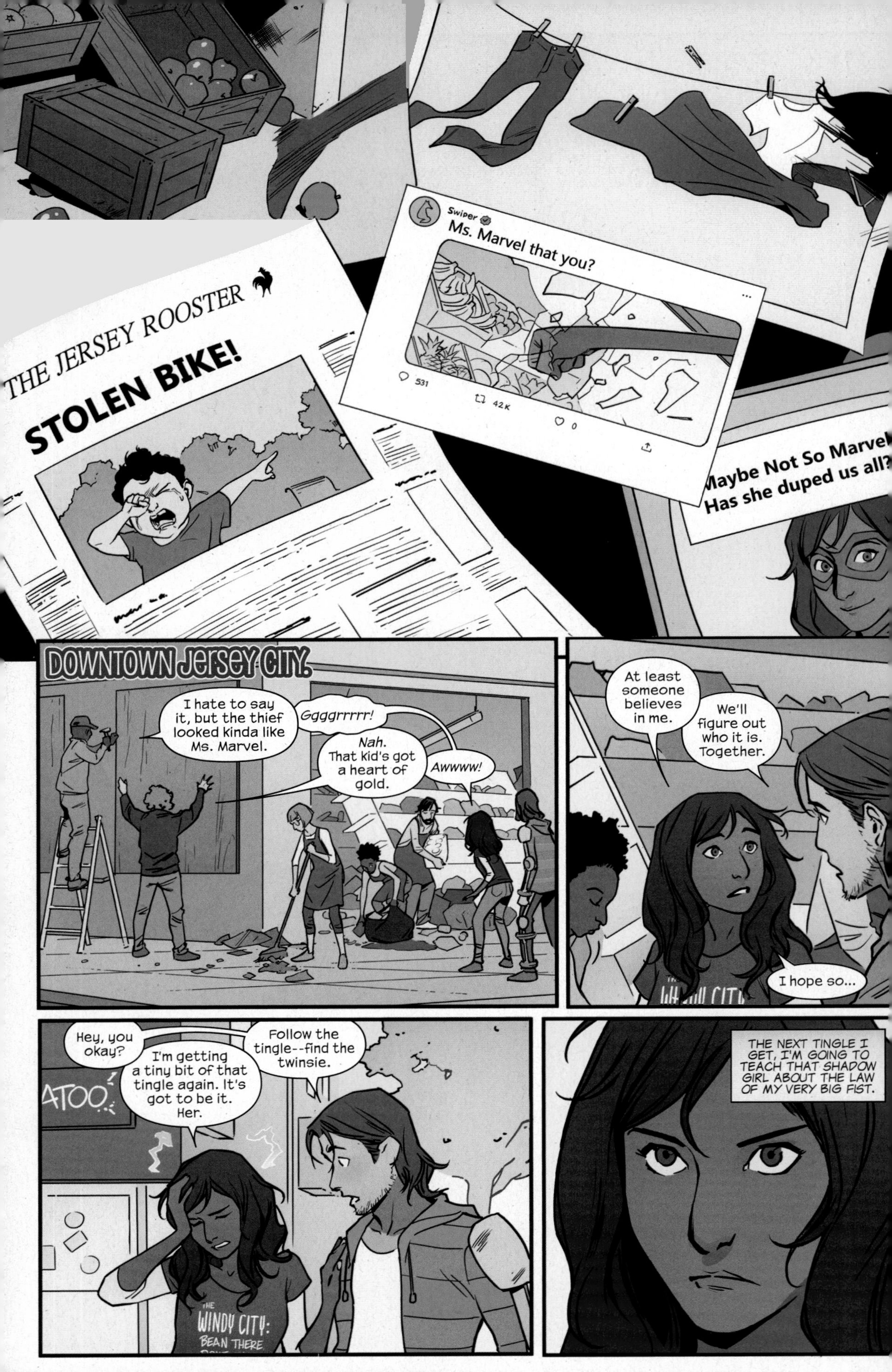
THE JERSEY ROOSTER
STOLEN BIKE!
Swiper
Ms. Marvel that you?
531
42K
0
Maybe Not So Marvel
Has she duped us all?
DOWNTOWN JERSEY CITY.
I hate to say it, but the thief looked kinda like Ms. Marvel.
Ggggrrrrr!
Nah. That kid's got a heart of gold.
Awwww!
At least someone believes in me.
We'll figure out who it is. Together.
I hope so...
Hey, you okay?
I'm getting a tiny bit of that tingle again. It's got to be it. Her.
Follow the tingle--find the twinsie.
THE WINDY CITY: BEAN THERE
THE NEXT TINGLE I GET, I'M GOING TO TEACH THAT SHADOW GIRL ABOUT THE LAW OF MY VERY BIG FIST.

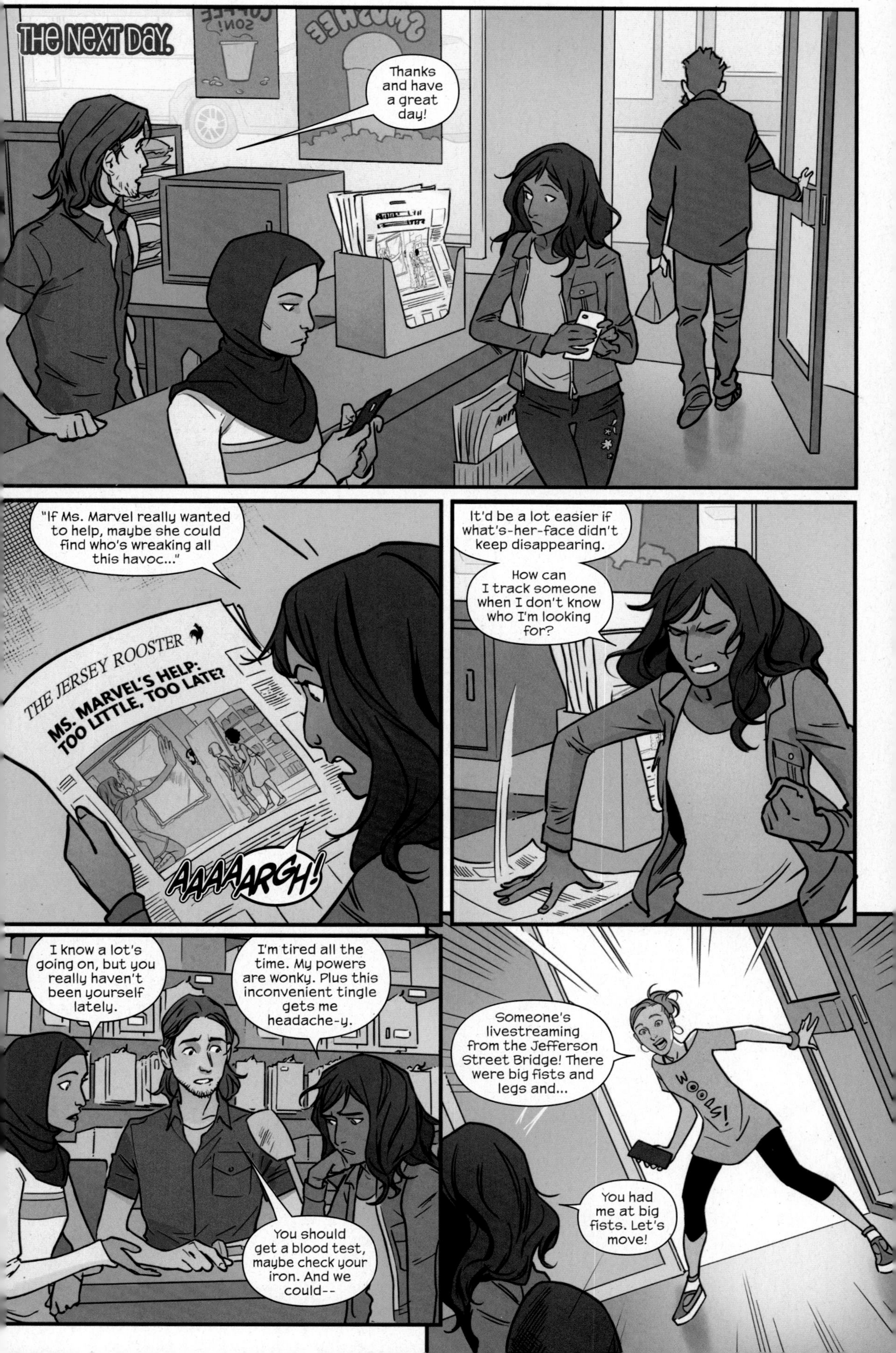
THE NEXT DAY.
COFFEE SON!
SMOOSHEE
Thanks and have a great day!
"If Ms. Marvel really wanted to help, maybe she could find who's wreaking all this havoc..."
THE JERSEY ROOSTER
MS. MARVEL'S HELP: TOO LITTLE, TOO LATE?
AAAAARGH!
It'd be a lot easier if what's-her-face didn't keep disappearing.
How can I track someone when I don't know who I'm looking for?
I know a lot's going on, but you really haven't been yourself lately.
I'm tired all the time. My powers are wonky. Plus this inconvenient tingle gets me headache-y.
You should get a blood test, maybe check your iron. And we could--
Someone's livestreaming from the Jefferson Street Bridge! There were big fists and legs and...
You had me at big fists. Let's move!

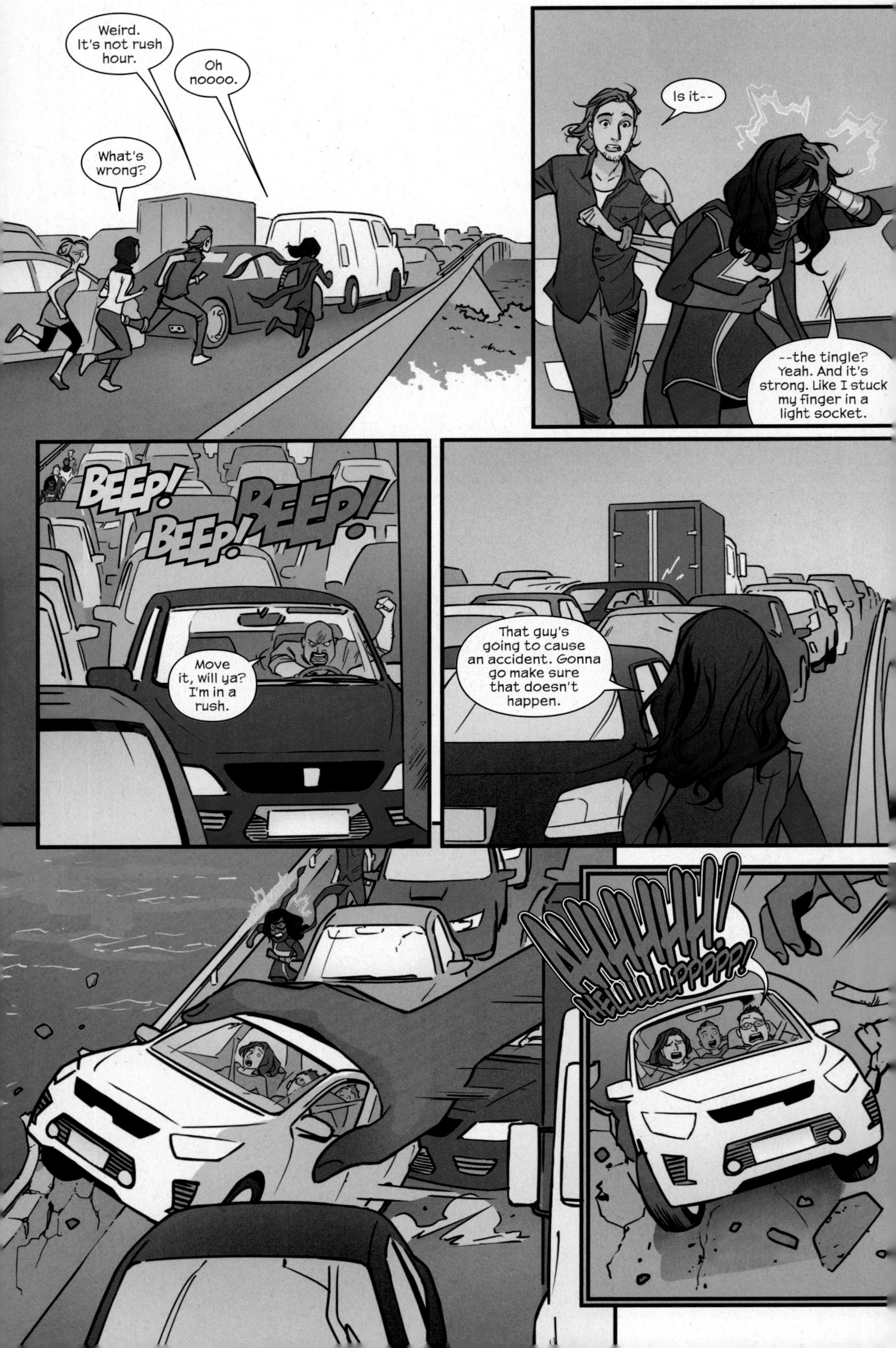

Weird. It's not rush hour.
Oh noooo.
What's wrong?
Is it--
--the tingle? Yeah. And it's strong. Like I stuck my finger in a light socket.
BEEP! BEEP! BEEP!
Move it, will ya? I'm in a rush.
That guy's going to cause an accident. Gonna go make sure that doesn't happen.
AHHHHHH! HELLLLLPPPPP!

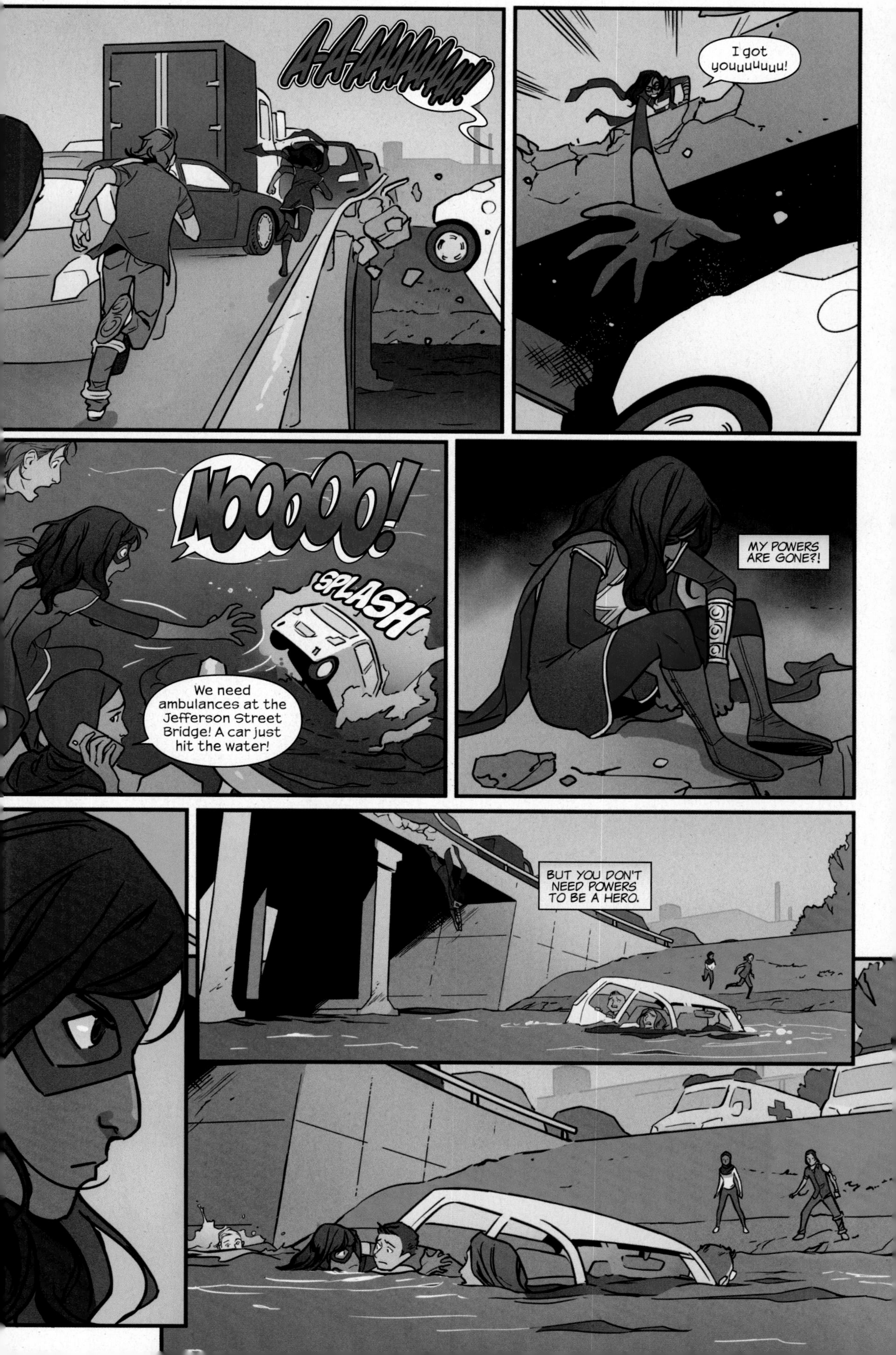

A-A-AAAAAAAAAH!!
I got youuuuuuu!
NOOOOO!
SPLASH
We need ambulances at the Jefferson Street Bridge! A car just hit the water!
MY POWERS ARE GONE?!
BUT YOU DON'T NEED POWERS TO BE A HERO.

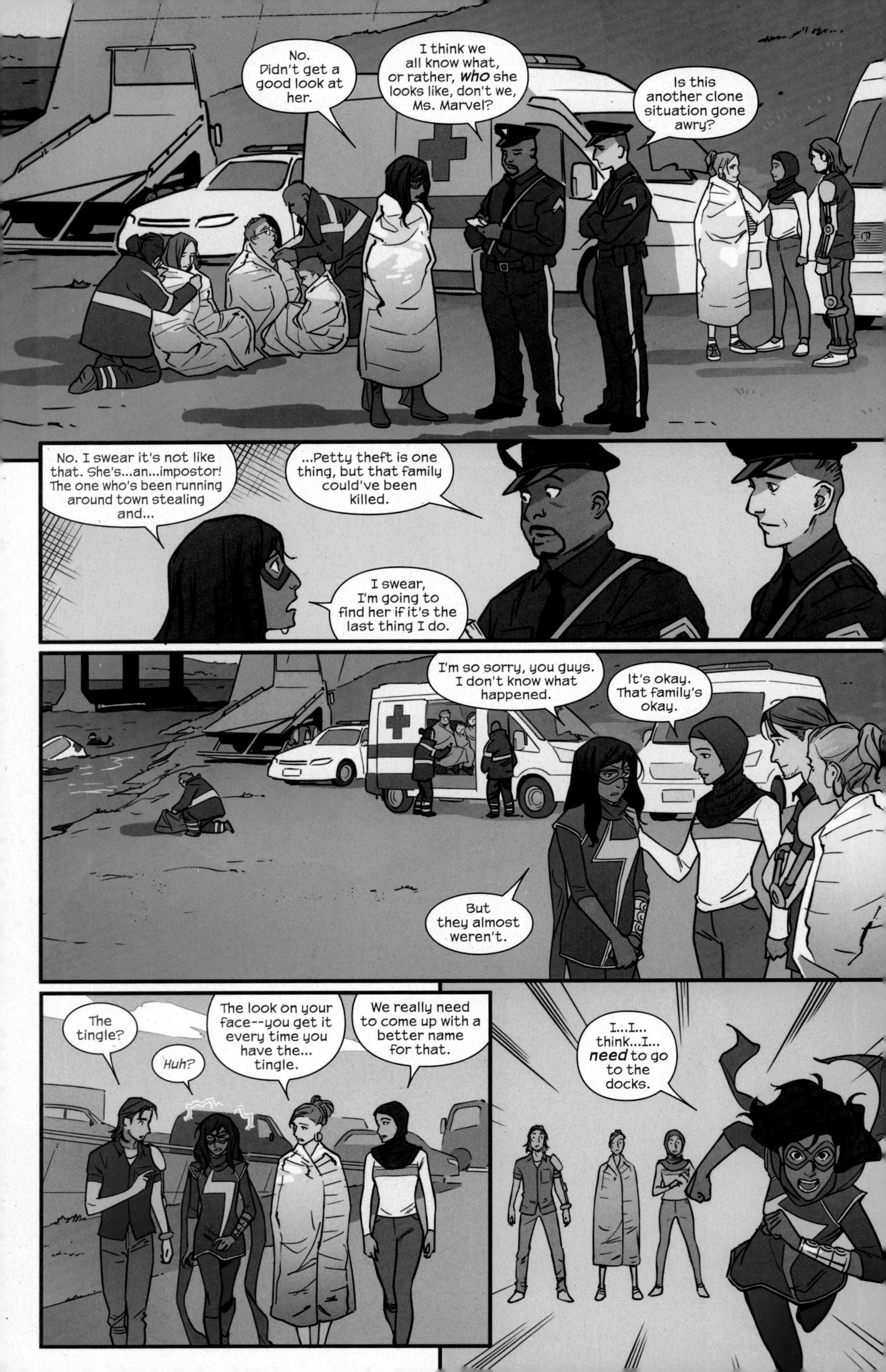
No. Didn't get a good look at her.
I think we all know what, or rather, who she looks like, don't we, Ms. Marvel?
Is this another clone situation gone awry?
No. I swear it's not like that. She's...an...impostor! The one who's been running around town stealing and...
...Petty theft is one thing, but that family could've been killed.
I swear, I'm going to find her if it's the last thing I do.
I'm so sorry, you guys. I don't know what happened.
It's okay. That family's okay.
But they almost weren't.
The tingle?
Huh?
The look on your face--you get it every time you have the... tingle.
We really need to come up with a better name for that.
I...I... think...I... need to go to the docks.

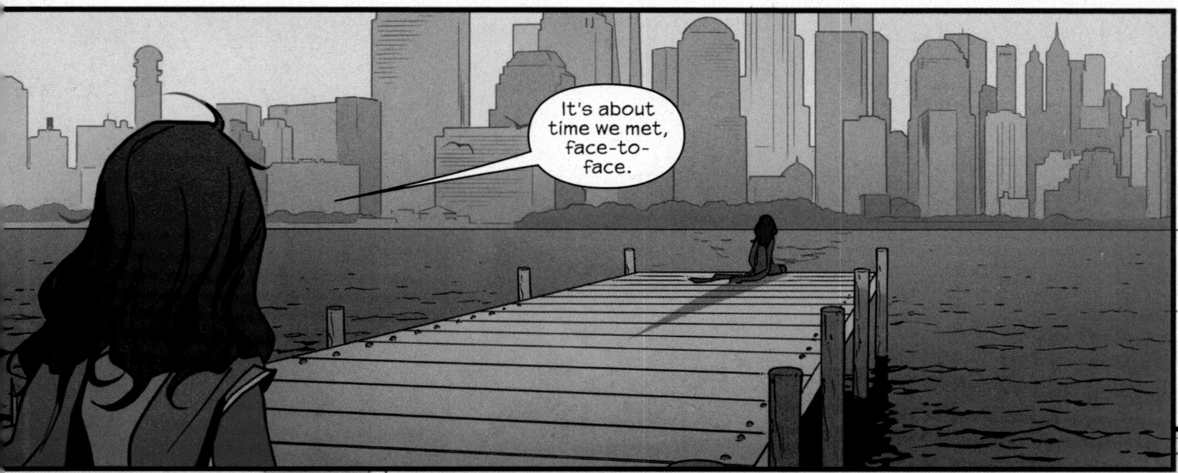
It's about time we met, face-to-face.

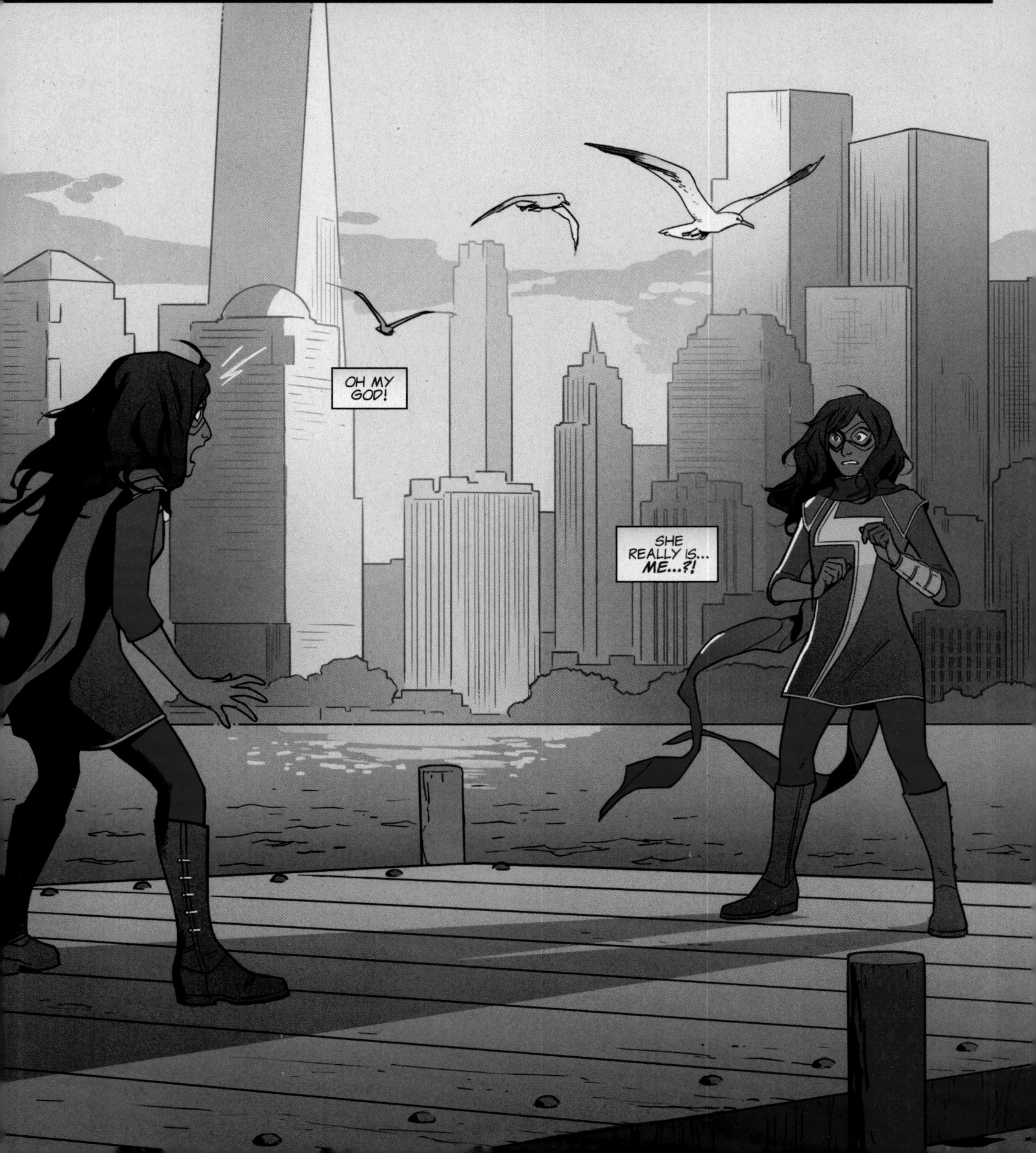
OH MY GOD!
SHE REALLY IS... ME...?!

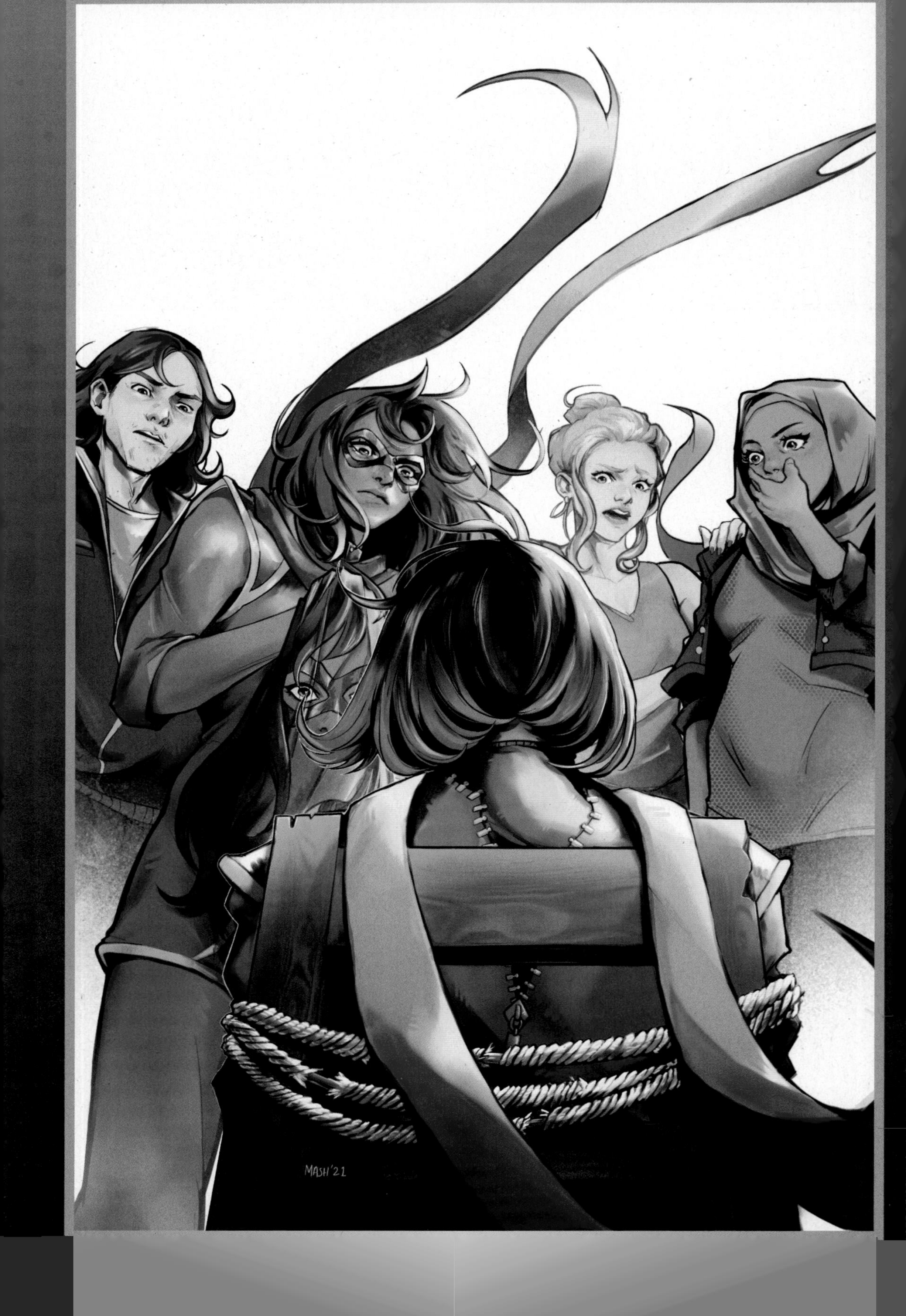
MASH'21

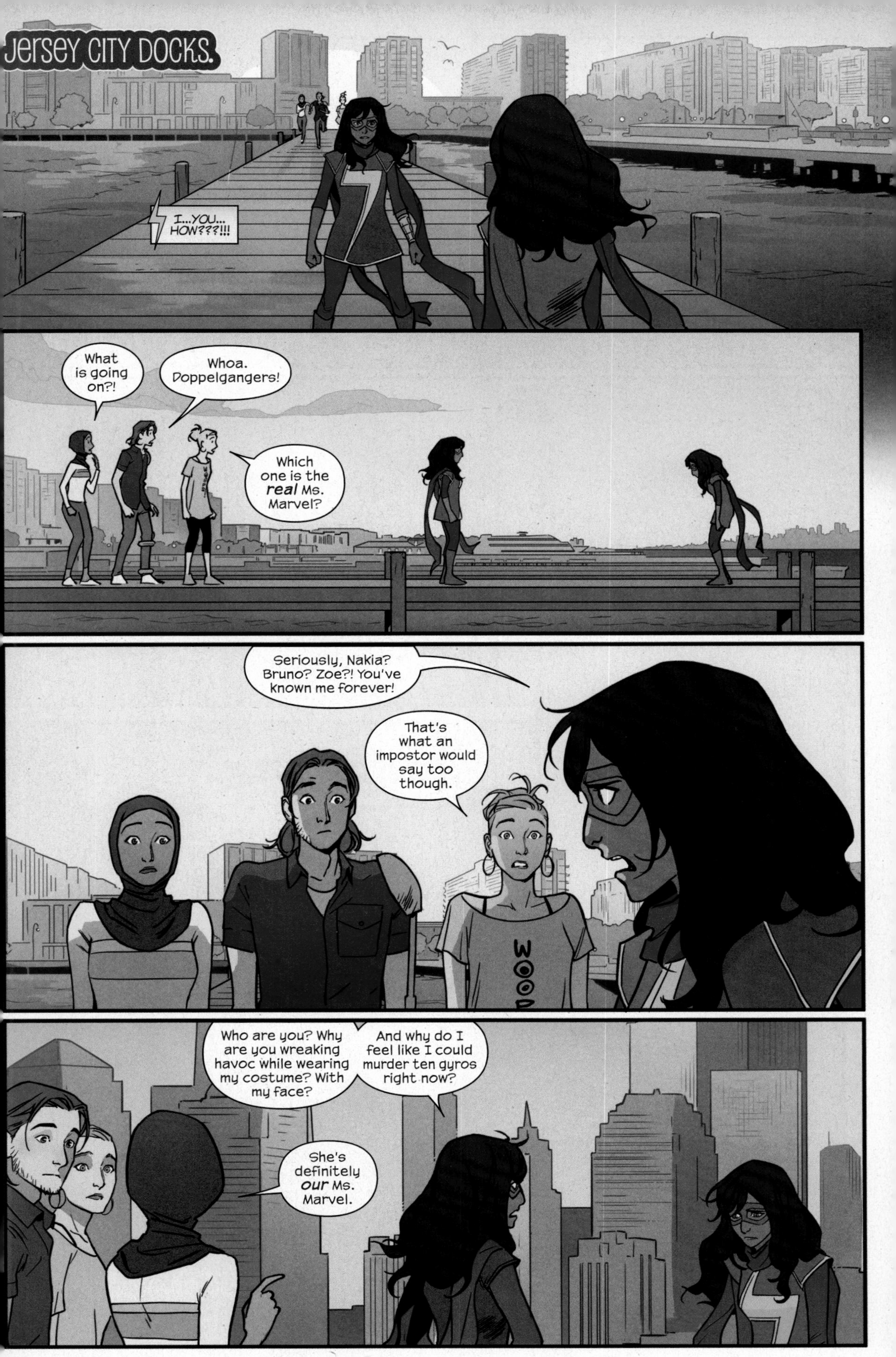
JERSEY CITY DOCKS.
I...YOU... HOW???!!!
What is going on?!
Whoa. Doppelgangers!
Which one is the *real* Ms. Marvel?
Seriously, Nakia? Bruno? Zoe?! You've known me forever!
That's what an impostor would say too though.
Who are you? Why are you wreaking havoc while wearing my costume? With my face?
And why do I feel like I could murder ten gyros right now?
She's definitely *our* Ms. Marvel.

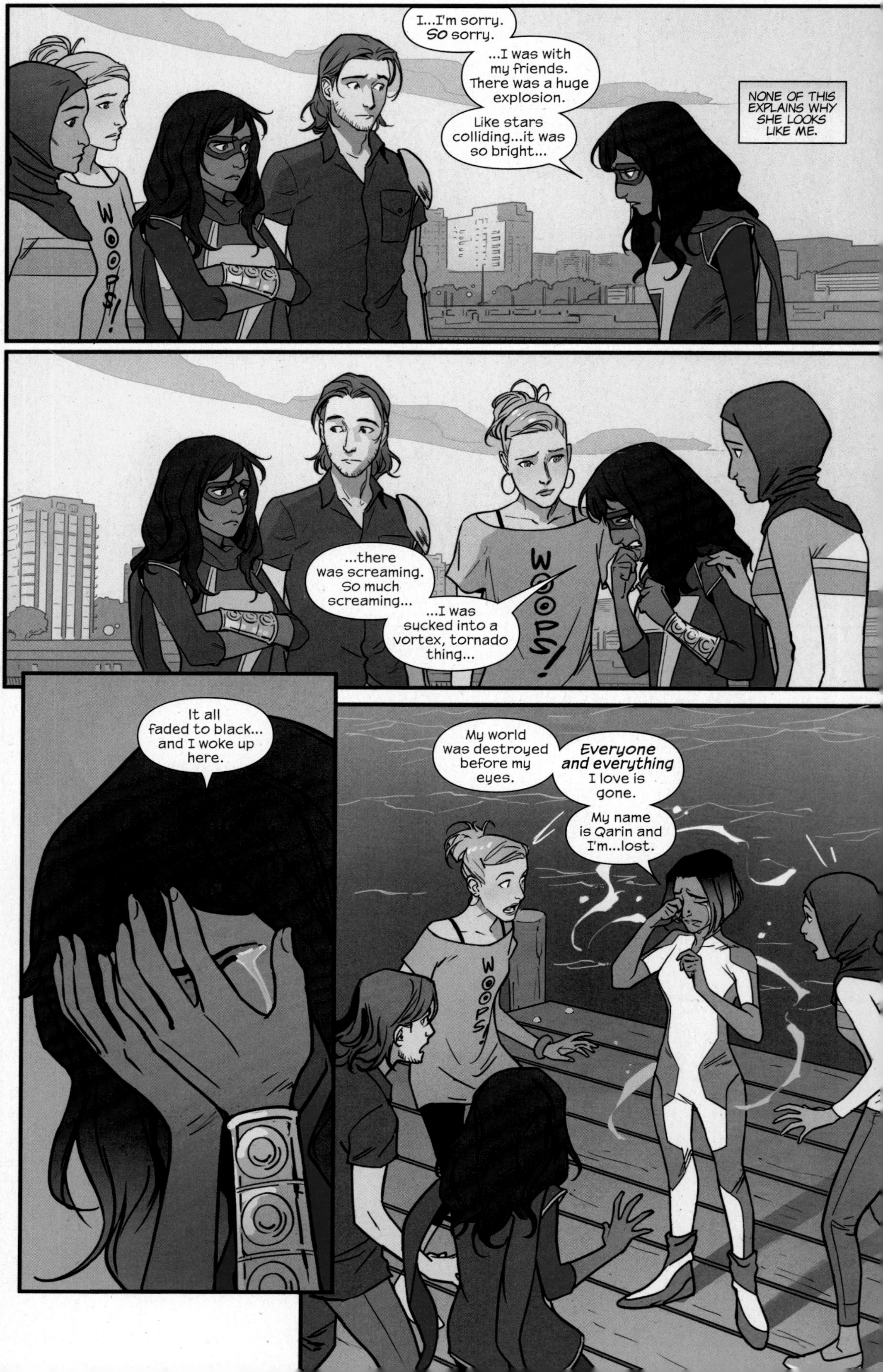

I...I'm sorry. *SO* sorry.
...I was with my friends. There was a huge explosion.
Like stars colliding...it was so bright...
NONE OF THIS EXPLAINS WHY SHE LOOKS LIKE ME.
...there was screaming. So much screaming...
...I was sucked into a vortex, tornado thing...
WOOPS!
It all faded to black... and I woke up here.
My world was destroyed before my eyes.
Everyone and everything I love is gone.
My name is Qarin and I'm...lost.

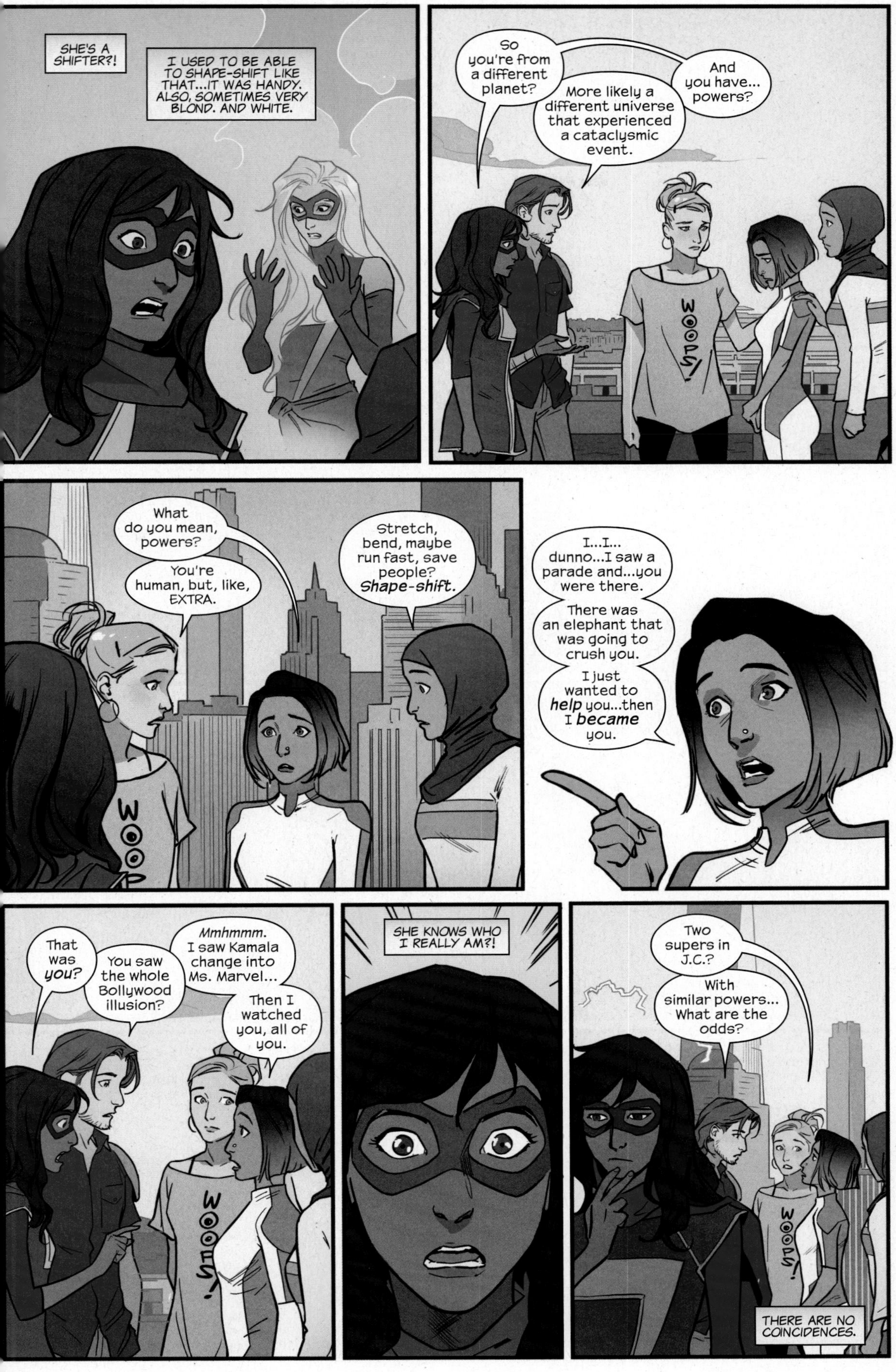

SHE'S A SHIFTER?!
I USED TO BE ABLE TO SHAPE-SHIFT LIKE THAT...IT WAS HANDY. ALSO, SOMETIMES VERY BLOND. AND WHITE.
So you're from a different planet?
And you have... powers?
More likely a different universe that experienced a cataclysmic event.
WOOPS!
What do you mean, powers?
You're human, but, like, EXTRA.
Stretch, bend, maybe run fast, save people? *Shape-shift.*
I...I... dunno...I saw a parade and...you were there.
There was an elephant that was going to crush you.
I just wanted to *help* you...then I *became* you.
That was *you?*
You saw the whole Bollywood illusion?
Mmhmmm. I saw Kamala change into Ms. Marvel...
Then I watched you, all of you.
WOOPS!
SHE KNOWS WHO I REALLY AM?!
Two supers in J.C.?
With similar powers... What are the odds?
WOOPS!
THERE ARE NO COINCIDENCES.

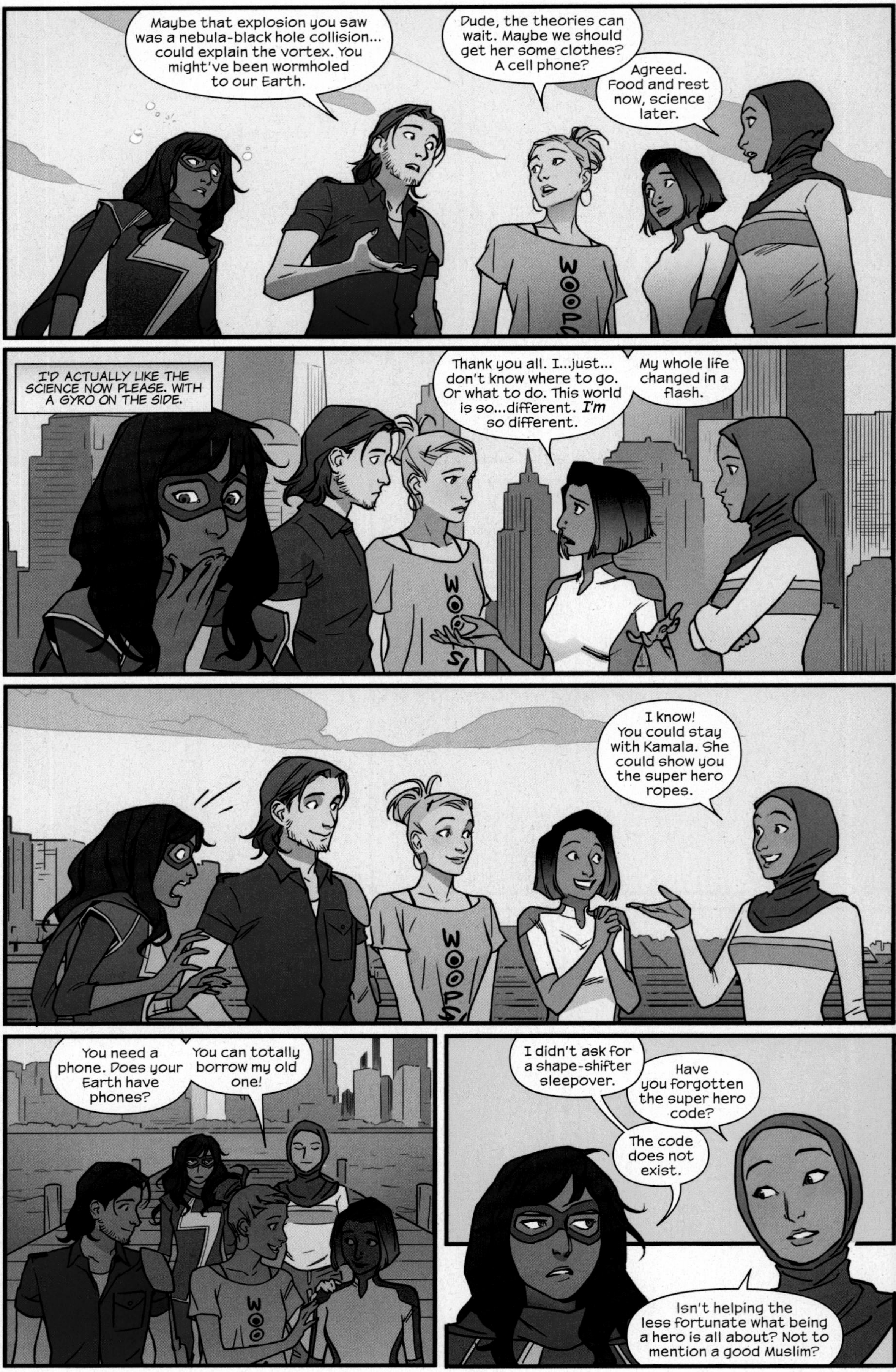
Maybe that explosion you saw was a nebula-black hole collision... could explain the vortex. You might've been wormholed to our Earth.
Dude, the theories can wait. Maybe we should get her some clothes? A cell phone?
Agreed. Food and rest now, science later.
I'D ACTUALLY LIKE THE SCIENCE NOW PLEASE. WITH A GYRO ON THE SIDE.
Thank you all. I...just... don't know where to go. Or what to do. This world is so...different. *I'm* so different.
My whole life changed in a flash.
I know! You could stay with Kamala. She could show you the super hero ropes.
WOOPS
You need a phone. Does your Earth have phones?
You can totally borrow my old one!
I didn't ask for a shape-shifter sleepover.
Have you forgotten the super hero code?
The code does not exist.
Isn't helping the less fortunate what being a hero is all about? Not to mention a good Muslim?

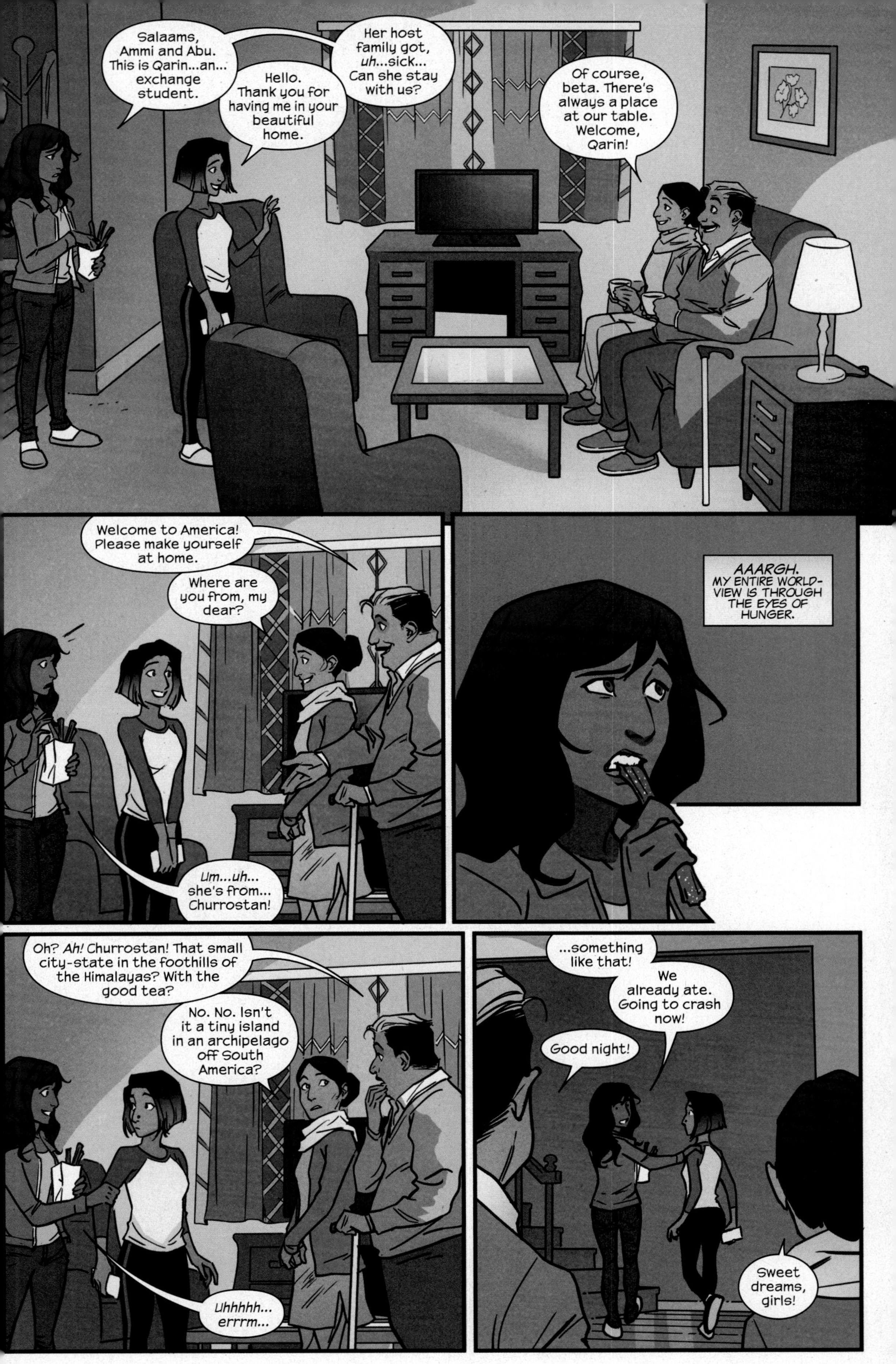
Salaams, Ammi and Abu. This is Qarin...an... exchange student.
Her host family got, *uh*...sick... Can she stay with us?
Hello. Thank you for having me in your beautiful home.
Of course, beta. There's always a place at our table. Welcome, Qarin!
Welcome to America! Please make yourself at home.
Where are you from, my dear?
Um...uh... she's from... Churrostan!
AAARGH. MY ENTIRE WORLD-VIEW IS THROUGH THE EYES OF HUNGER.
Oh? *Ah!* Churrostan! That small city-state in the foothills of the Himalayas? With the good tea?
No. No. Isn't it a tiny island in an archipelago off South America?
Uhhhhh... errrm...
...something like that!
We already ate. Going to crash now!
Good night!
Sweet dreams, girls!

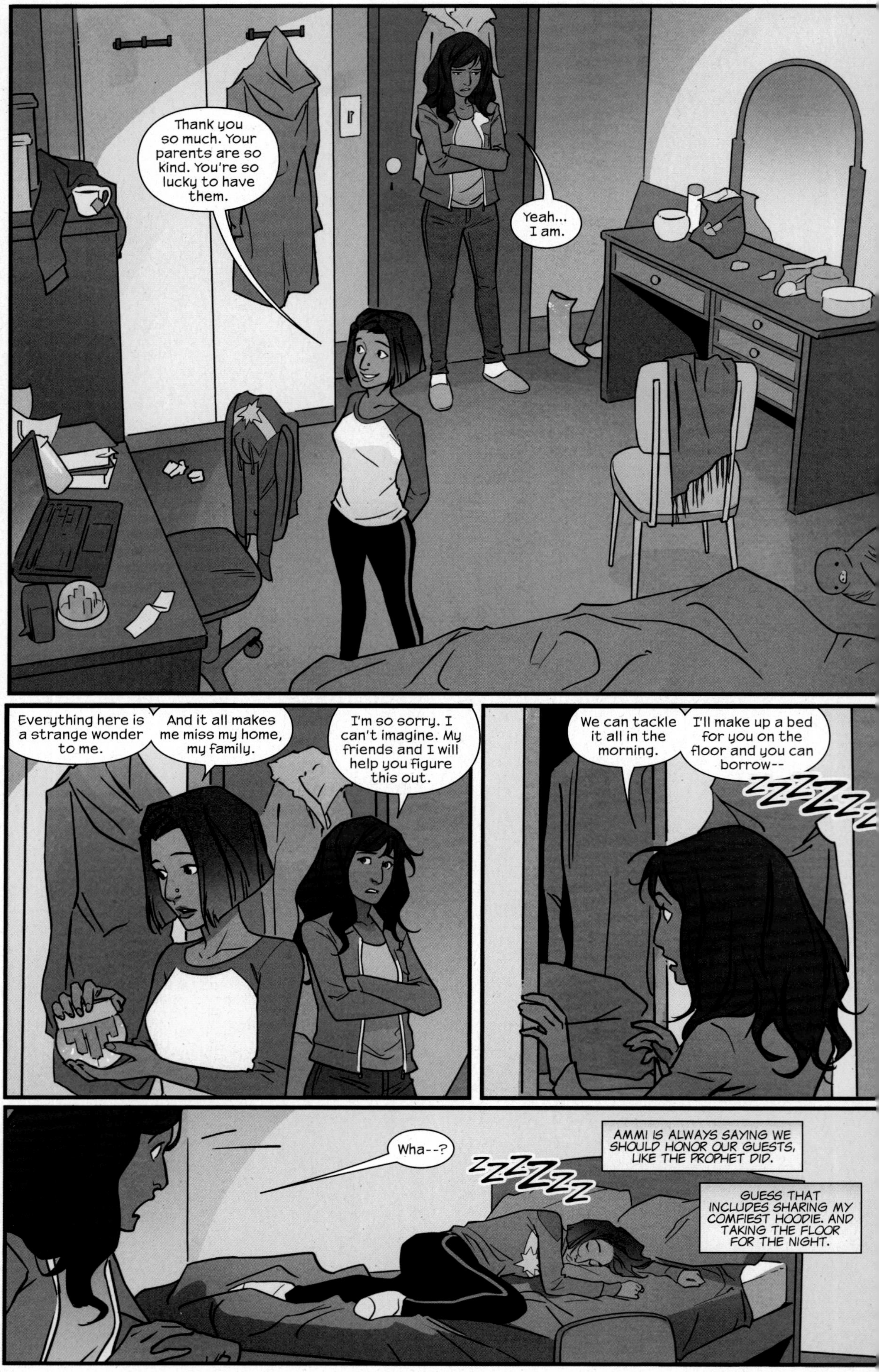

Thank you so much. Your parents are so kind. You're so lucky to have them.
Yeah... I am.
Everything here is a strange wonder to me.
And it all makes me miss my home, my family.
I'm so sorry. I can't imagine. My friends and I will help you figure this out.
We can tackle it all in the morning.
I'll make up a bed for you on the floor and you can borrow--
ZZZZZZ
Wha--?
ZZZZZZ
AMMI IS ALWAYS SAYING WE SHOULD HONOR OUR GUESTS, LIKE THE PROPHET DID.
GUESS THAT INCLUDES SHARING MY COMFIEST HOODIE. AND TAKING THE FLOOR FOR THE NIGHT.

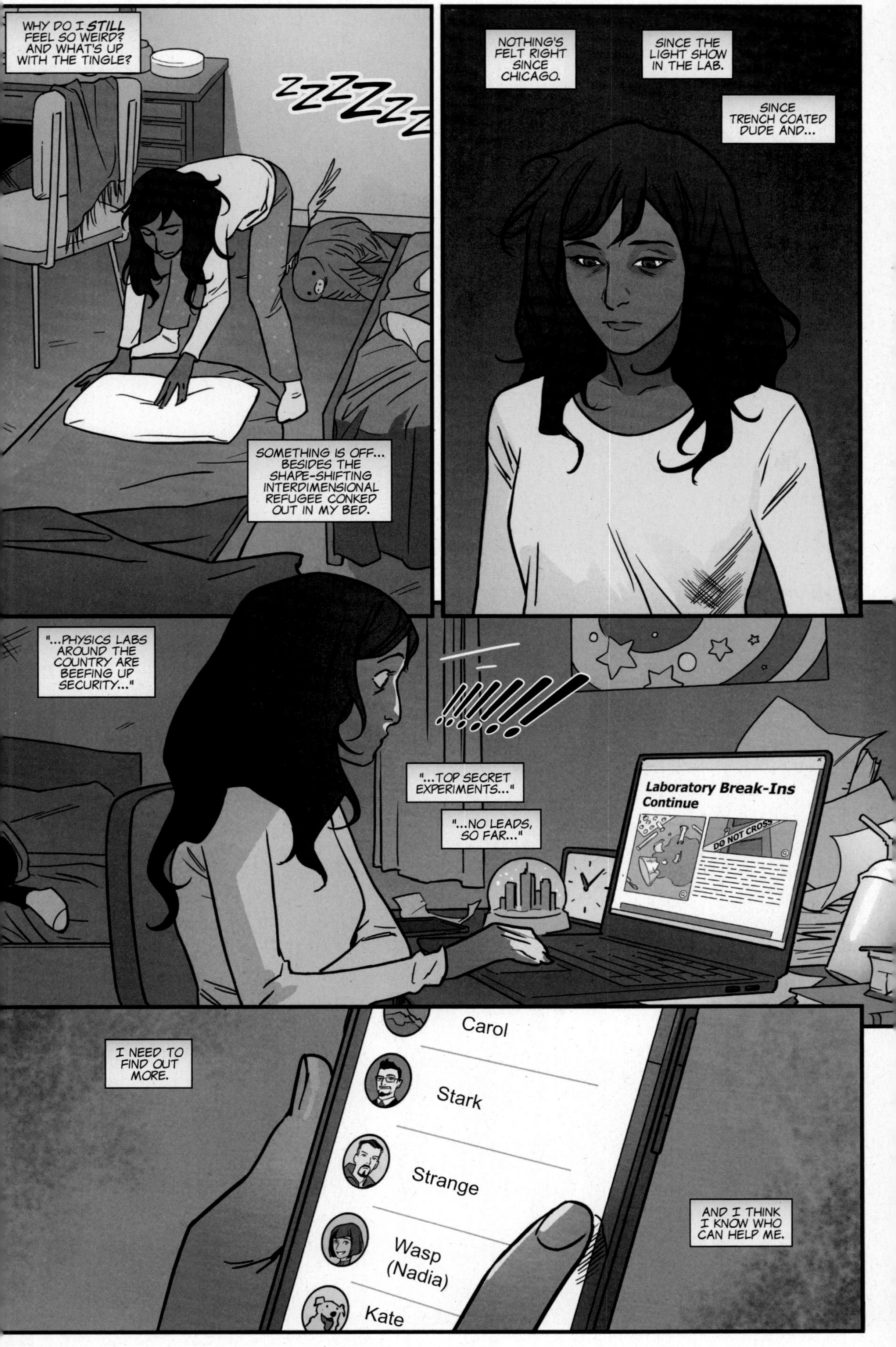
WHY DO I STILL FEEL SO WEIRD? AND WHAT'S UP WITH THE TINGLE?
ZZZZZZZ
SOMETHING IS OFF... BESIDES THE SHAPE-SHIFTING INTERDIMENSIONAL REFUGEE CONKED OUT IN MY BED.
NOTHING'S FELT RIGHT SINCE CHICAGO.
SINCE THE LIGHT SHOW IN THE LAB.
SINCE TRENCH COATED DUDE AND...
"...PHYSICS LABS AROUND THE COUNTRY ARE BEEFING UP SECURITY..."
!!!!!!
"...TOP SECRET EXPERIMENTS..."
"...NO LEADS, SO FAR..."
Laboratory Break-Ins Continue
DO NOT CROSS
I NEED TO FIND OUT MORE.
Carol
Stark
Strange
Wasp (Nadia)
Kate
AND I THINK I KNOW WHO CAN HELP ME.

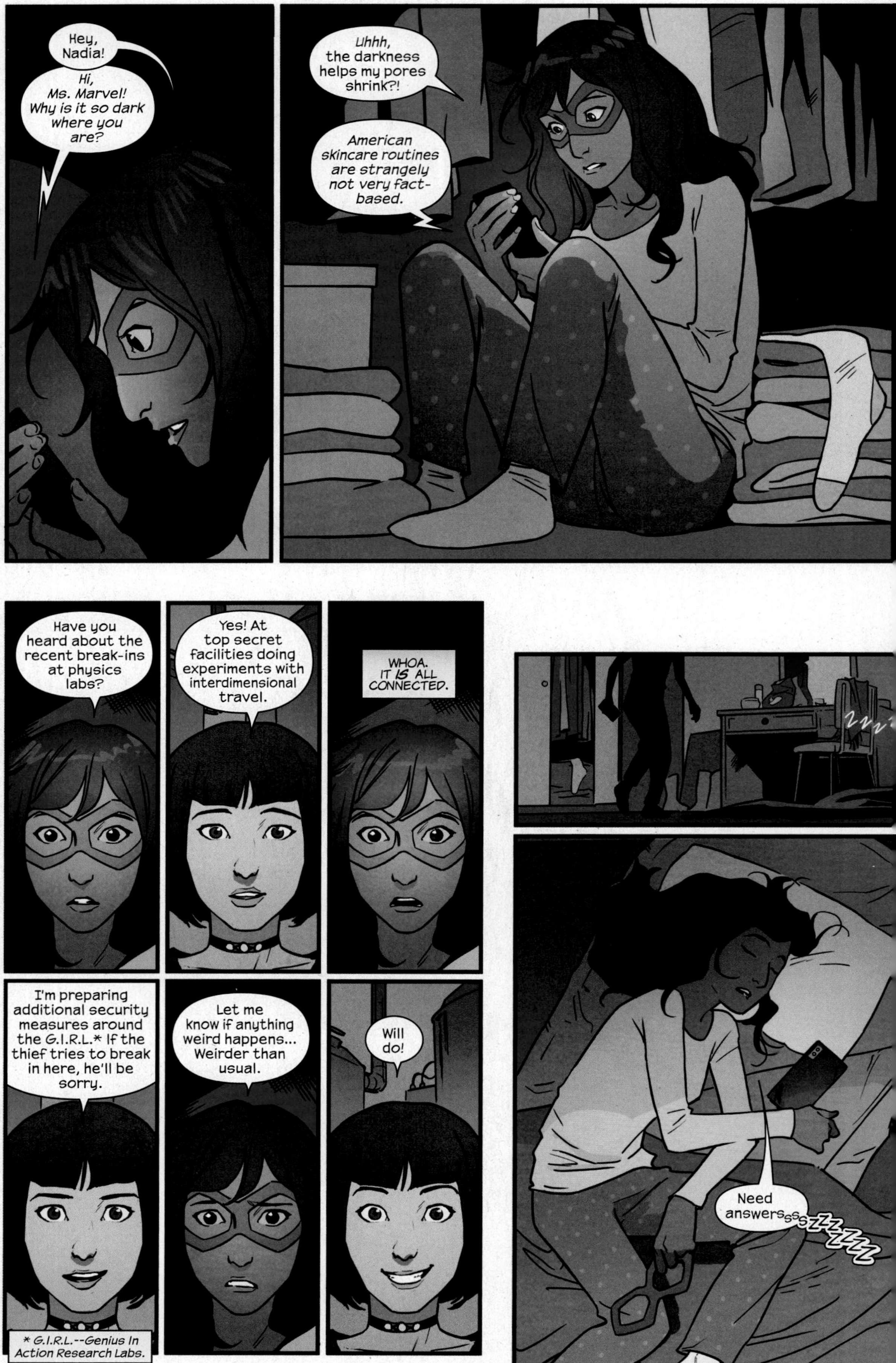
Hey, Nadia!
Hi, Ms. Marvel! Why is it so dark where you are?
Uhhh, the darkness helps my pores shrink?!
American skincare routines are strangely not very fact-based.
Have you heard about the recent break-ins at physics labs?
Yes! At top secret facilities doing experiments with interdimensional travel.
WHOA. IT IS ALL CONNECTED.
I'm preparing additional security measures around the G.I.R.L.* If the thief tries to break in here, he'll be sorry.
Let me know if anything weird happens... Weirder than usual.
Will do!
* G.I.R.L.--Genius In Action Research Labs.
ZZZ
Need answerssssZZZZZZ

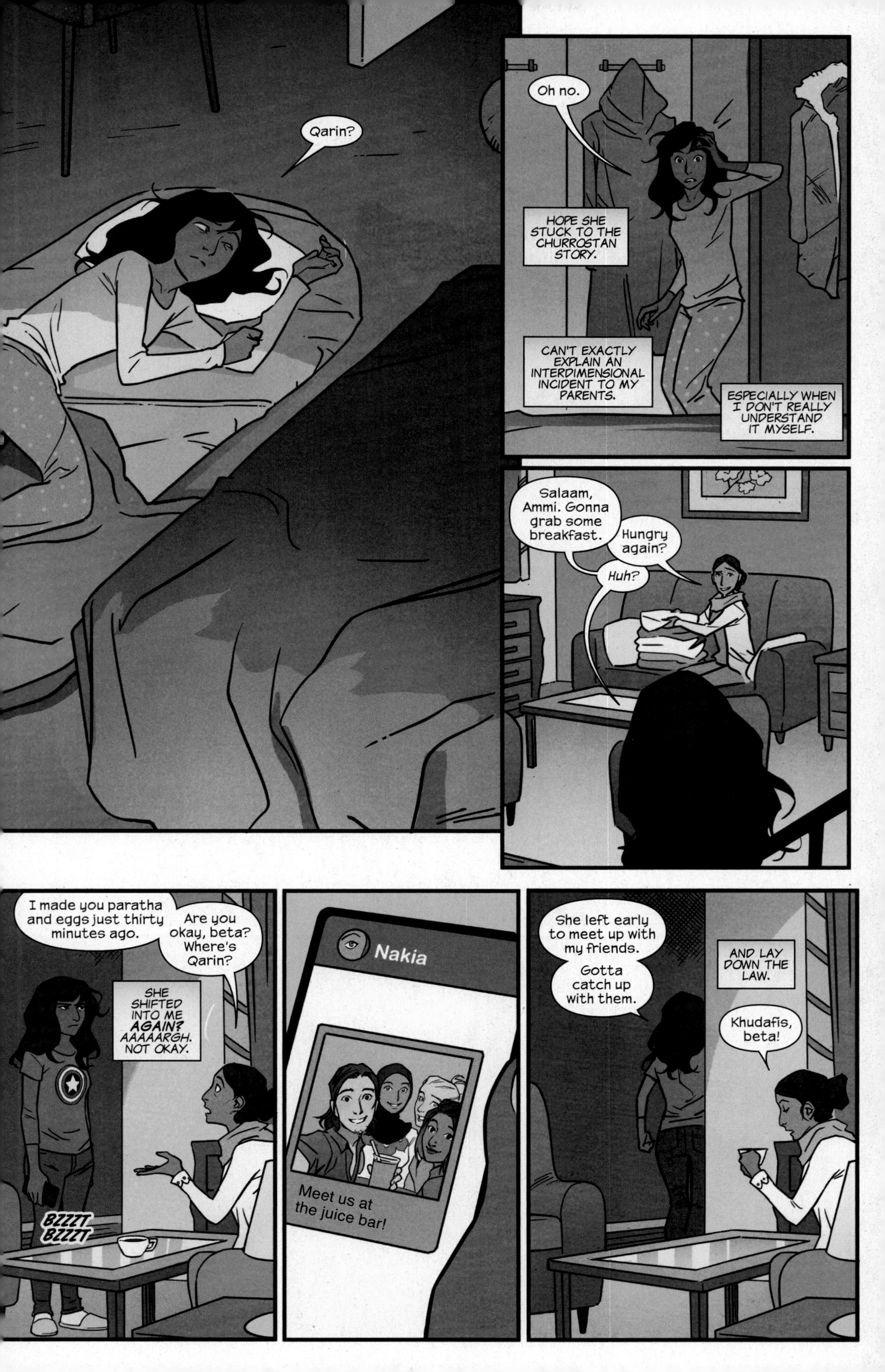
Qarin?
Oh no.
HOPE SHE STUCK TO THE CHURROSTAN STORY.
CAN'T EXACTLY EXPLAIN AN INTERDIMENSIONAL INCIDENT TO MY PARENTS.
ESPECIALLY WHEN I DON'T REALLY UNDERSTAND IT MYSELF.
Salaam, Ammi. Gonna grab some breakfast.
Hungry again?
Huh?
I made you paratha and eggs just thirty minutes ago.
Are you okay, beta? Where's Qarin?
SHE SHIFTED INTO ME AGAIN? AAAAARGH. NOT OKAY.
BZZZT BZZZT
Nakia
Meet us at the juice bar!
She left early to meet up with my friends.
Gotta catch up with them.
AND LAY DOWN THE LAW.
Khudafis, beta!

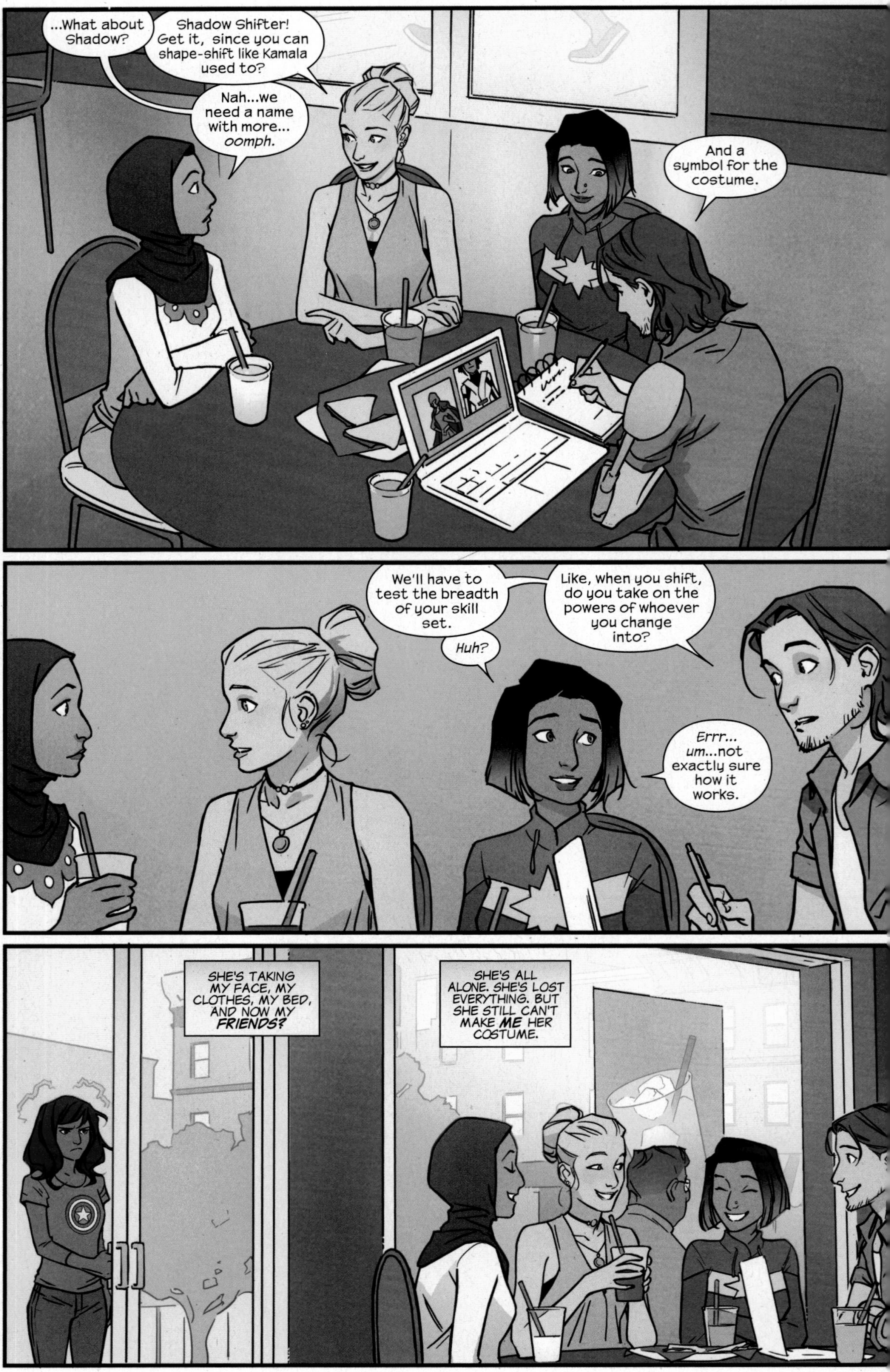

...What about Shadow?
Shadow Shifter! Get it, since you can shape-shift like Kamala used to?
Nah...we need a name with more... *oomph.*
And a symbol for the costume.
We'll have to test the breadth of your skill set.
Like, when you shift, do you take on the powers of whoever you change into?
Huh?
*Errr... um...*not exactly sure how it works.
SHE'S TAKING MY FACE, MY CLOTHES, MY BED, AND NOW MY *FRIENDS?*
SHE'S ALL ALONE. SHE'S LOST EVERYTHING. BUT SHE STILL CAN'T MAKE *ME* HER COSTUME.

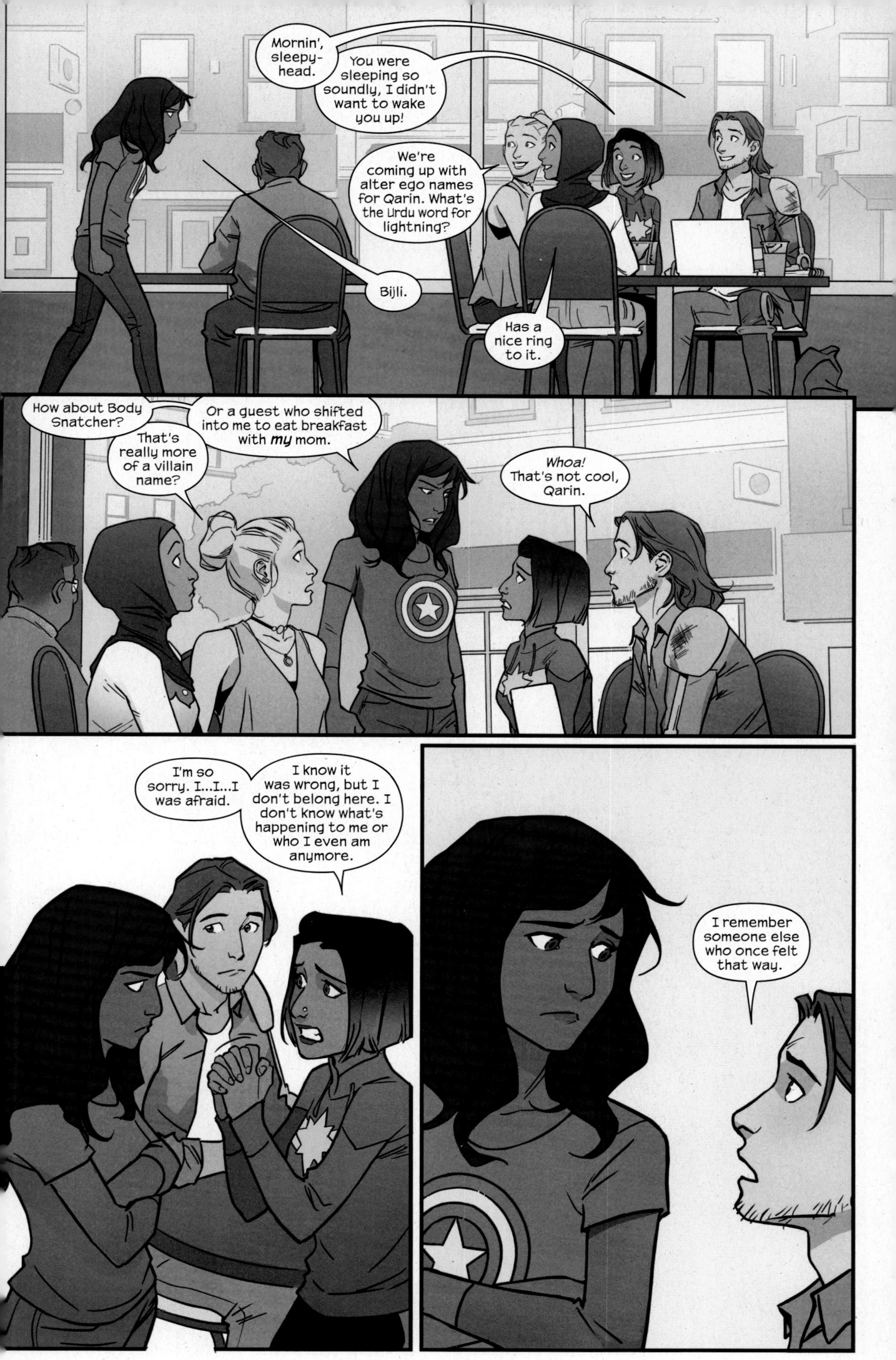
Mornin', sleepy-head.
You were sleeping so soundly, I didn't want to wake you up!
We're coming up with alter ego names for Qarin. What's the Urdu word for lightning?
Bijli.
Has a nice ring to it.
How about Body Snatcher?
That's really more of a villain name?
Or a guest who shifted into me to eat breakfast with *my* mom.
Whoa! That's not cool, Qarin.
I'm so sorry. I...I...I was afraid.
I know it was wrong, but I don't belong here. I don't know what's happening to me or who I even am anymore.
I remember someone else who once felt that way.

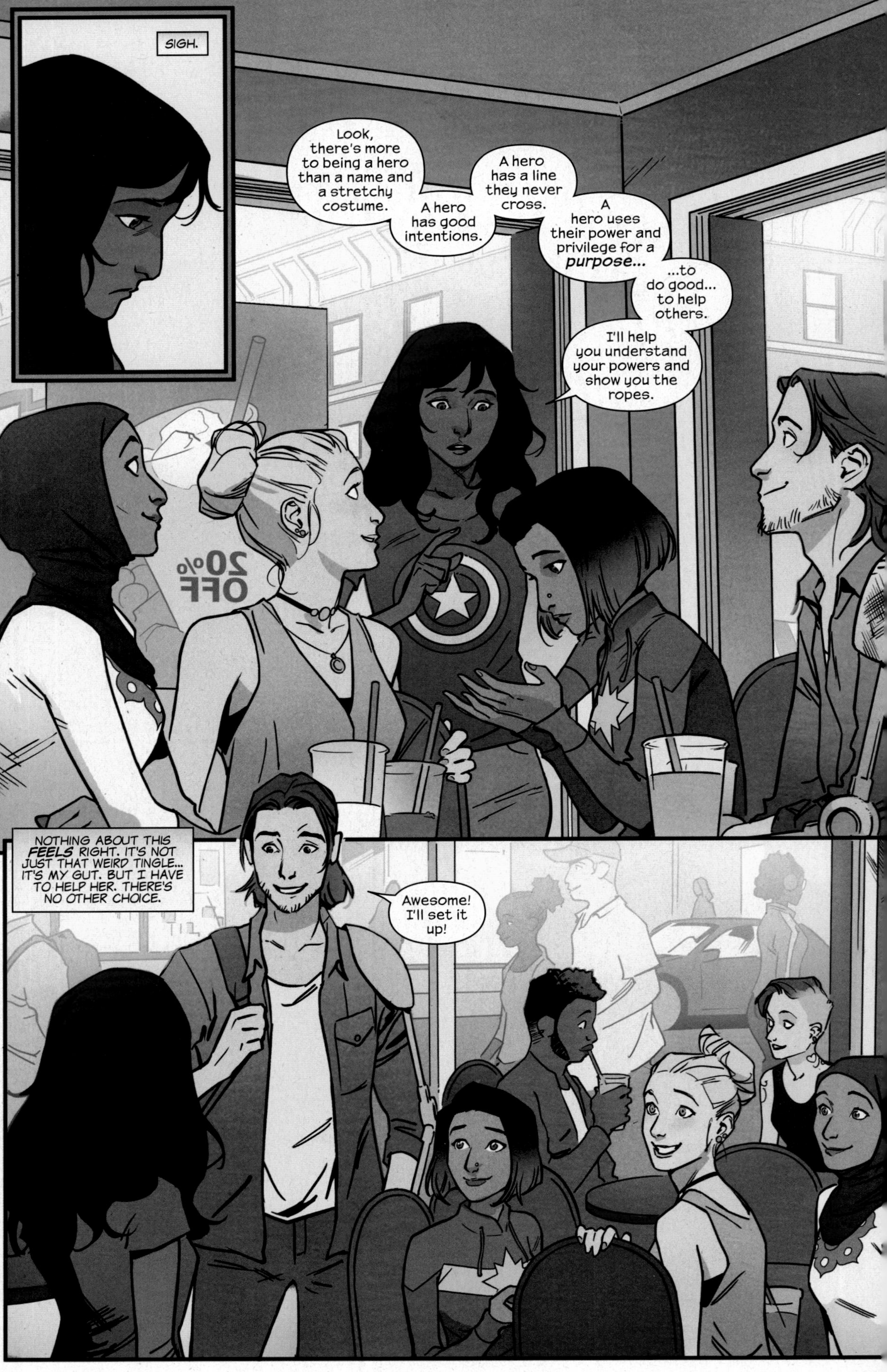
SIGH.
Look, there's more to being a hero than a name and a stretchy costume.
A hero has good intentions.
A hero has a line they never cross.
A hero uses their power and privilege for a *purpose...*
...to do good... to help others.
I'll help you understand your powers and show you the ropes.
20% OFF
NOTHING ABOUT THIS *FEELS* RIGHT. IT'S NOT JUST THAT WEIRD TINGLE... IT'S MY GUT. BUT I HAVE TO HELP HER. THERE'S NO OTHER CHOICE.
Awesome! I'll set it up!

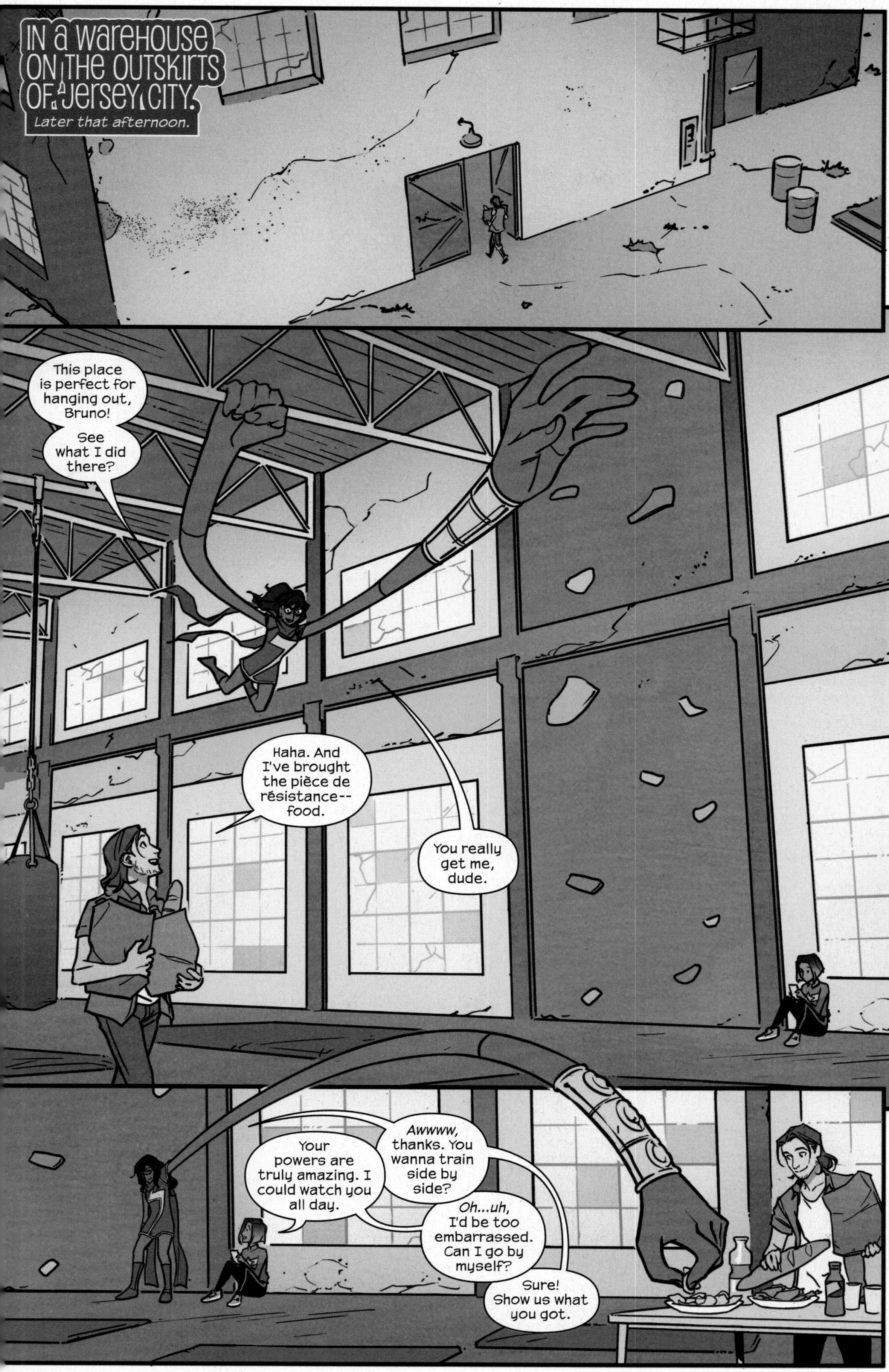
IN A WAREHOUSE ON THE OUTSKIRTS OF JERSEY CITY.
Later that afternoon.
This place is perfect for hanging out, Bruno!
See what I did there?
Haha. And I've brought the pièce de résistance-- food.
You really get me, dude.
Your powers are truly amazing. I could watch you all day.
Awwww, thanks. You wanna train side by side?
Oh...uh, I'd be too embarrassed. Can I go by myself?
Sure! Show us what you got.

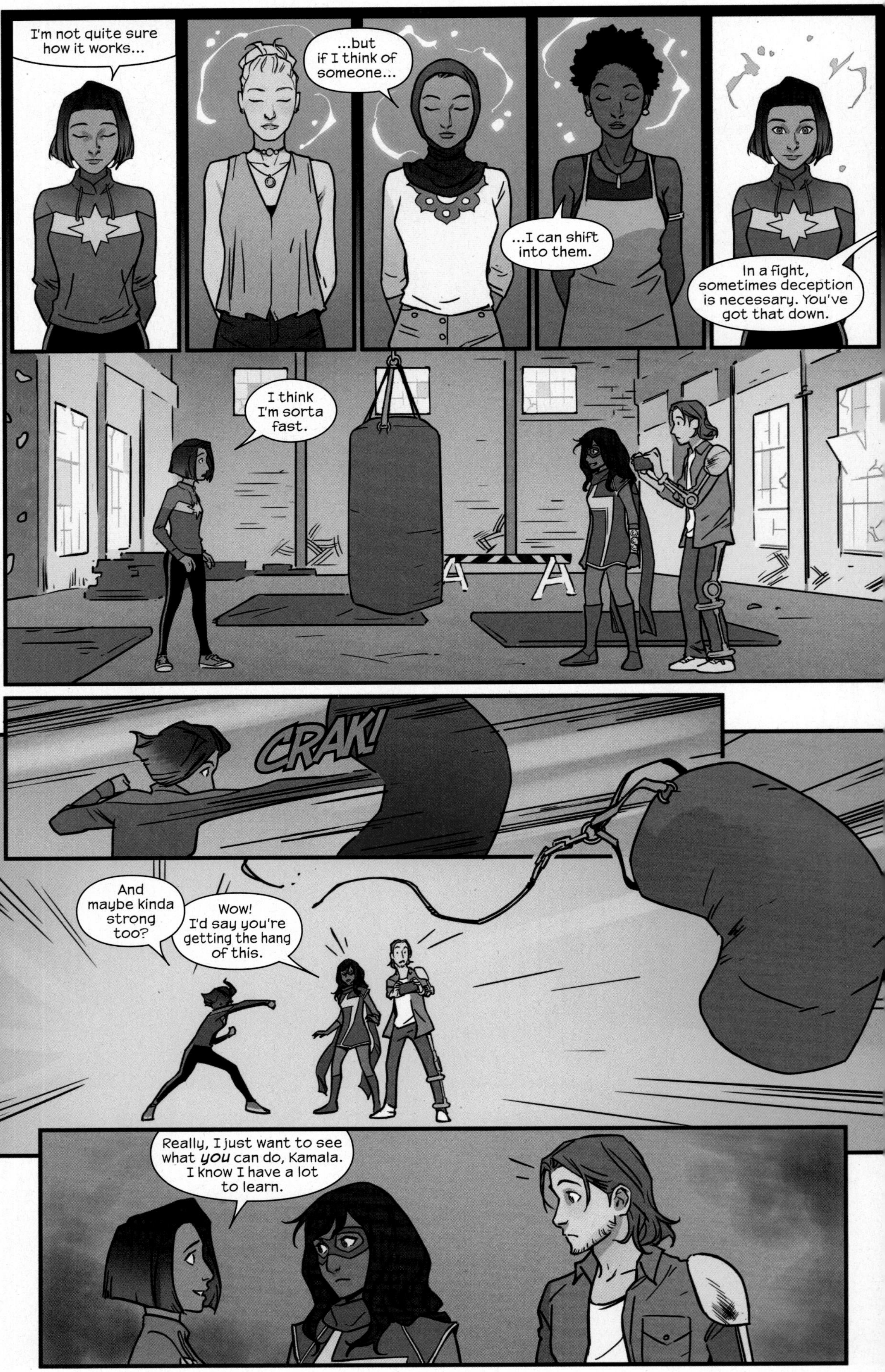
I'm not quite sure how it works...
...but if I think of someone...
...I can shift into them.
In a fight, sometimes deception is necessary. You've got that down.
I think I'm sorta fast.
CRAK!
And maybe kinda strong too?
Wow! I'd say you're getting the hang of this.
Really, I just want to see what *you* can do, Kamala. I know I have a lot to learn.

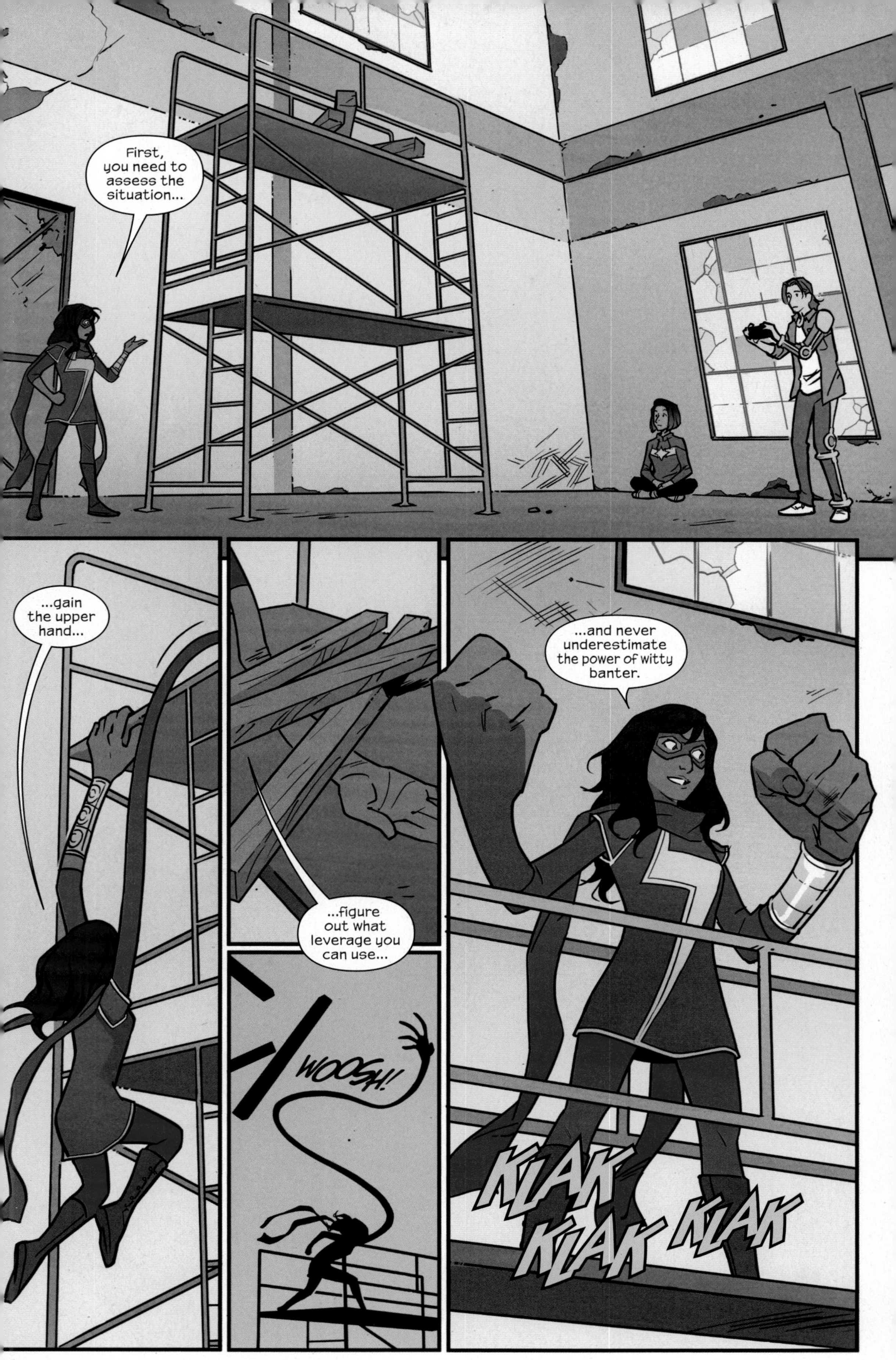
First, you need to assess the situation...
...gain the upper hand...
...figure out what leverage you can use...
WOOSH!
...and never underestimate the power of witty banter.
KLAK KLAK KLAK KLAK

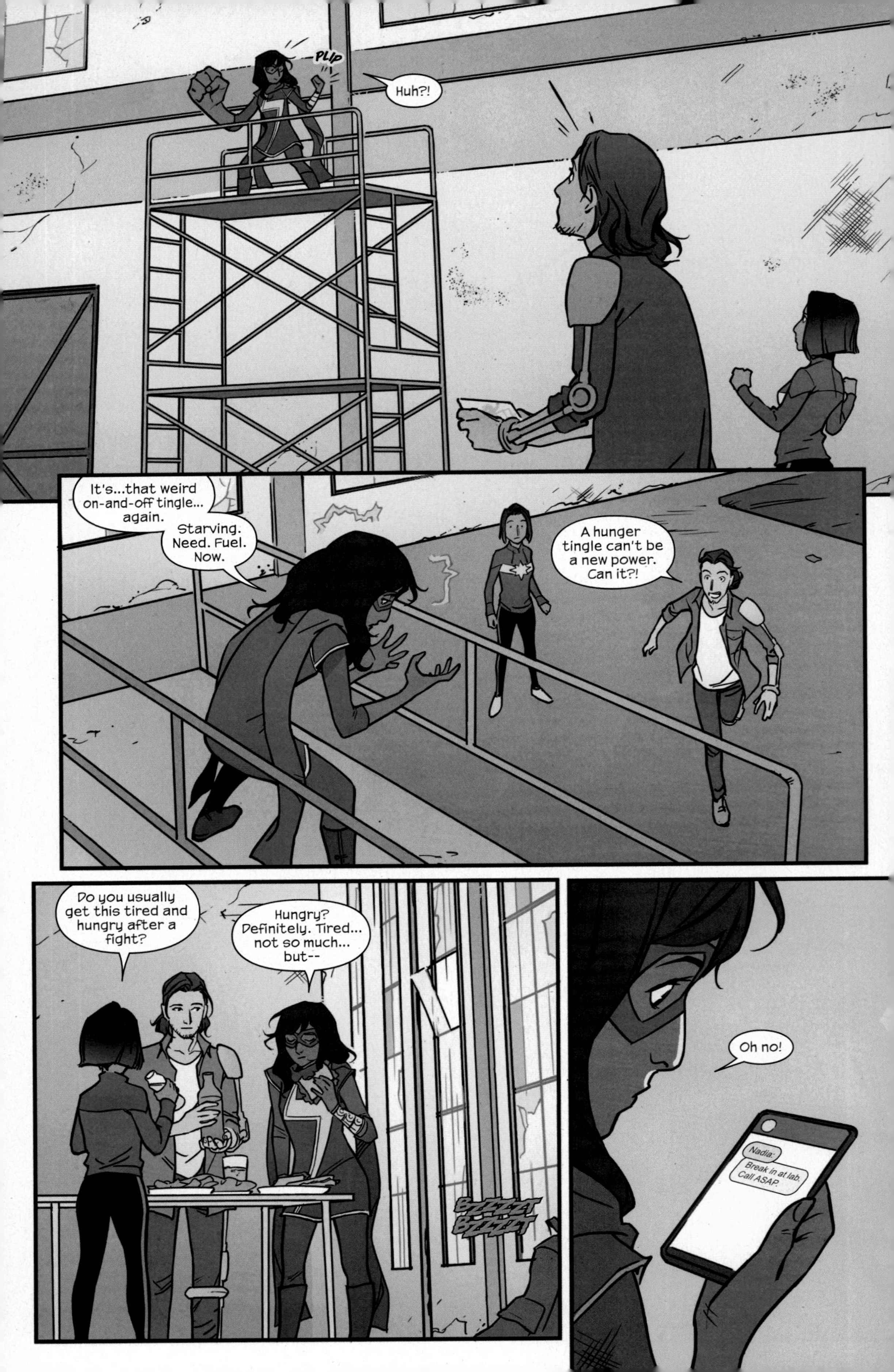
PLIP
Huh?!
It's...that weird on-and-off tingle... again.
Starving. Need. Fuel. Now.
A hunger tingle can't be a new power. Can it?!
Do you usually get this tired and hungry after a fight?
Hungry? Definitely. Tired... not so much... but--
BZZZZT BZZZZT
Oh no!
Nadia:
Break in at lab. Call ASAP.

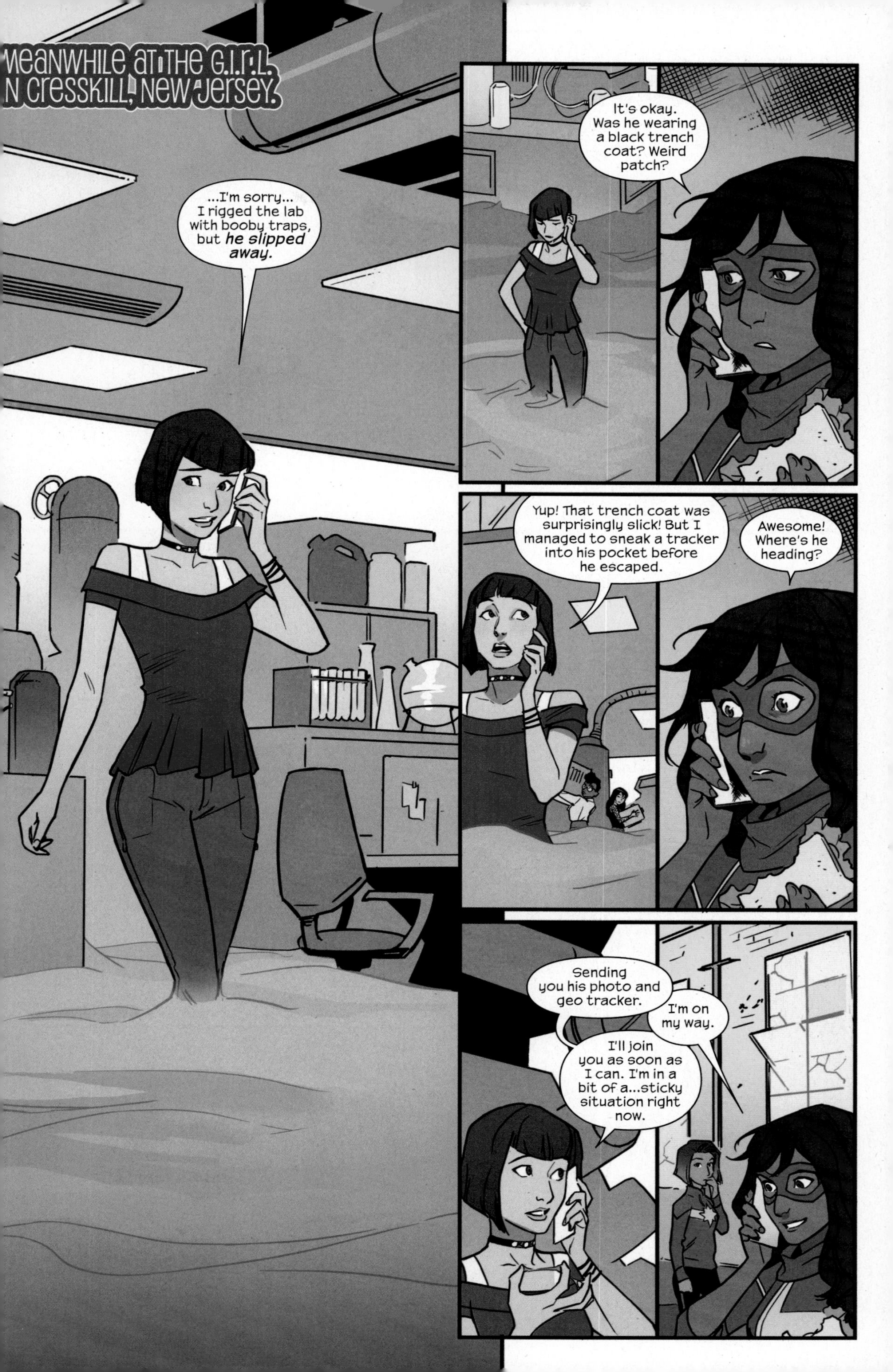
MEANWHILE AT THE G.I.R.L. IN CRESSKILL, NEW JERSEY.
...I'm sorry... I rigged the lab with booby traps, but *he slipped away.*
It's okay. Was he wearing a black trench coat? Weird patch?
Yup! That trench coat was surprisingly slick! But I managed to sneak a tracker into his pocket before he escaped.
Awesome! Where's he heading?
Sending you his photo and geo tracker.
I'm on my way.
I'll join you as soon as I can. I'm in a bit of a...sticky situation right now.

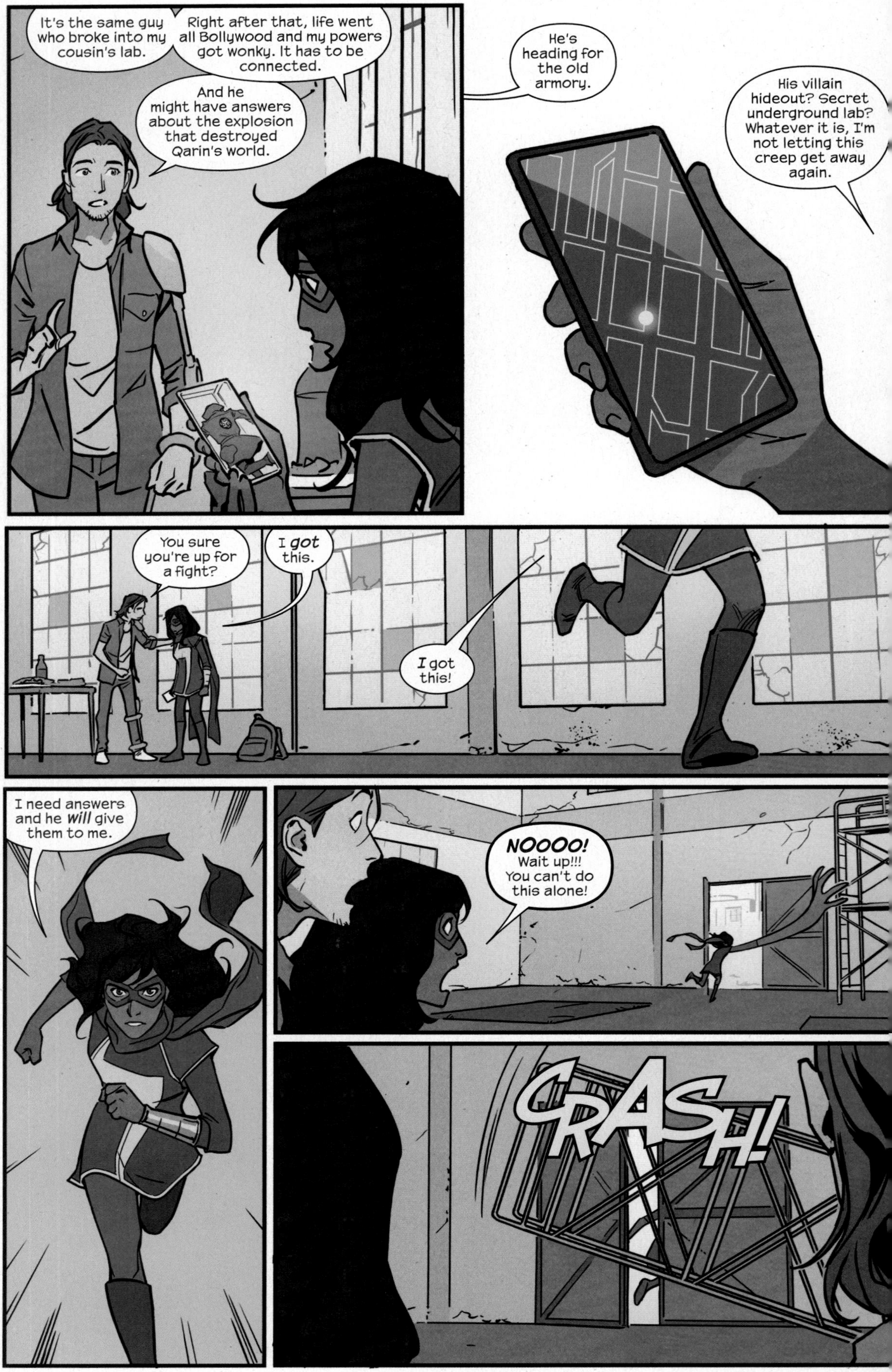
It's the same guy who broke into my cousin's lab.
Right after that, life went all Bollywood and my powers got wonky. It has to be connected.
And he might have answers about the explosion that destroyed Qarin's world.
He's heading for the old armory.
His villain hideout? Secret underground lab? Whatever it is, I'm not letting this creep get away again.
You sure you're up for a fight?
I got this.
I got this!
I need answers and he will give them to me.
NOOOO! Wait up!!! You can't do this alone!
CRASH!

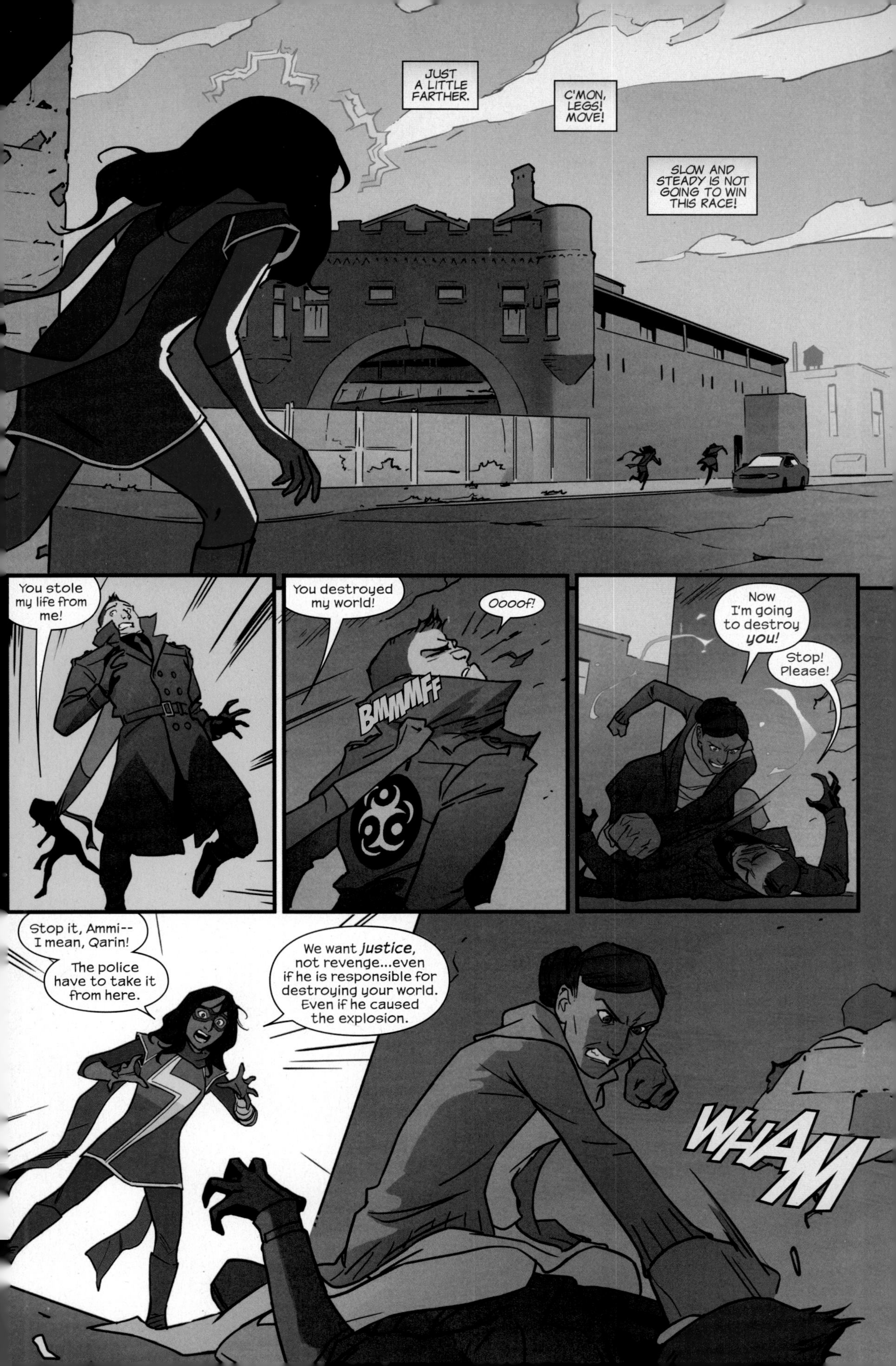

JUST A LITTLE FARTHER.
C'MON, LEGS! MOVE!
SLOW AND STEADY IS NOT GOING TO WIN THIS RACE!
You stole my life from me!
You destroyed my world!
BMMMFF
Ooof!
Now I'm going to destroy *you!*
Stop! Please!
Stop it, Ammi-- I mean, Qarin!
The police have to take it from here.
We want *justice*, not revenge...even if he is responsible for destroying your world. Even if he caused the explosion.
WHAM

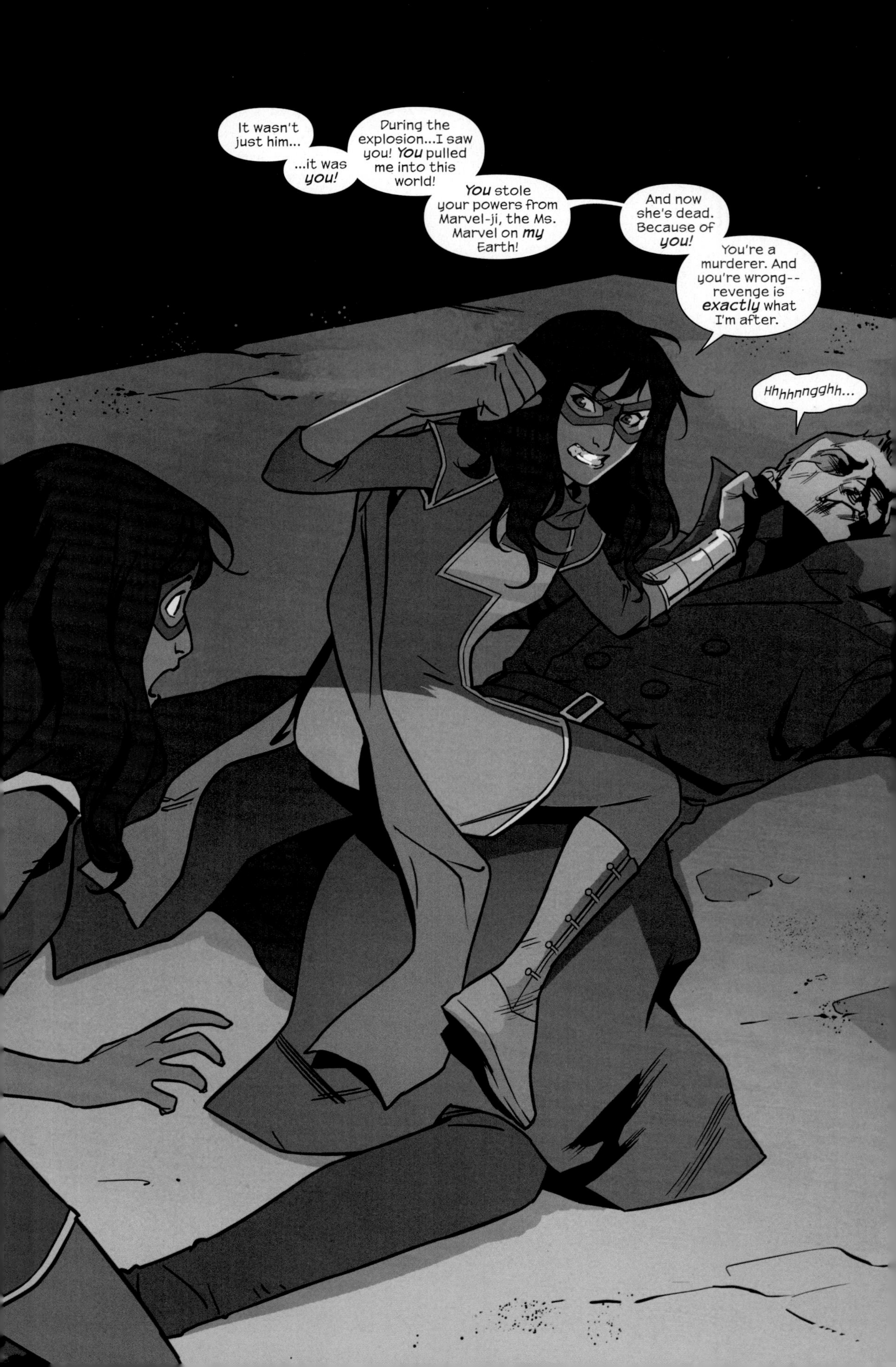

It wasn't just him...
...it was *you!*
During the explosion...I saw you! *You* pulled me into this world!
You stole your powers from Marvel-ji, the Ms. Marvel on *my* Earth!
And now she's dead. Because of *you!*
You're a murderer. And you're wrong--revenge is *exactly* what I'm after.
Hhhhnngghh...

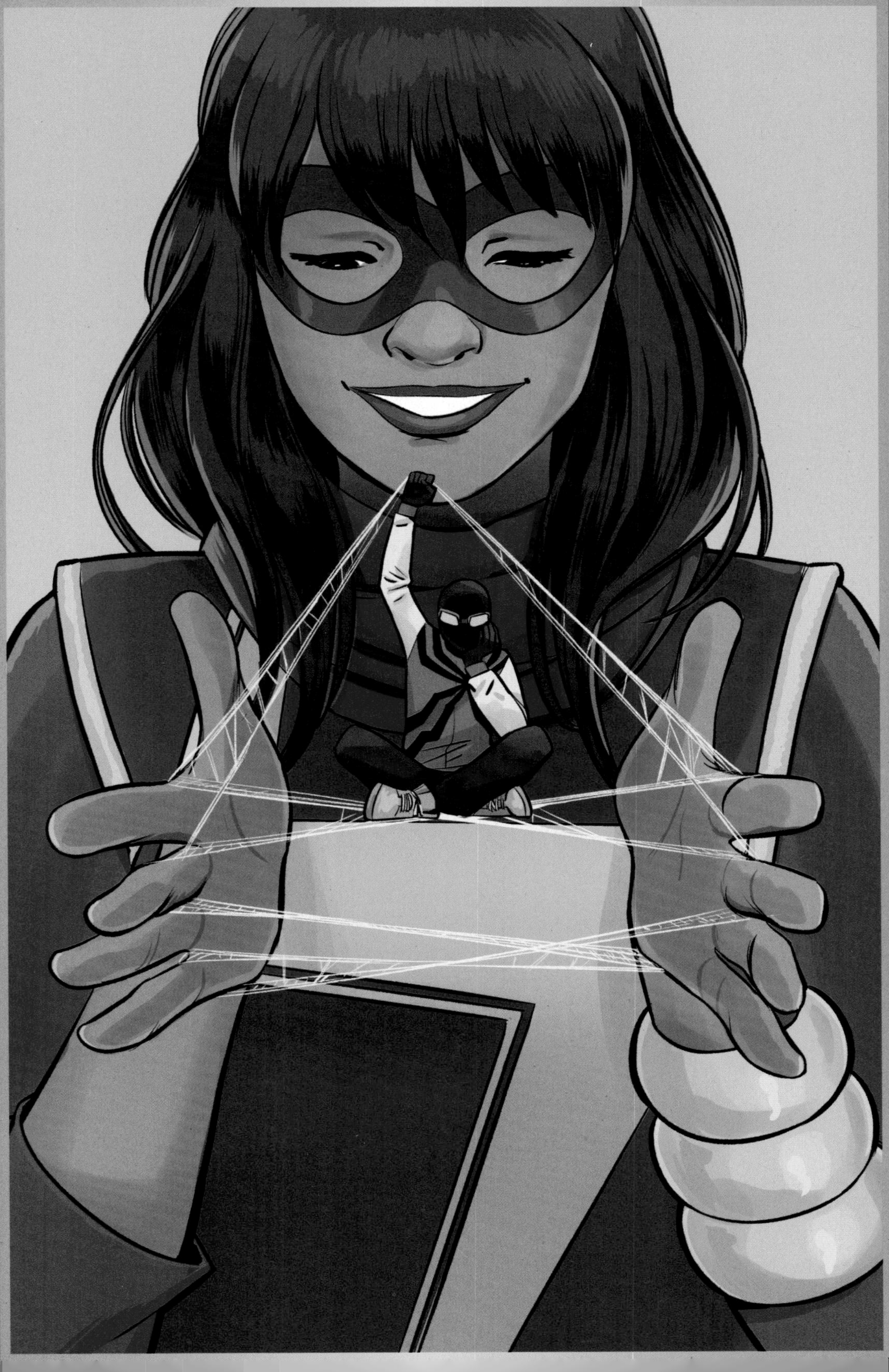

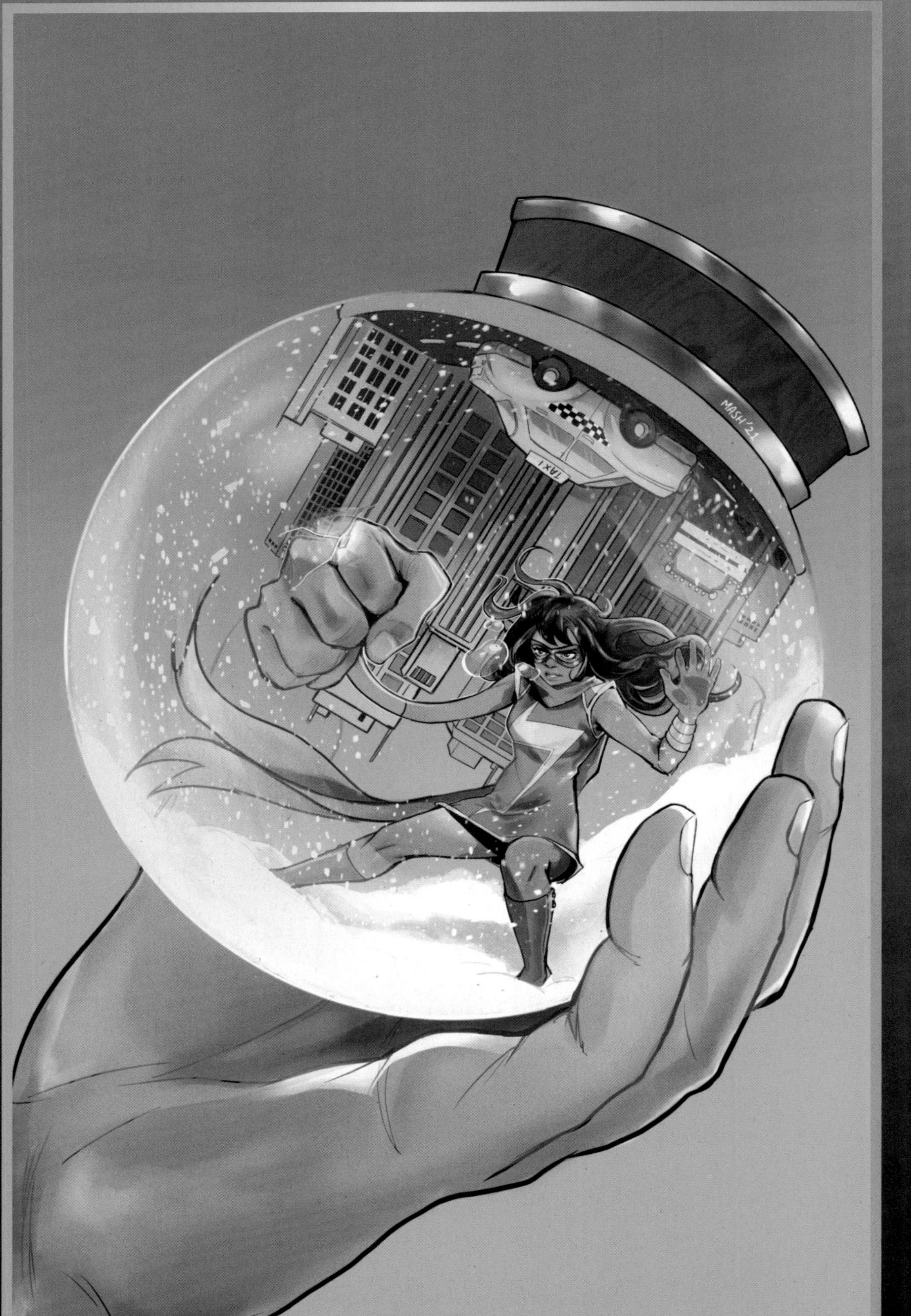
TAXI
MASH '21

4

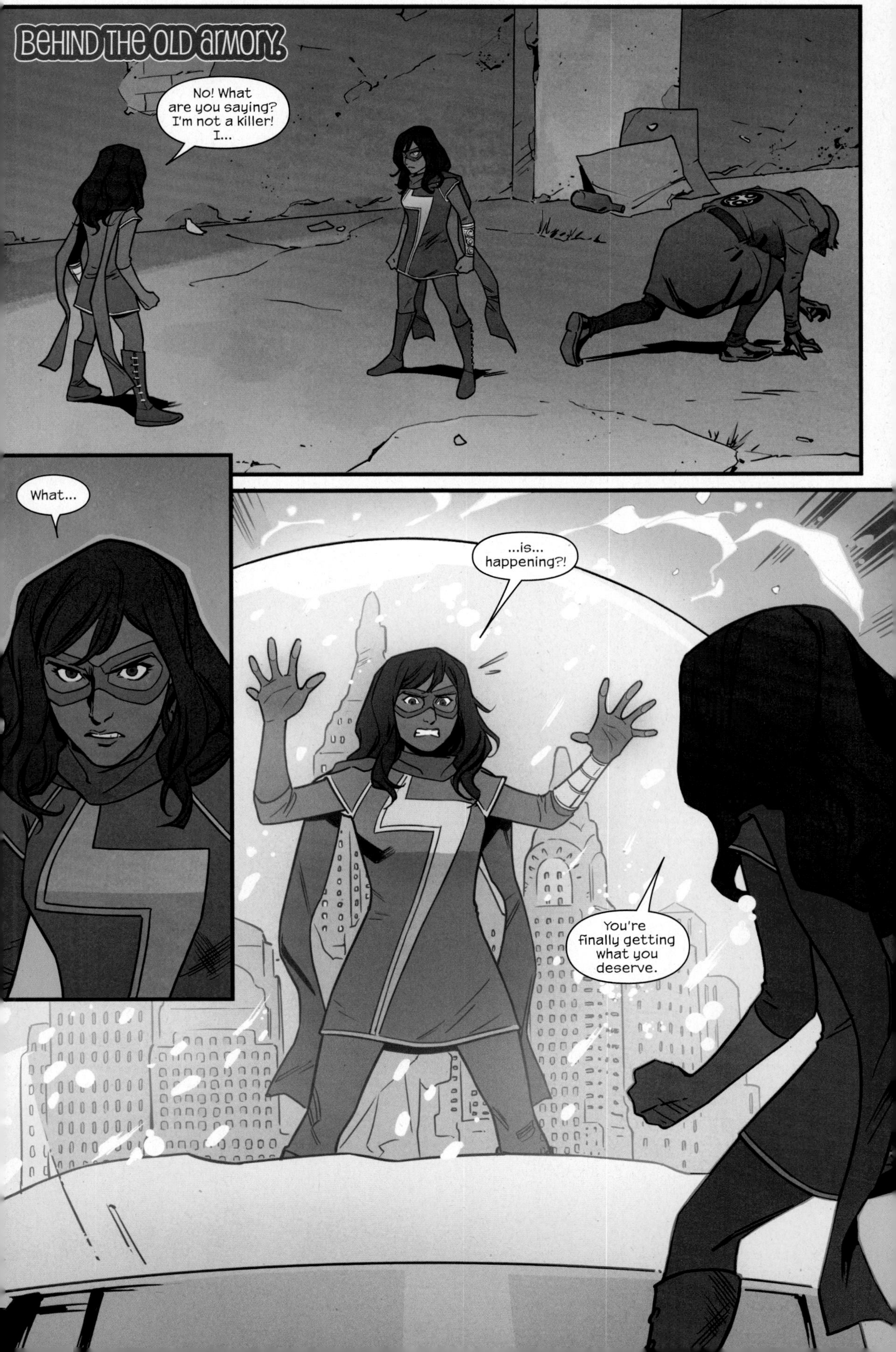

BEHIND THE OLD ARMORY.
No! What are you saying? I'm not a killer! I...
What...
...is... happening?!
You're finally getting what you deserve.

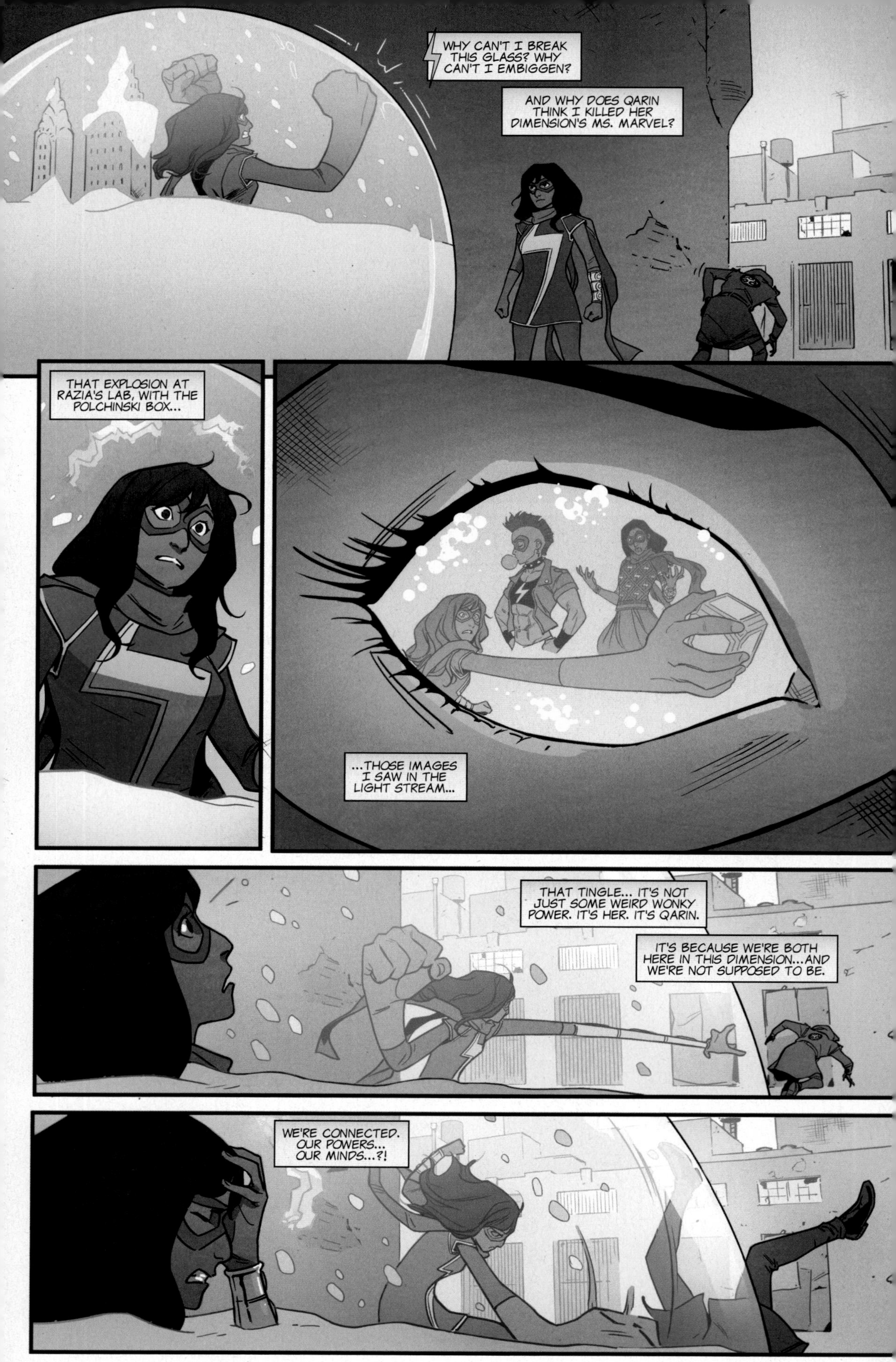
WHY CAN'T I BREAK THIS GLASS? WHY CAN'T I EMBIGGEN?
AND WHY DOES QARIN THINK I KILLED HER DIMENSION'S MS. MARVEL?
THAT EXPLOSION AT RAZIA'S LAB, WITH THE POLCHINSKI BOX...
...THOSE IMAGES I SAW IN THE LIGHT STREAM...
THAT TINGLE... IT'S NOT JUST SOME WEIRD WONKY POWER. IT'S HER. IT'S QARIN.
IT'S BECAUSE WE'RE BOTH HERE IN THIS DIMENSION...AND WE'RE NOT SUPPOSED TO BE.
WE'RE CONNECTED. OUR POWERS... OUR MINDS...?!

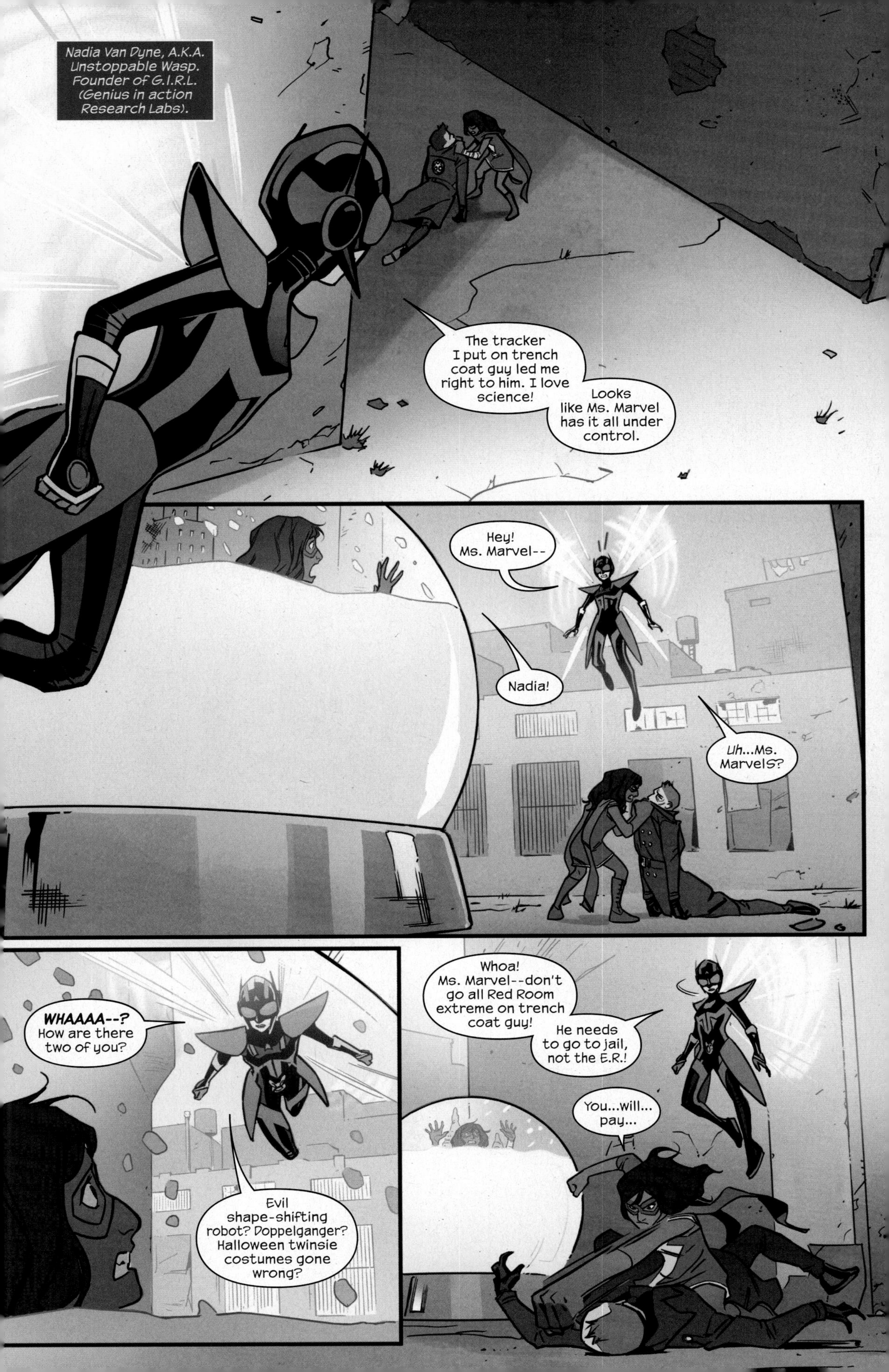
Nadia Van Dyne, A.K.A. Unstoppable Wasp. Founder of G.I.R.L. (Genius in action Research Labs).
The tracker I put on trench coat guy led me right to him. I love science!
Looks like Ms. Marvel has it all under control.
Hey! Ms. Marvel--
Nadia!
Uh...Ms. MarvelS?
WHAAAA--? How are there two of you?
Evil shape-shifting robot? Doppelganger? Halloween twinsie costumes gone wrong?
Whoa! Ms. Marvel--don't go all Red Room extreme on trench coat guy!
He needs to go to jail, not the E.R.!
You...will... pay...

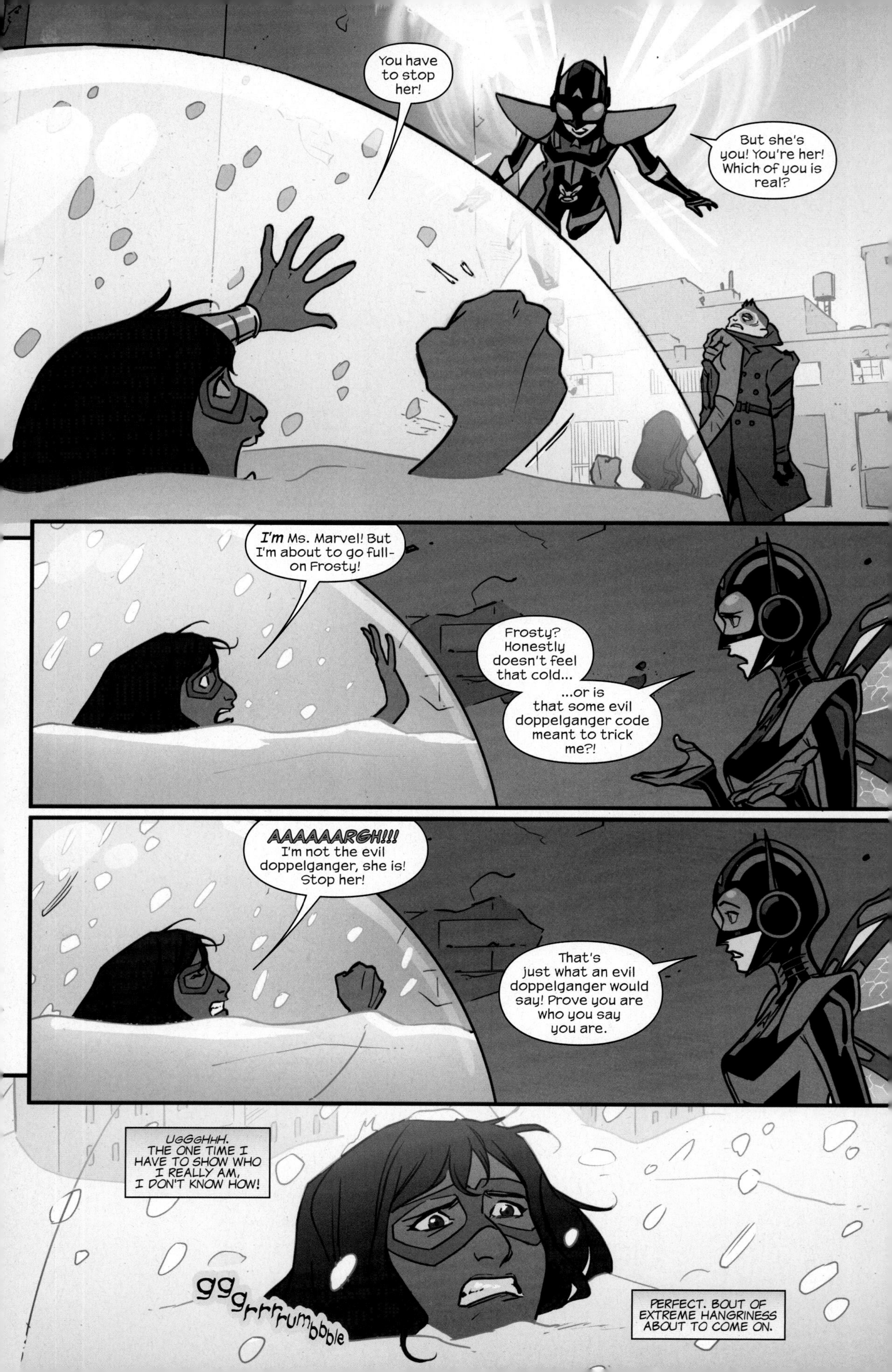
You have to stop her!
But she's you! You're her! Which of you is real?
I'm Ms. Marvel! But I'm about to go full-on Frosty!
Frosty? Honestly doesn't feel that cold...
...or is that some evil doppelganger code meant to trick me?!
AAAAAARGH!!! I'm not the evil doppelganger, she is! Stop her!
That's just what an evil doppelganger would say! Prove you are who you say you are.
UGGGHHH. THE ONE TIME I HAVE TO SHOW WHO I REALLY AM, I DON'T KNOW HOW!
ggrrrrumbbble
PERFECT. BOUT OF EXTREME HANGRINESS ABOUT TO COME ON.

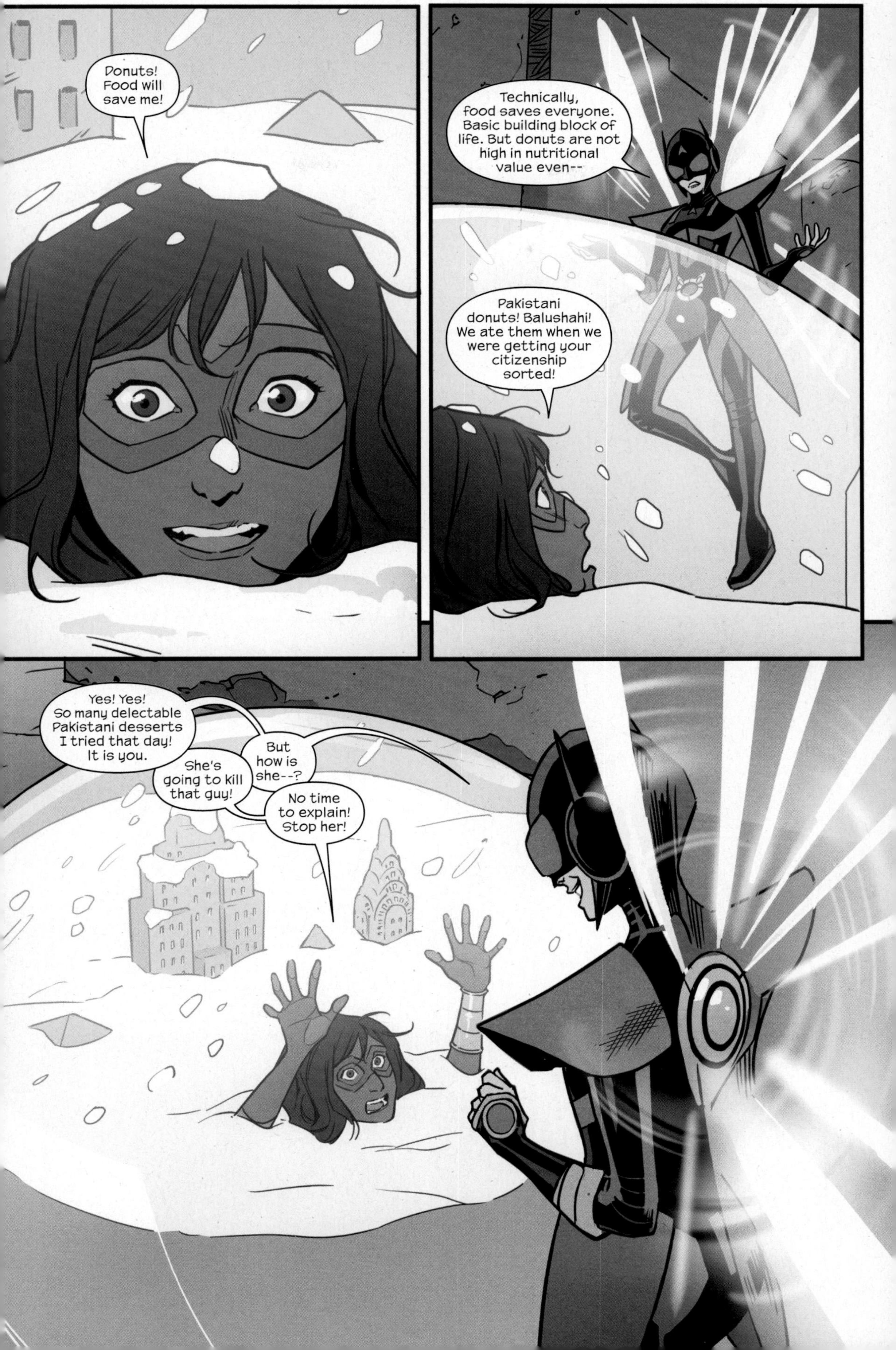
Donuts! Food will save me!
Technically, food saves everyone. Basic building block of life. But donuts are not high in nutritional value even--
Pakistani donuts! Balushahi! We ate them when we were getting your citizenship sorted!
Yes! Yes! So many delectable Pakistani desserts I tried that day! It is you.
But how is she--?
She's going to kill that guy!
No time to explain! Stop her!

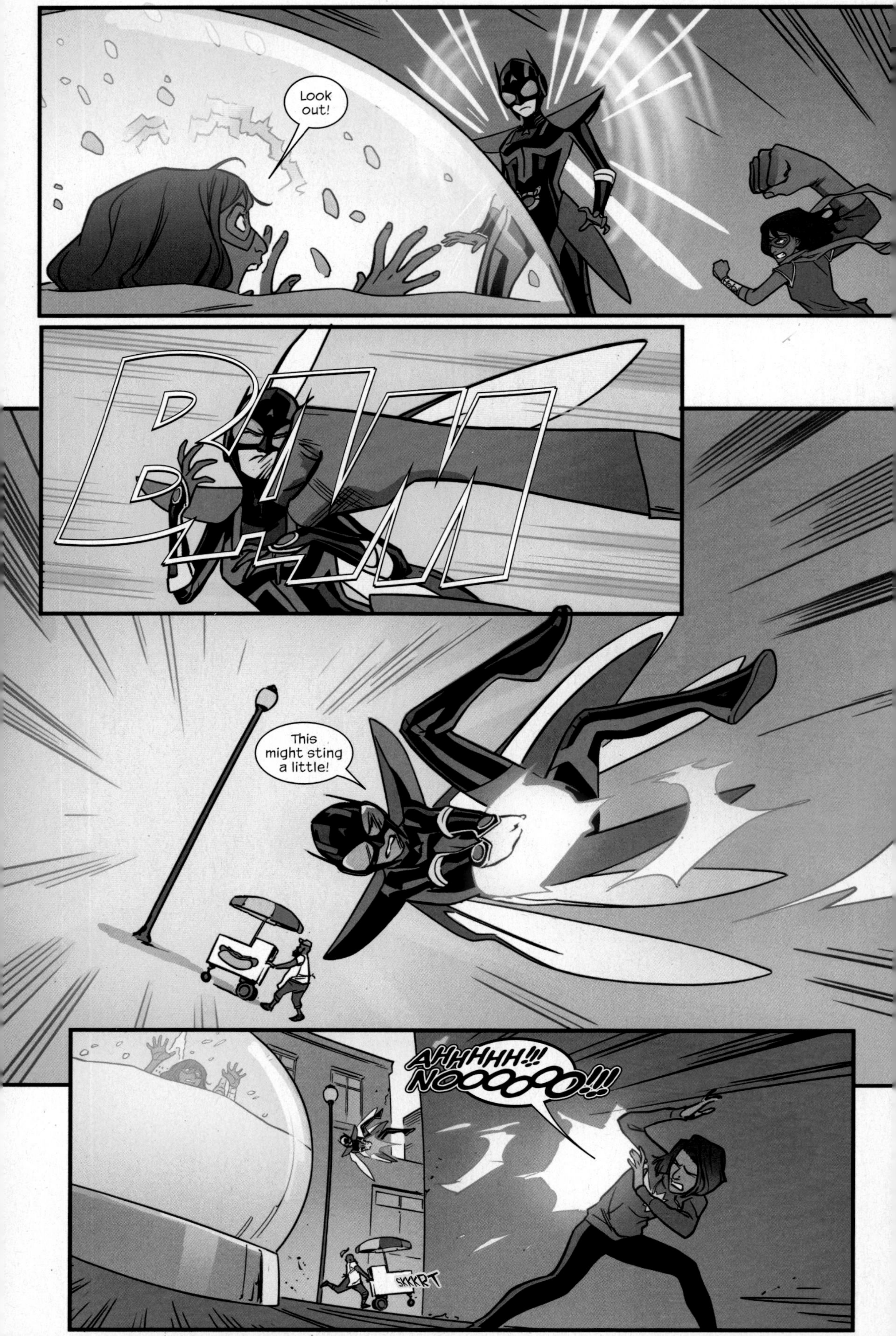
Look out!
BAM
This might sting a little!
AHHHHH!!! NOOOOOO!!!
SKKKRT

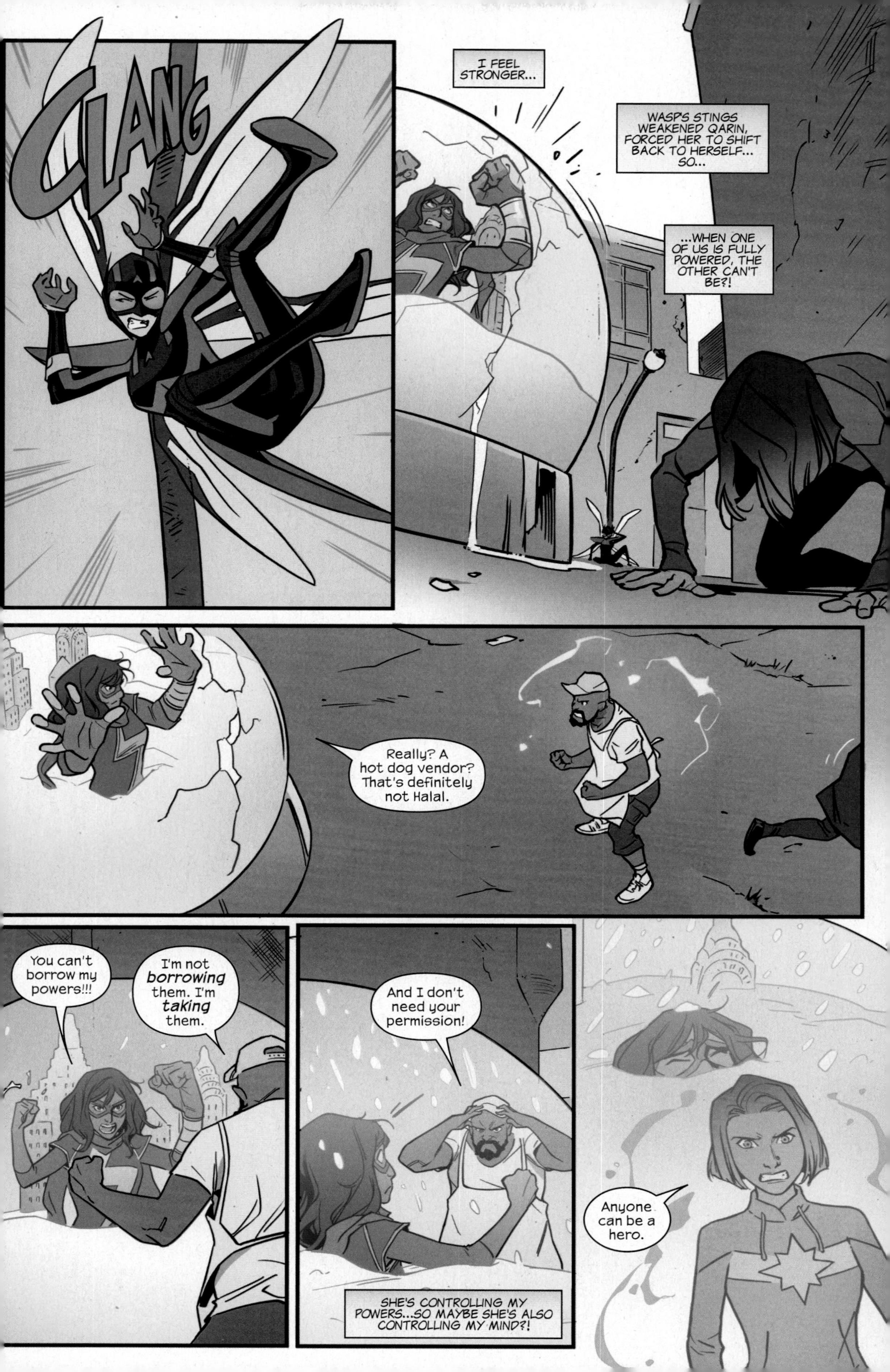
CLANG
I FEEL STRONGER...
WASP'S STINGS WEAKENED QARIN, FORCED HER TO SHIFT BACK TO HERSELF... SO...
...WHEN ONE OF US IS FULLY POWERED, THE OTHER CAN'T BE?!
Really? A hot dog vendor? That's definitely not Halal.
You can't borrow my powers!!!
I'm not *borrowing* them. I'm *taking* them.
And I don't need your permission!
SHE'S CONTROLLING MY POWERS...SO MAYBE SHE'S ALSO CONTROLLING MY MIND?!
Anyone can be a hero.

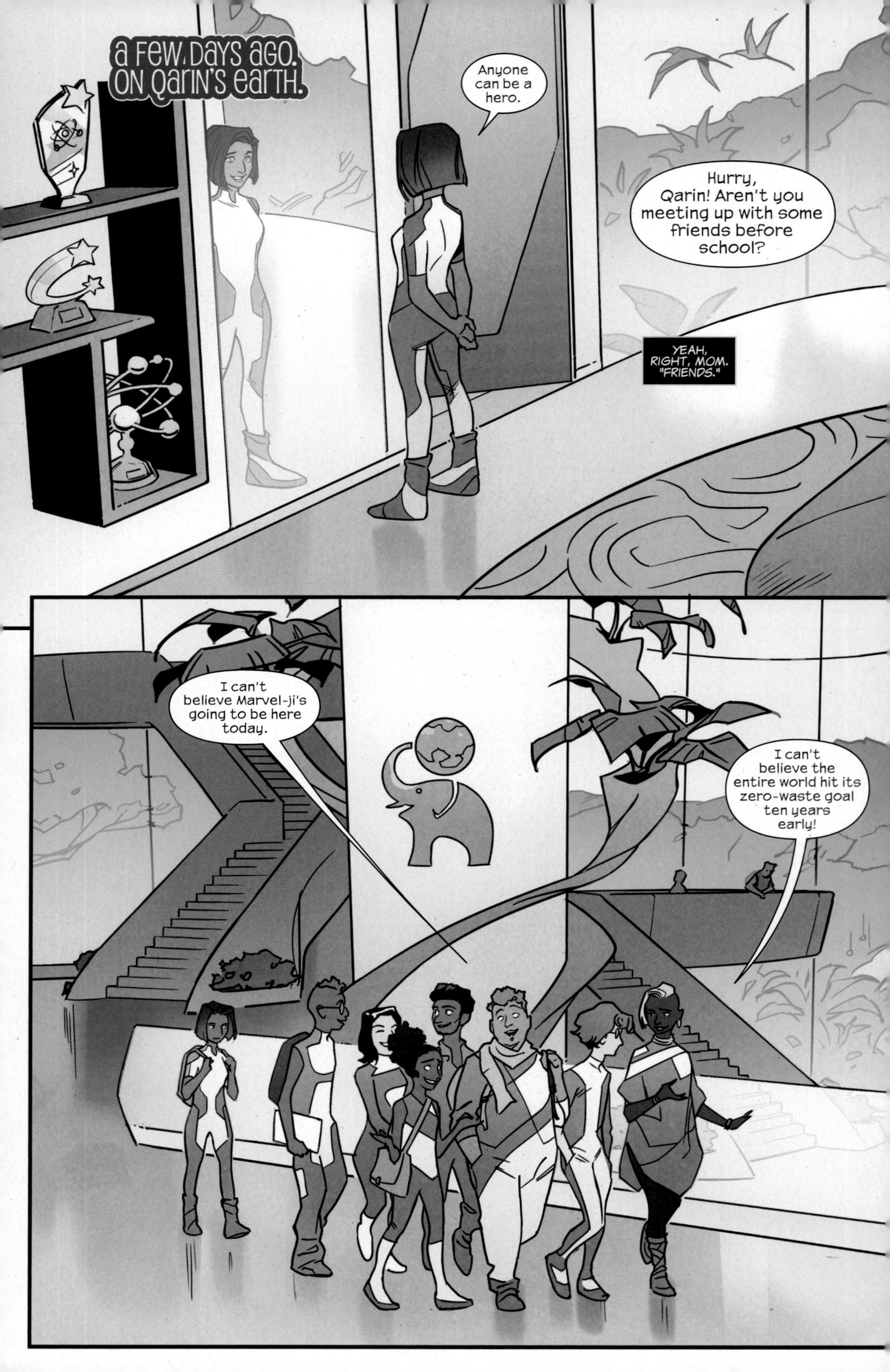
A FEW DAYS AGO. ON QARIN'S EARTH.
Anyone can be a hero.
Hurry, Qarin! Aren't you meeting up with some friends before school?
YEAH, RIGHT, MOM. "FRIENDS."
I can't believe Marvel-ji's going to be here today.
I can't believe the entire world hit its zero-waste goal ten years early!

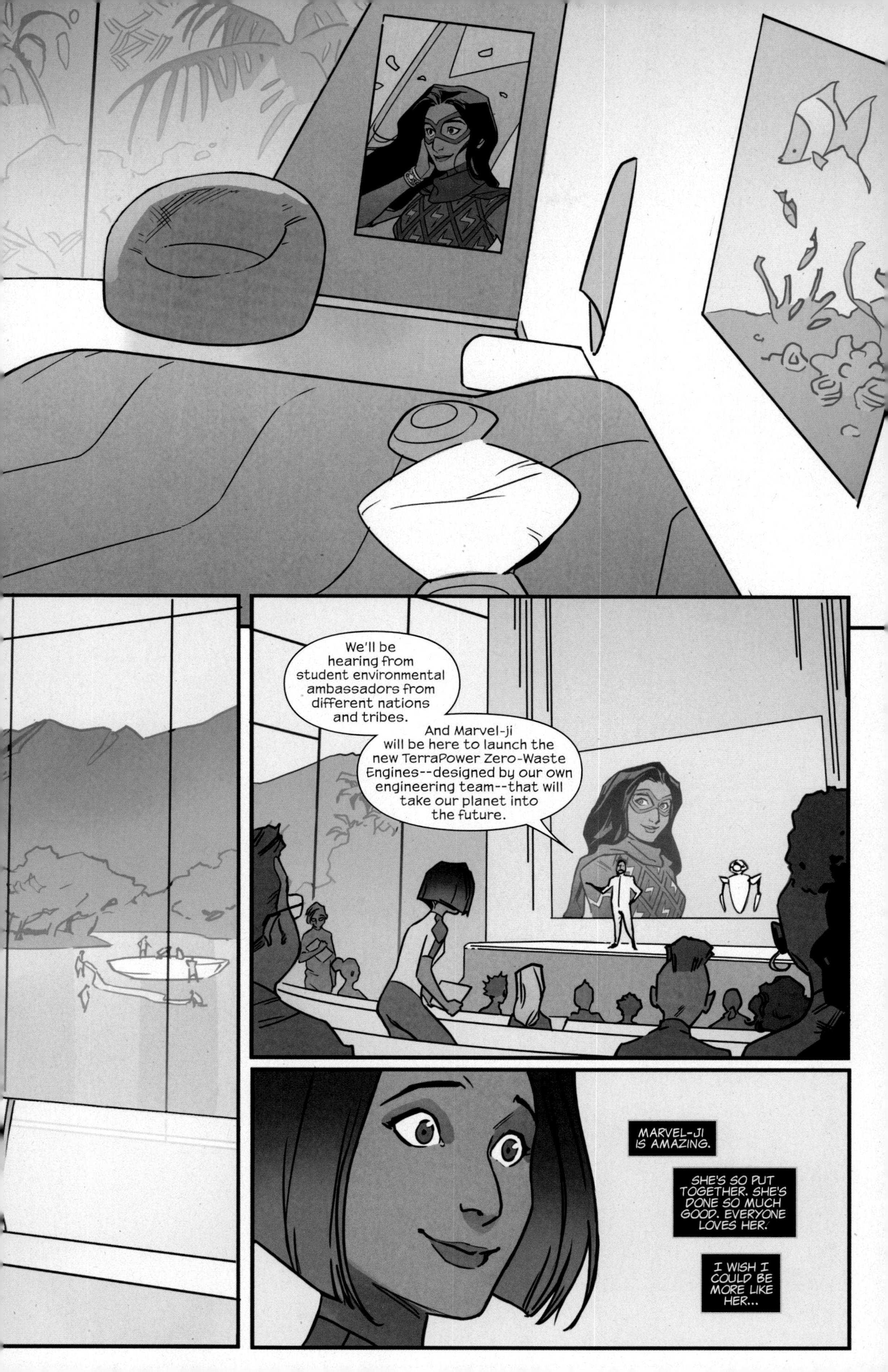

We'll be hearing from student environmental ambassadors from different nations and tribes.
And Marvel-ji will be here to launch the new TerraPower Zero-Waste Engines--designed by our own engineering team--that will take our planet into the future.
MARVEL-JI IS AMAZING.
SHE'S SO PUT TOGETHER. SHE'S DONE SO MUCH GOOD. EVERYONE LOVES HER.
I WISH I COULD BE MORE LIKE HER...

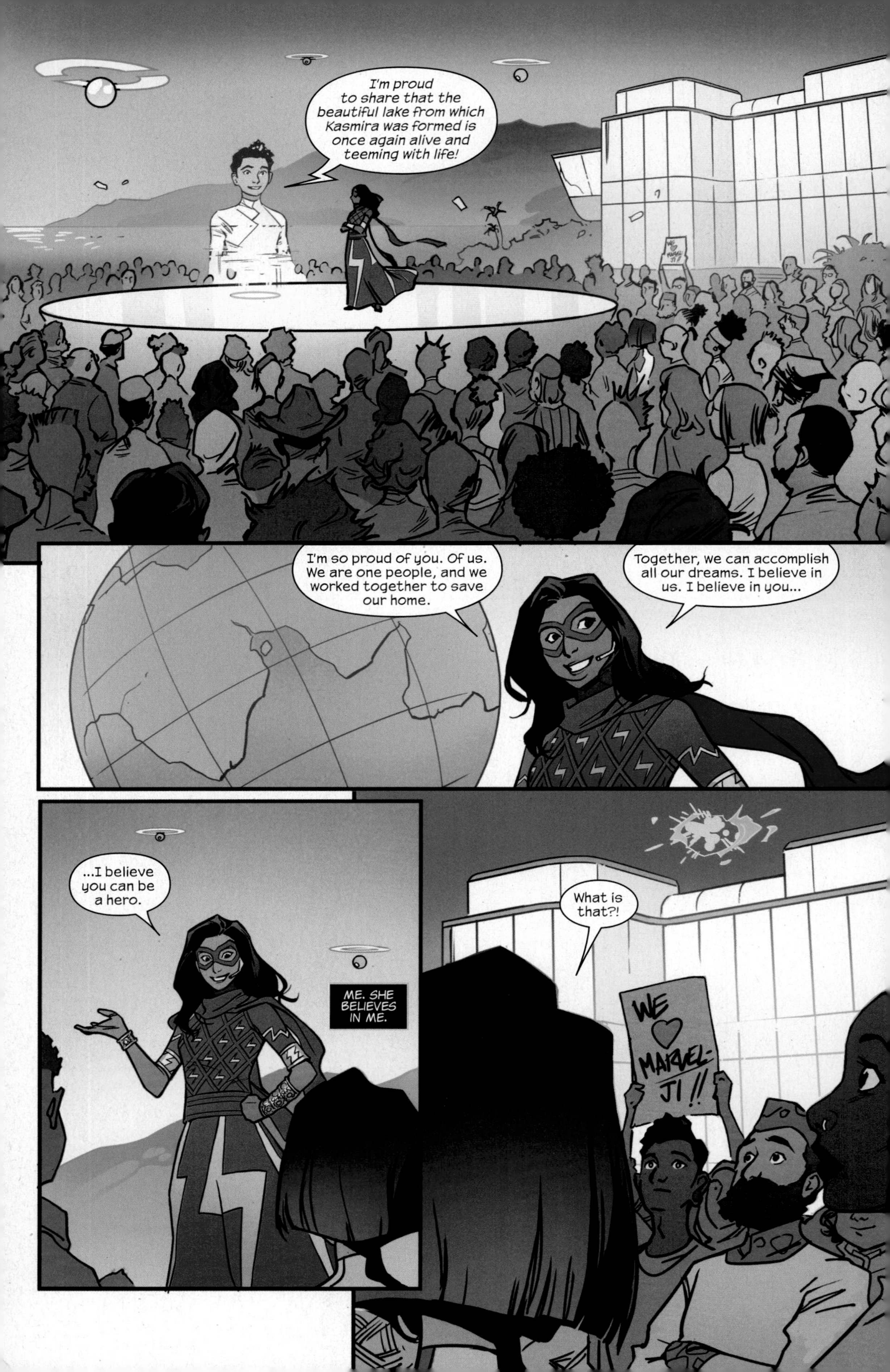
I'm proud to share that the beautiful lake from which Kasmira was formed is once again alive and teeming with life!
I'm so proud of you. Of us. We are one people, and we worked together to save our home.
Together, we can accomplish all our dreams. I believe in us. I believe in you...
...I believe you can be a hero.
ME. SHE BELIEVES IN ME.
What is that?!
WE ♥ MARVEL-JI!!

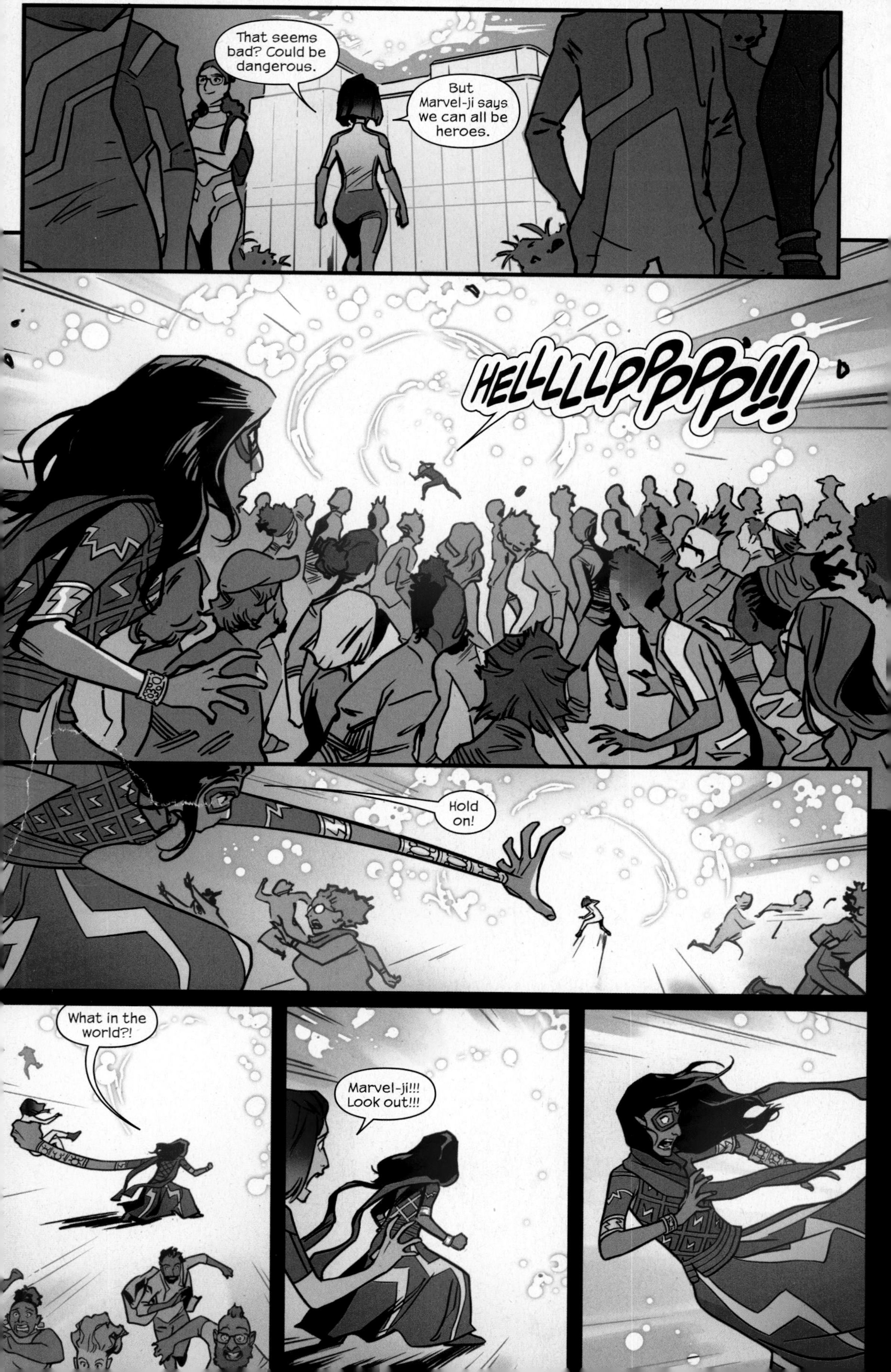

That seems bad? Could be dangerous.
But Marvel-ji says we can all be heroes.
HELLLLLLPPPPP!!!
Hold on!
What in the world?!
Marvel-ji!!! Look out!!!

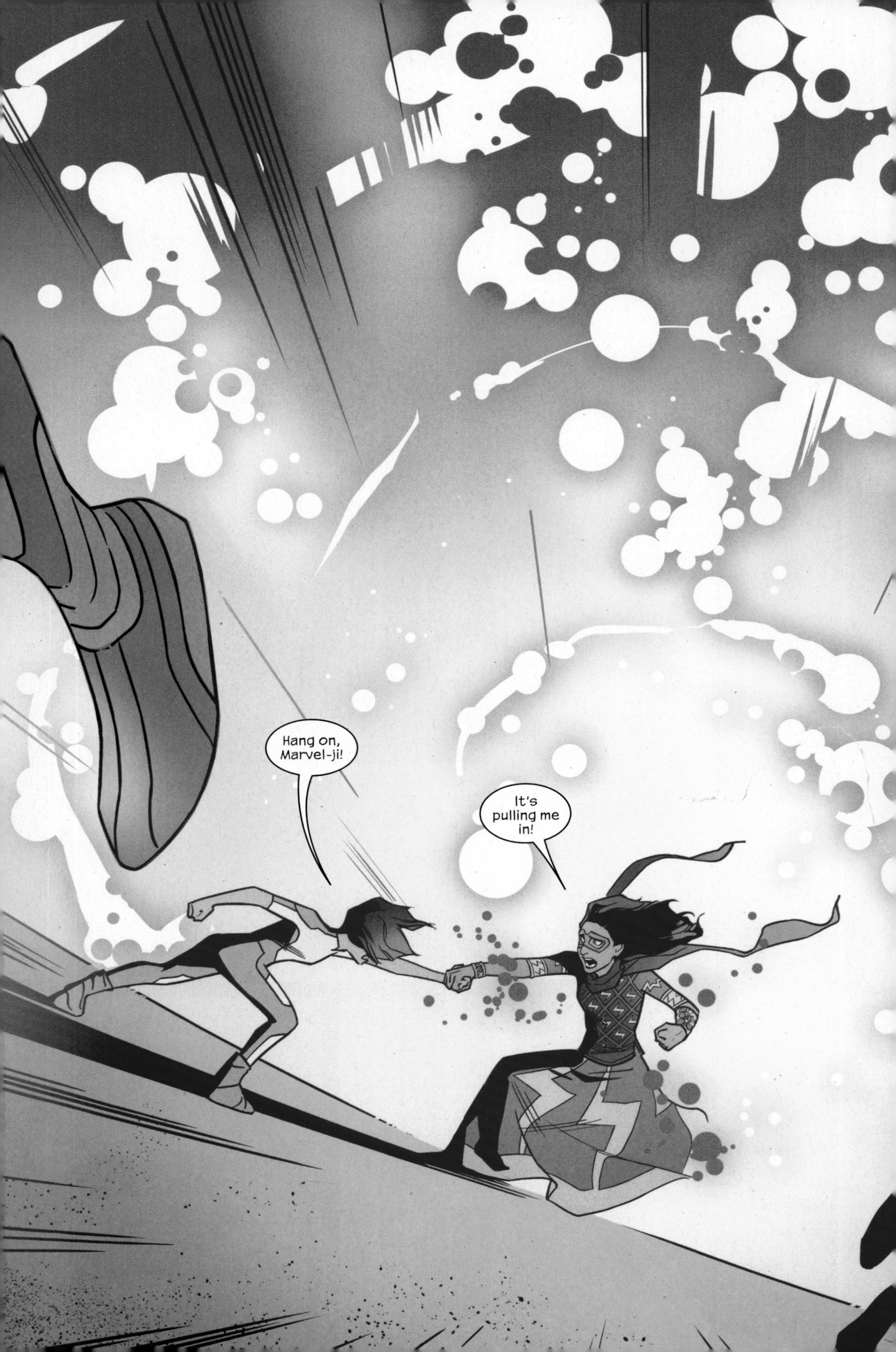
Hang on, Marvel-ji!
It's pulling me in!

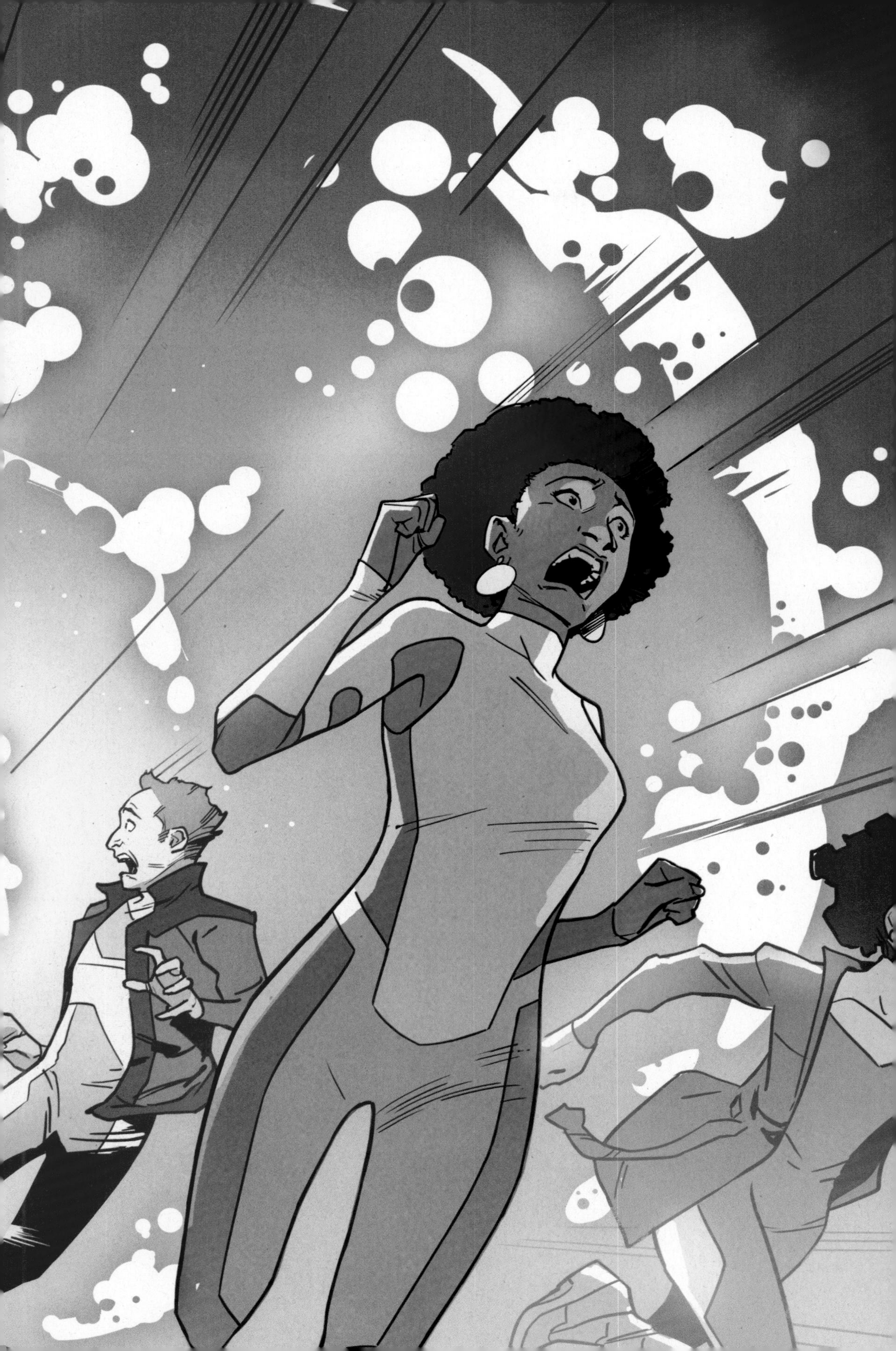

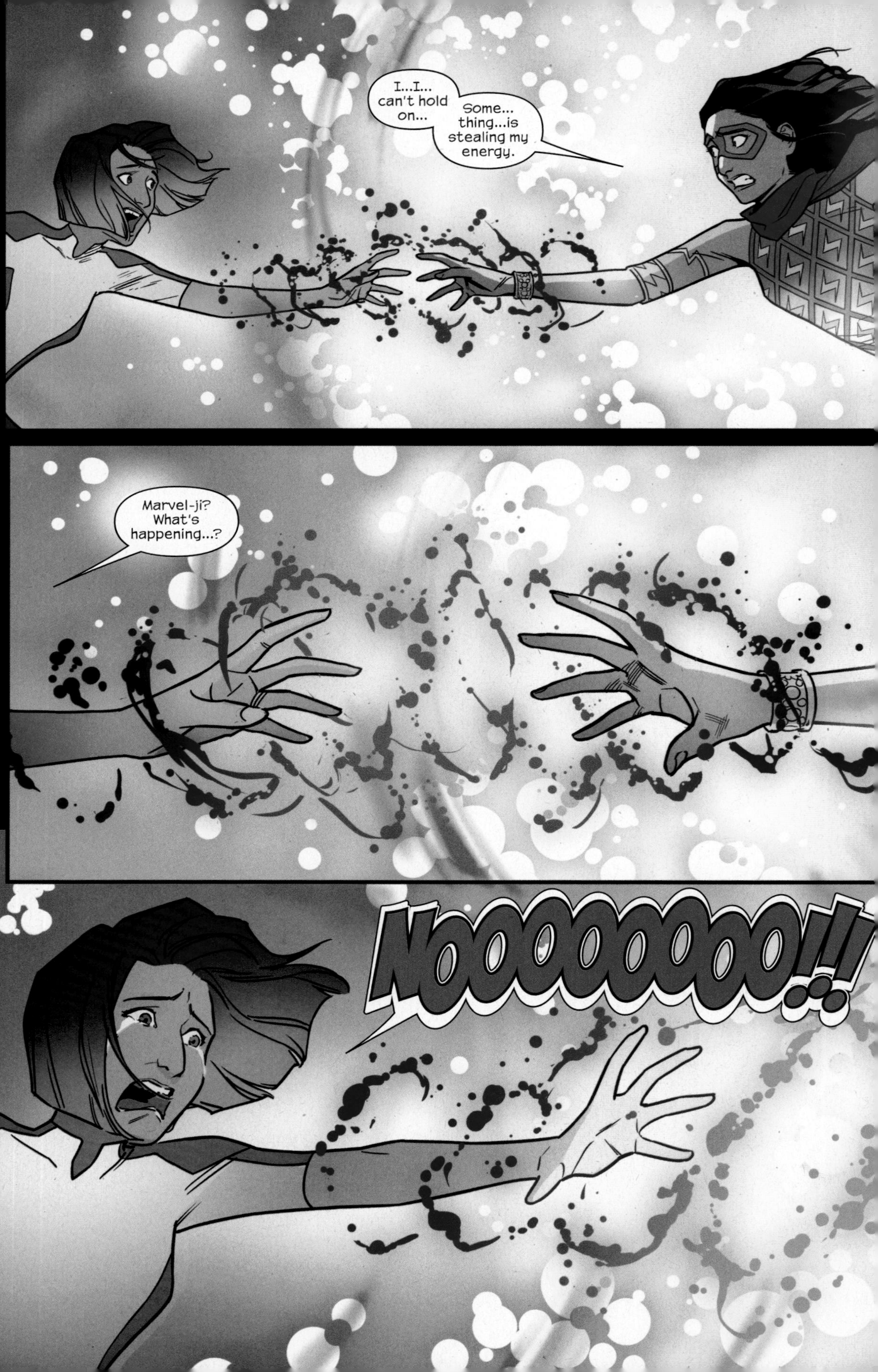
I...I... can't hold on...
Some... thing...is stealing my energy.
Marvel-ji? What's happening...?
NOOOOOOOO!!!

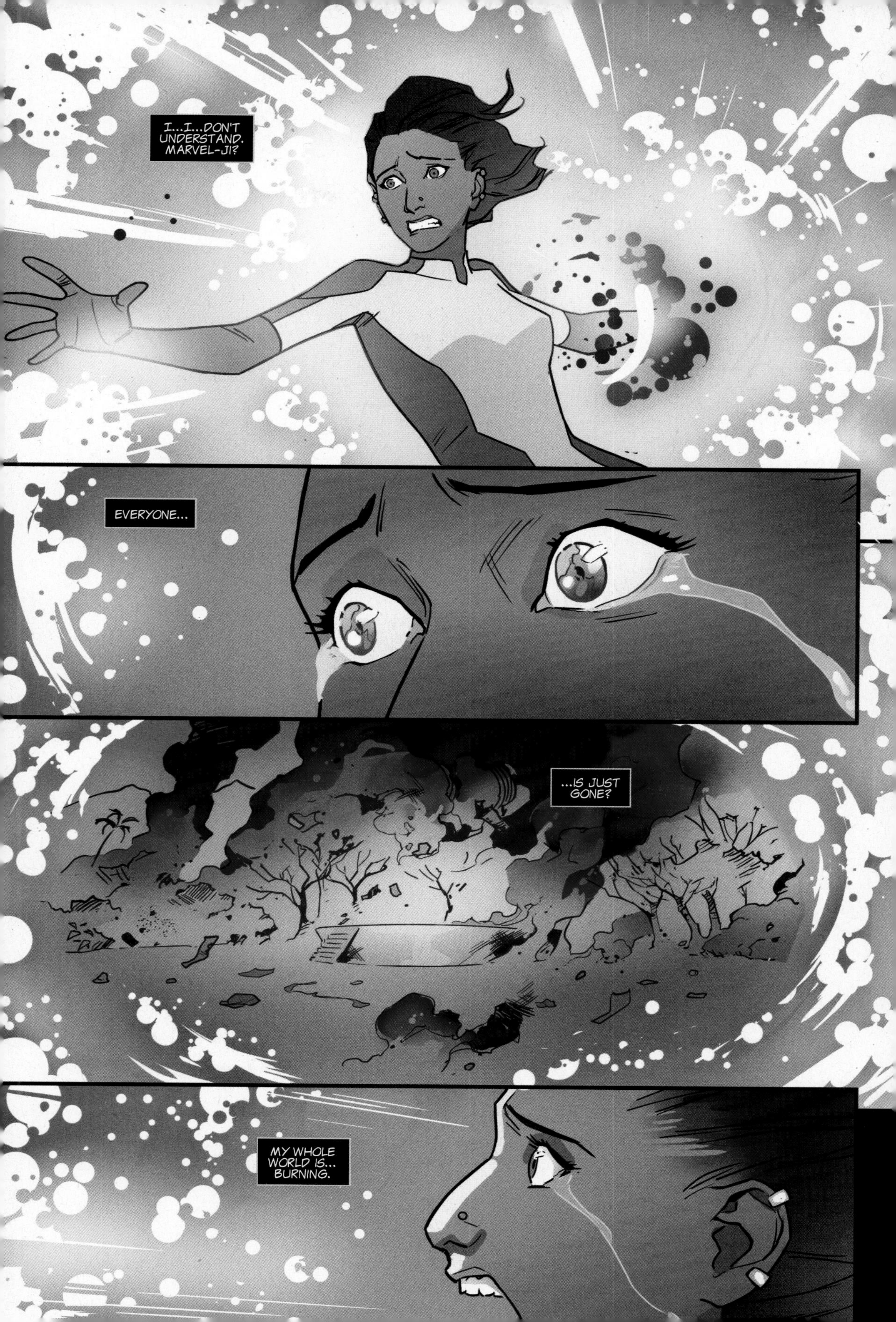
I...I...DON'T UNDERSTAND. MARVEL-JI?
EVERYONE...
...IS JUST GONE?
MY WHOLE WORLD IS... BURNING.

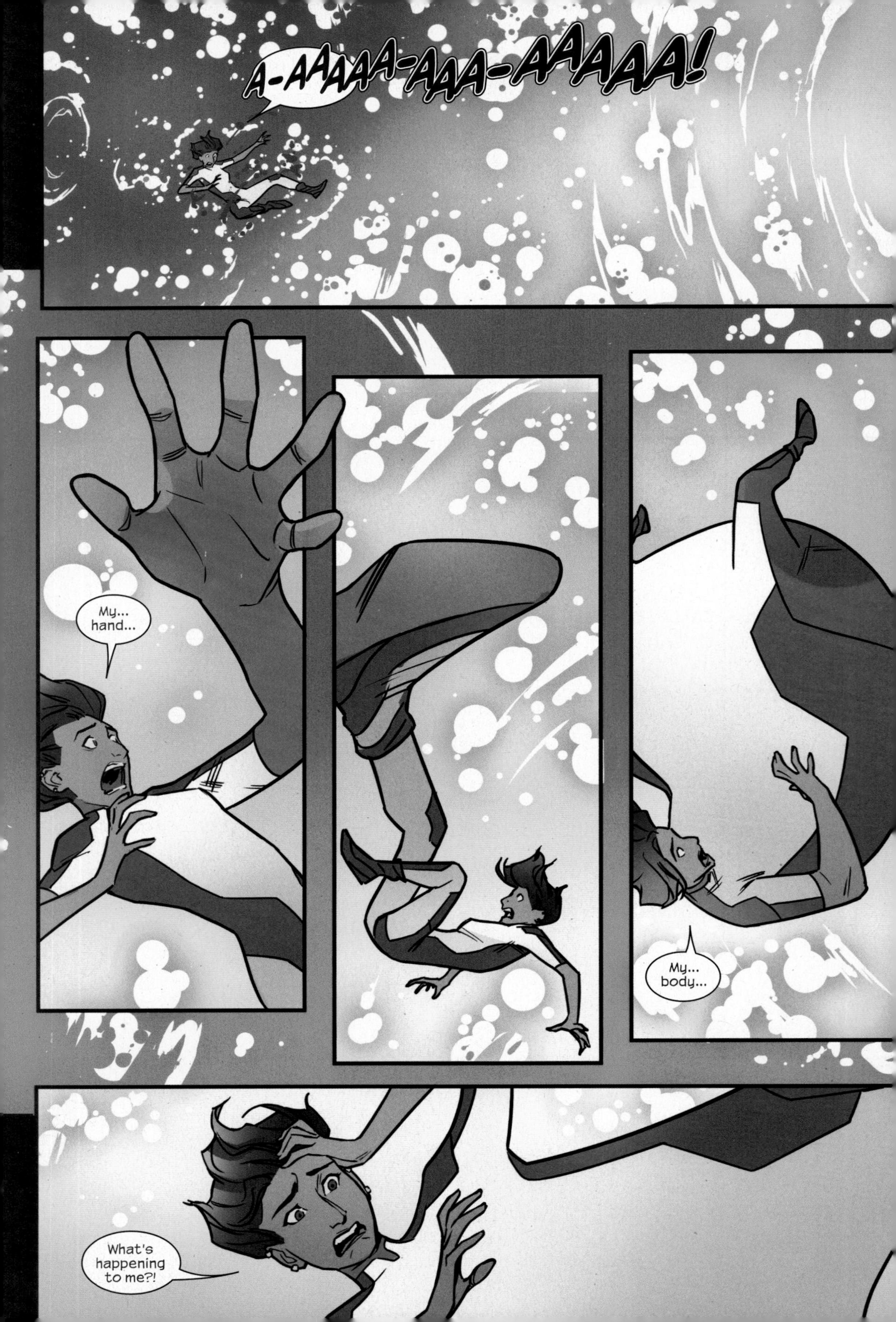
A-AAAAA-AAA-AAAAAA!
My... hand...
My... body...
What's happening to me?!

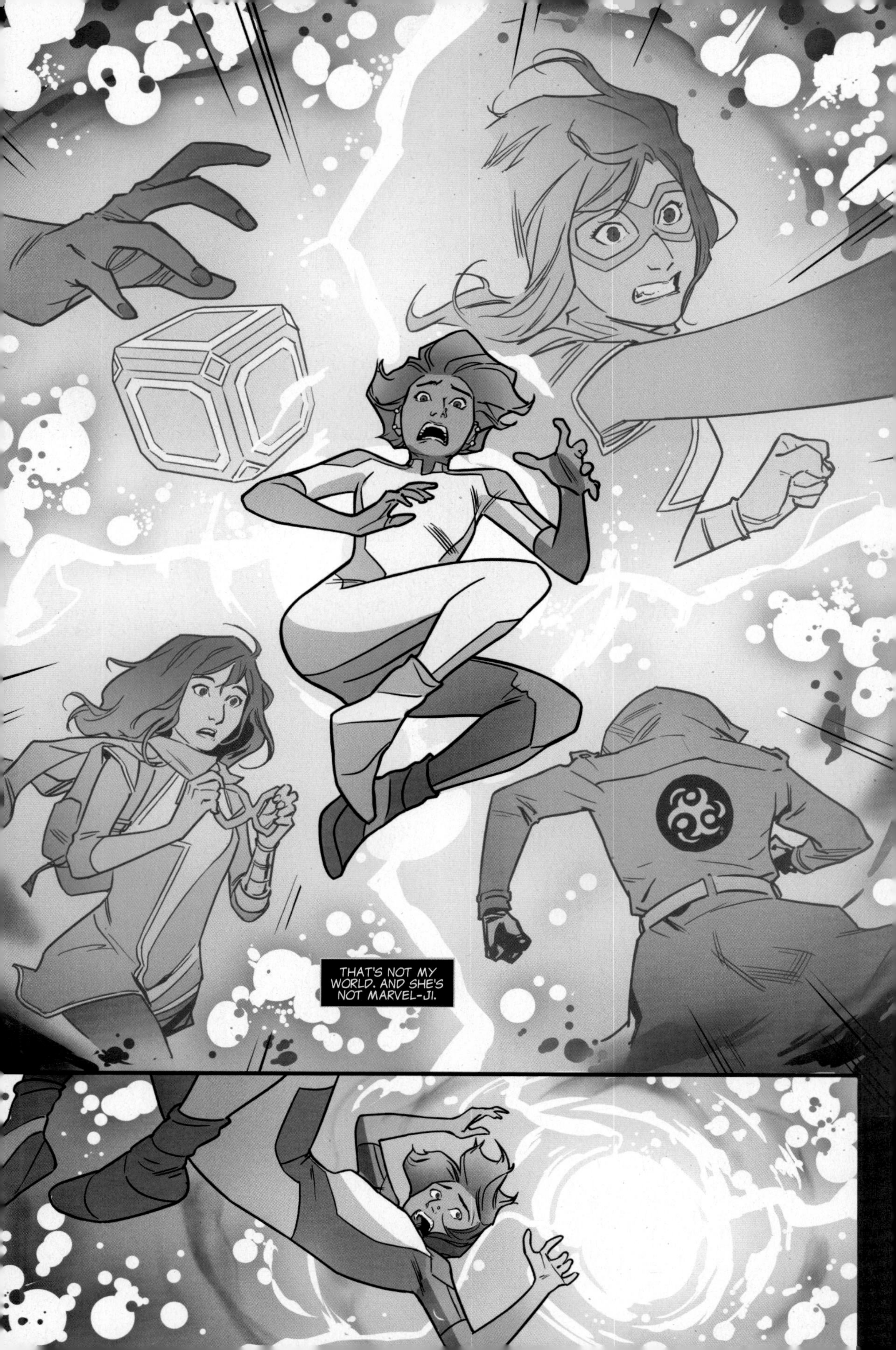
THAT'S NOT MY WORLD. AND SHE'S NOT MARVEL-JI.

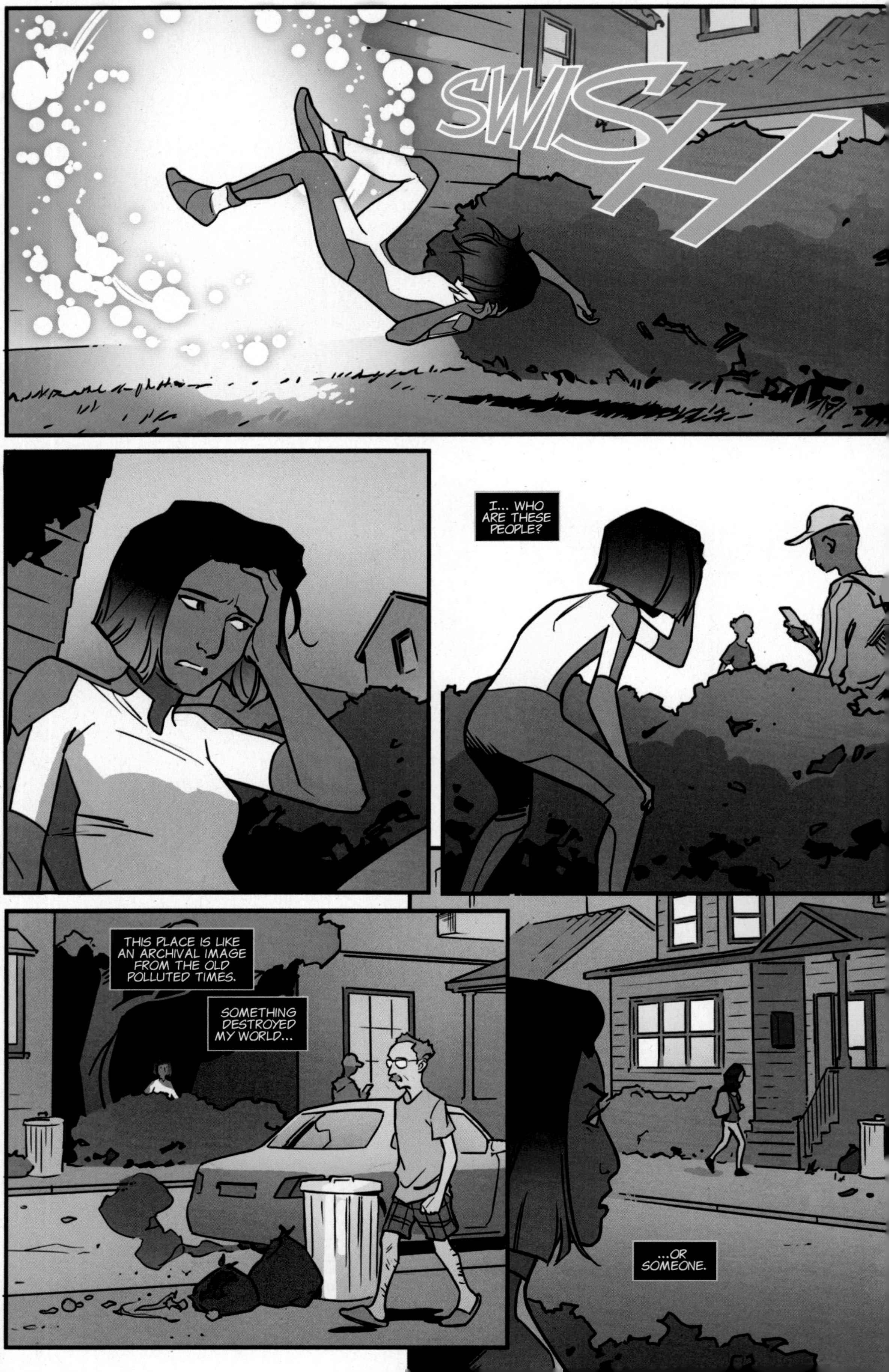
SWISH
I... WHO ARE THESE PEOPLE?
THIS PLACE IS LIKE AN ARCHIVAL IMAGE FROM THE OLD POLLUTED TIMES.
SOMETHING DESTROYED MY WORLD...
...OR SOMEONE.

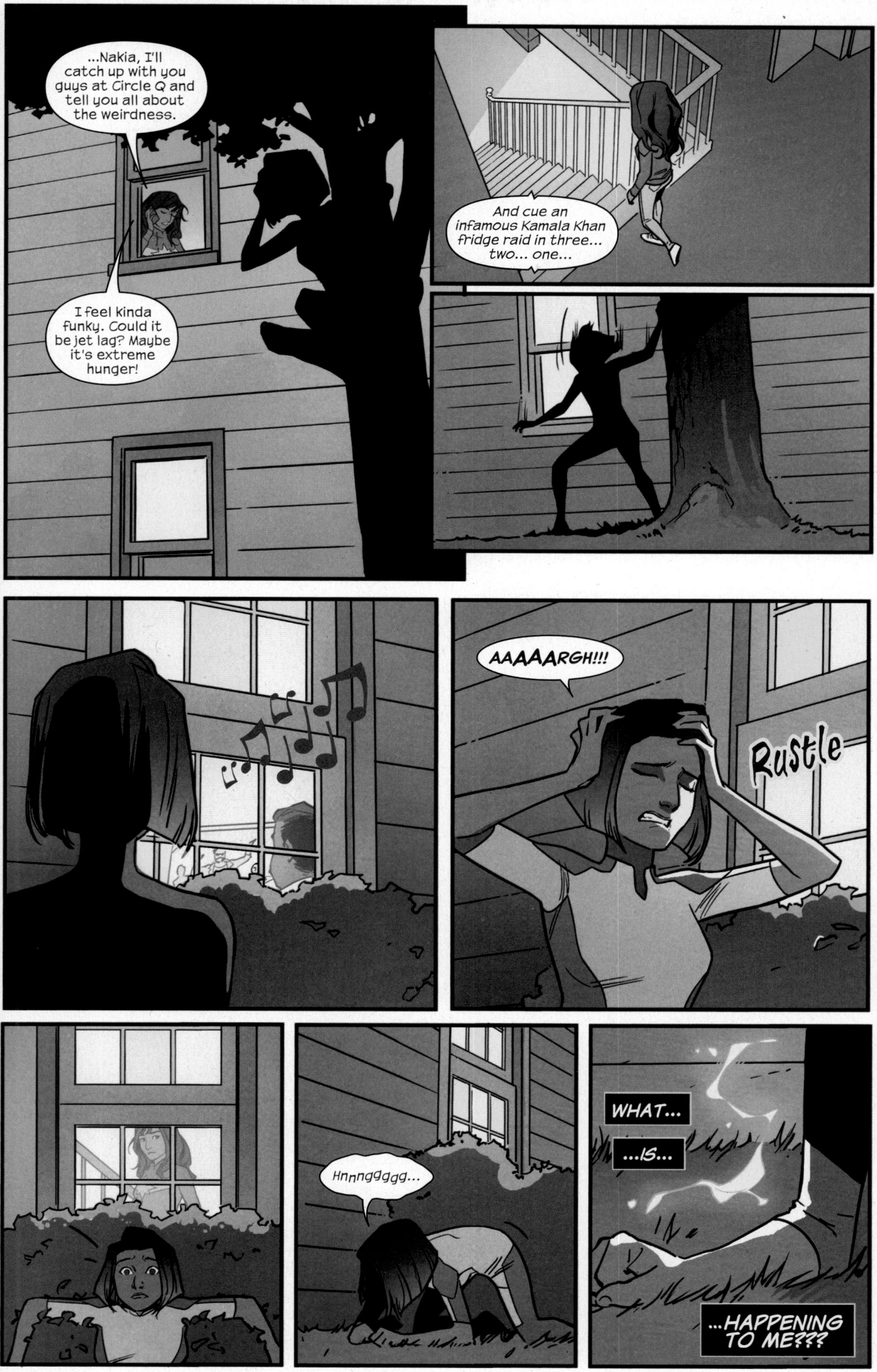

...Nakia, I'll catch up with you guys at Circle Q and tell you all about the weirdness.
I feel kinda funky. Could it be jet lag? Maybe it's extreme hunger!
And cue an infamous Kamala Khan fridge raid in three... two... one...
AAAAARGH!!!
Rustle
Hnnngggg...
WHAT...
...IS...
...HAPPENING TO ME???

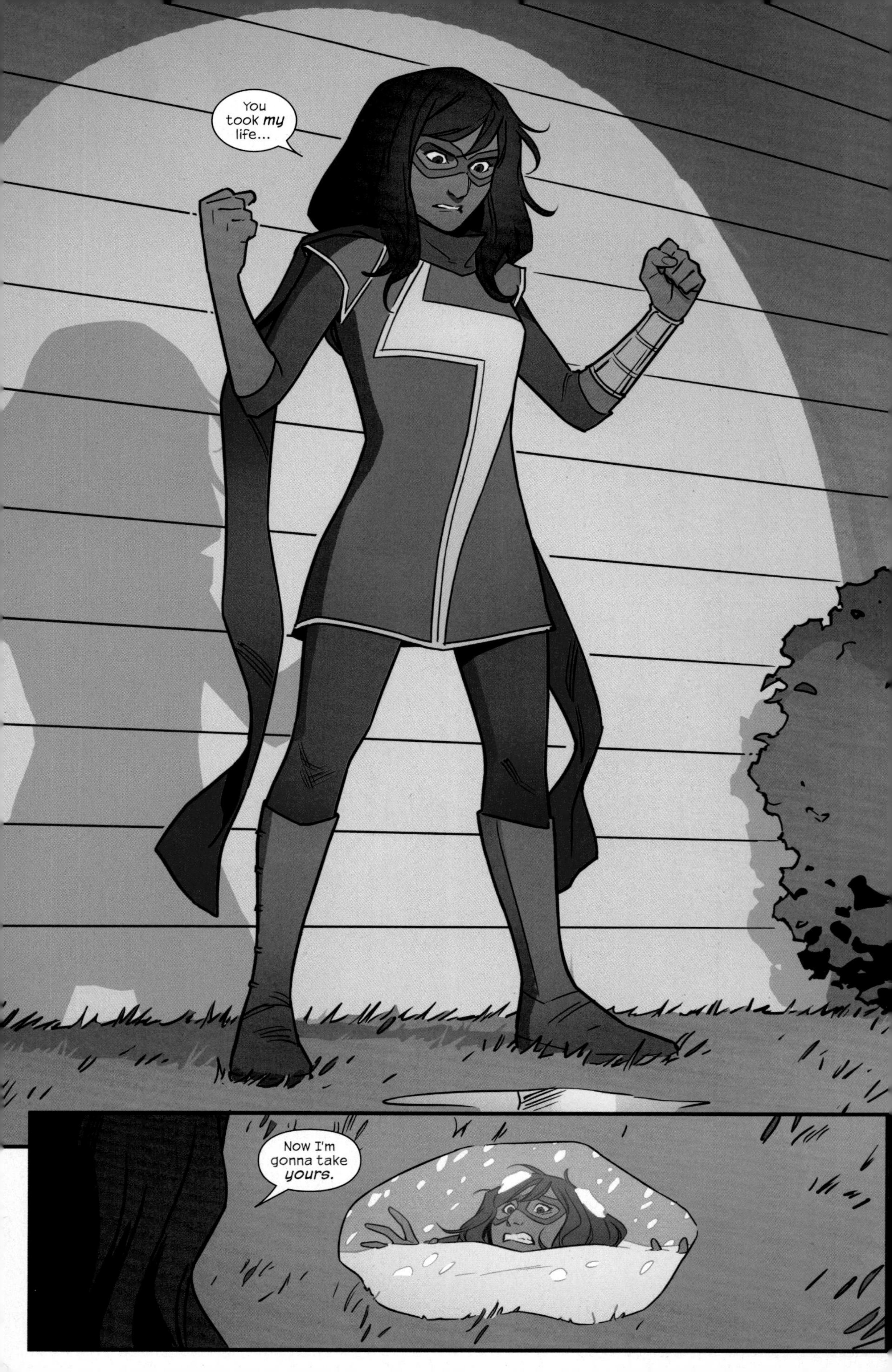
You took *my* life...
Now I'm gonna take *yours*.

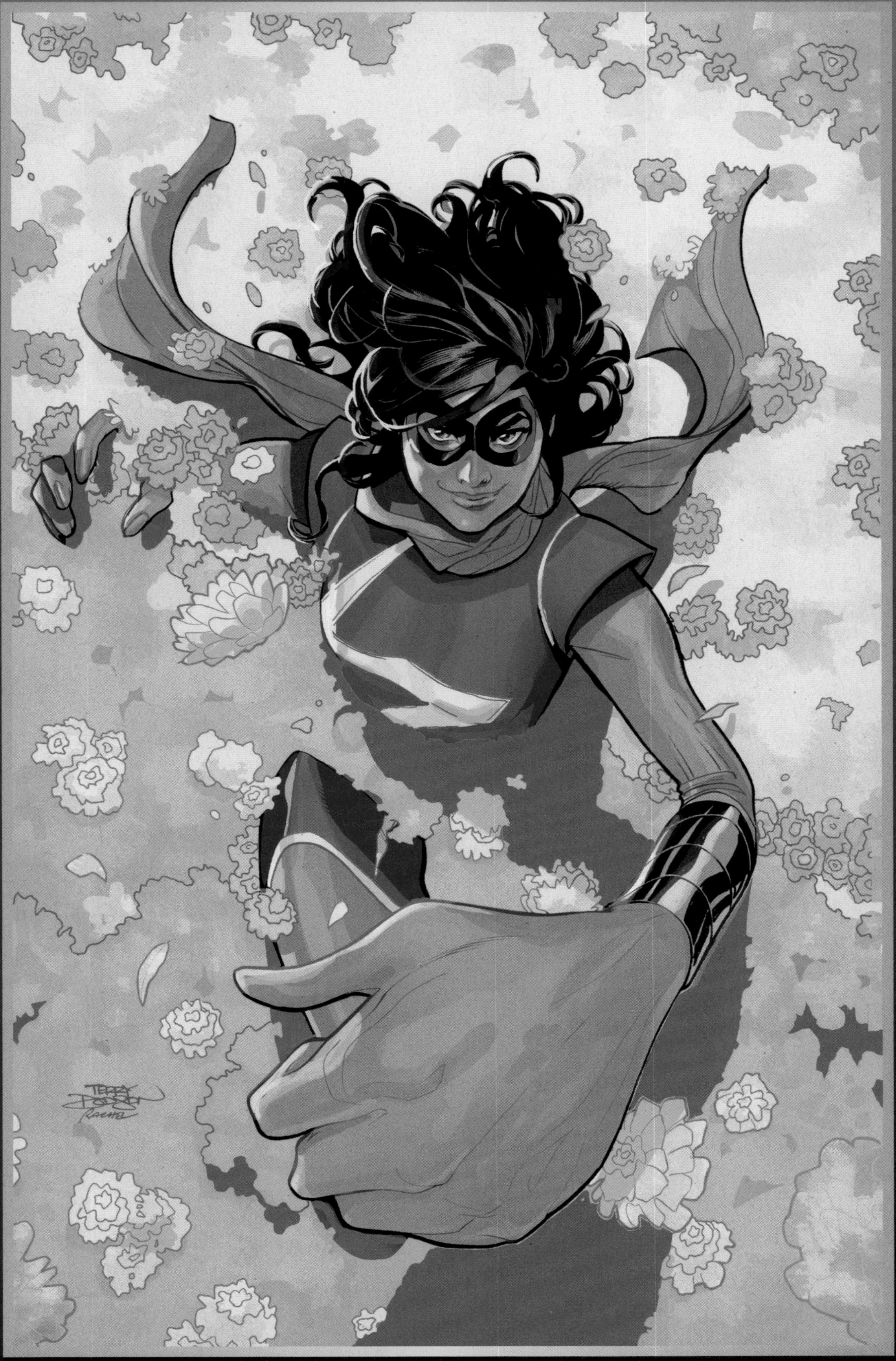

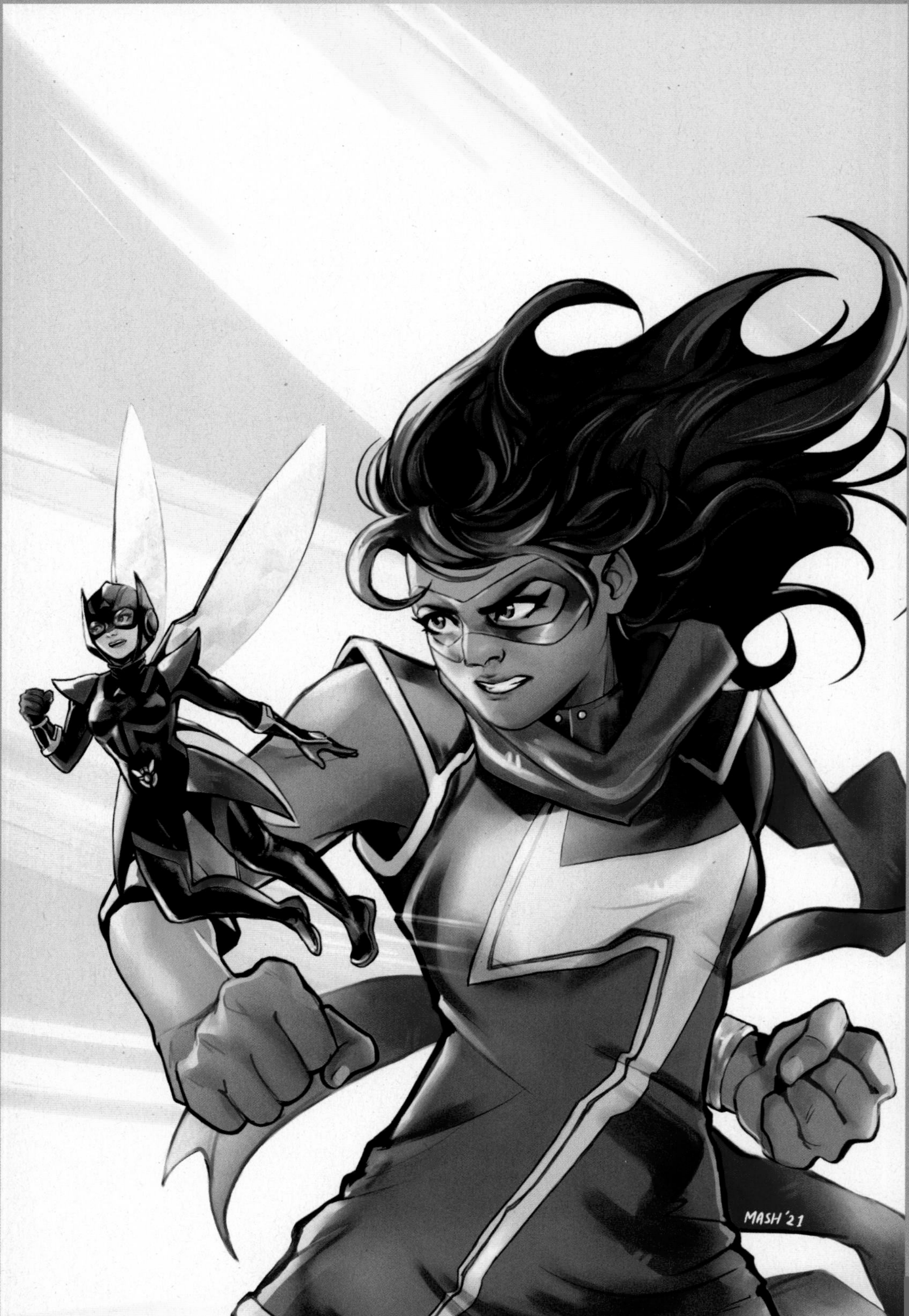
MASH '21

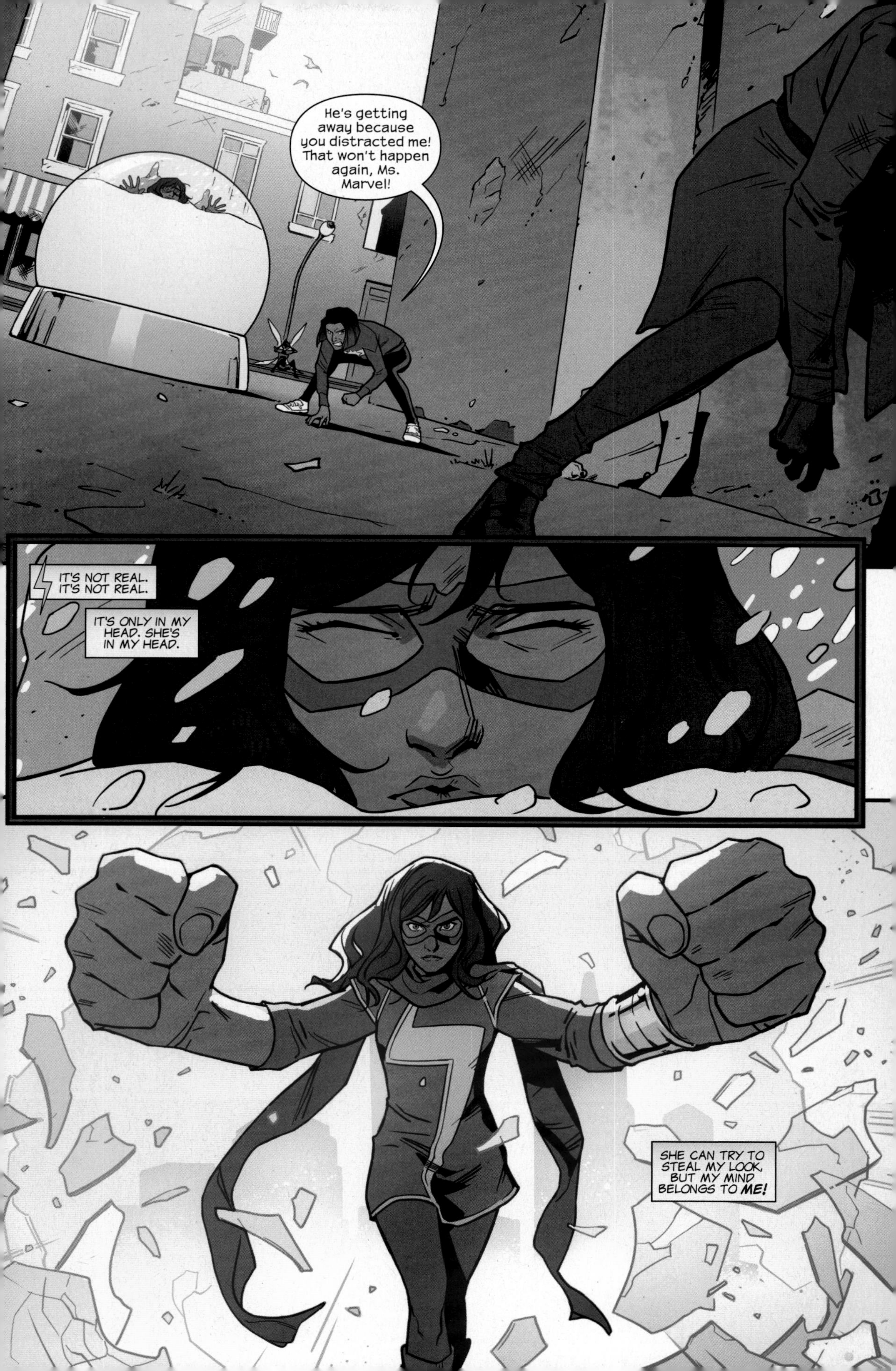
He's getting away because you distracted me! That won't happen again, Ms. Marvel!
IT'S NOT REAL. IT'S NOT REAL.
IT'S ONLY IN MY HEAD. SHE'S IN MY HEAD.
SHE CAN TRY TO STEAL MY LOOK, BUT MY MIND BELONGS TO ME!

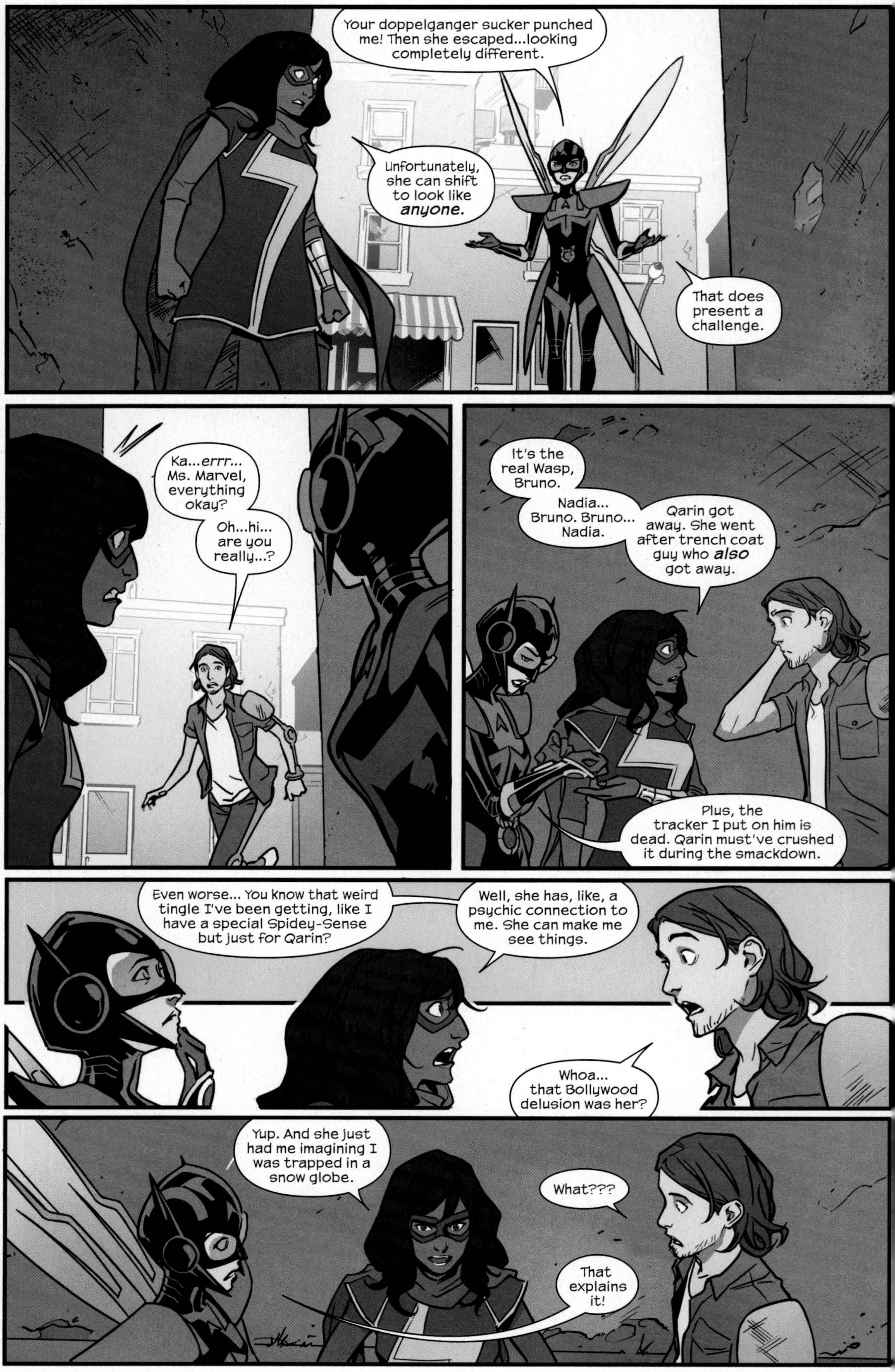

Your doppelganger sucker punched me! Then she escaped...looking completely different.
Unfortunately, she can shift to look like *anyone.*
That does present a challenge.
Ka...*errr...* Ms. Marvel, everything okay?
Oh...hi... are you really...?
It's the real Wasp, Bruno.
Nadia... Bruno. Bruno... Nadia.
Qarin got away. She went after trench coat guy who *also* got away.
Plus, the tracker I put on him is dead. Qarin must've crushed it during the smackdown.
Even worse... You know that weird tingle I've been getting, like I have a special Spidey-Sense but just for Qarin?
Well, she has, like, a psychic connection to me. She can make me see things.
Whoa... that Bollywood delusion was her?
Yup. And she just had me imagining I was trapped in a snow globe.
What???
That explains it!

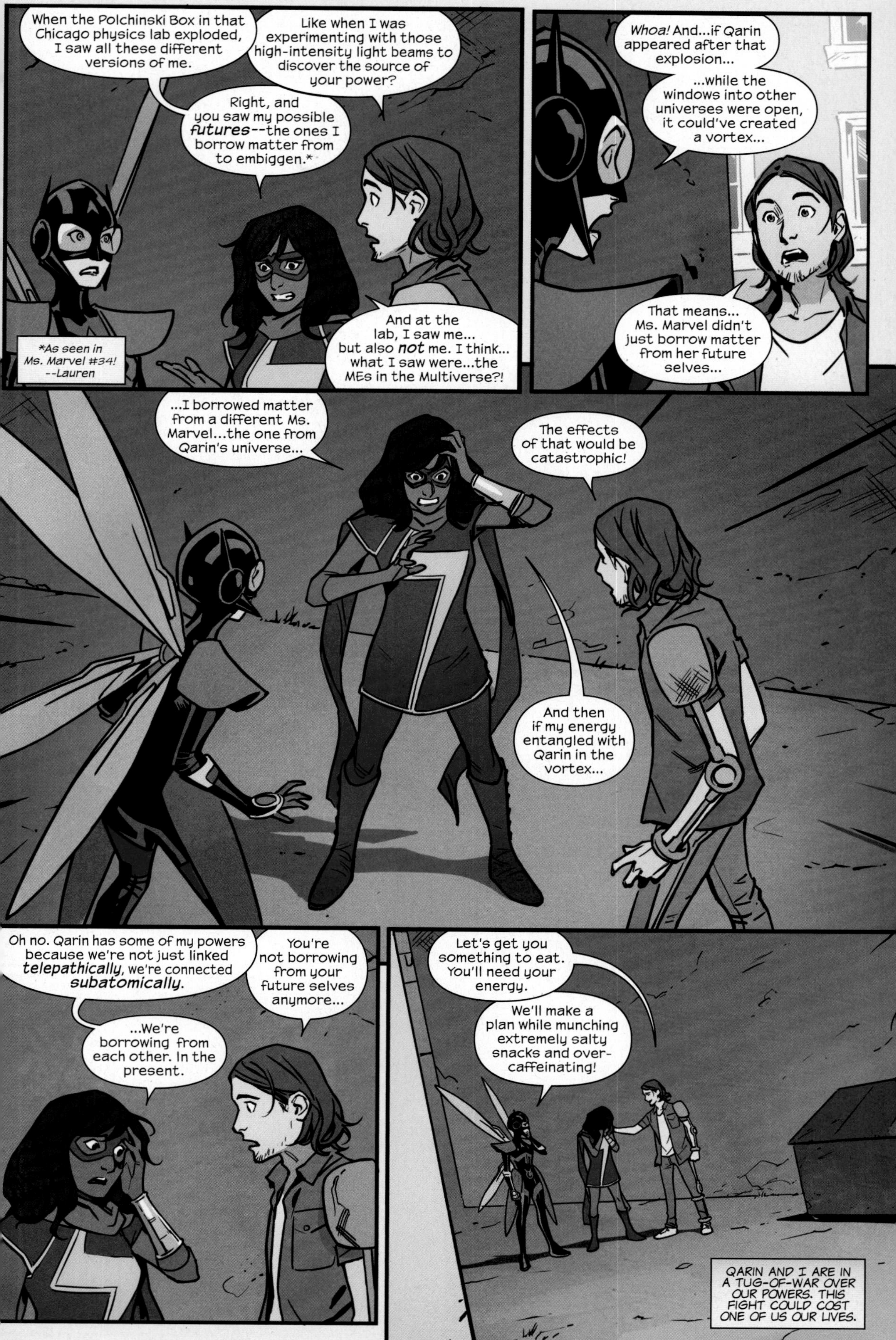
When the Polchinski Box in that Chicago physics lab exploded, I saw all these different versions of me.
Like when I was experimenting with those high-intensity light beams to discover the source of your power?
Right, and you saw my possible *futures*--the ones I borrow matter from to embiggen.*
And at the lab, I saw me... but also *not* me. I think... what I saw were...the MEs in the Multiverse?!
*As seen in Ms. Marvel #34! --Lauren
Whoa! And...if Qarin appeared after that explosion...
...while the windows into other universes were open, it could've created a vortex...
That means... Ms. Marvel didn't just borrow matter from her future selves...
...I borrowed matter from a different Ms. Marvel...the one from Qarin's universe...
The effects of that would be catastrophic!
And then if my energy entangled with Qarin in the vortex...
Oh no. Qarin has some of my powers because we're not just linked *telepathically*, we're connected *subatomically*.
You're not borrowing from your future selves anymore...
...We're borrowing from each other. In the present.
Let's get you something to eat. You'll need your energy.
We'll make a plan while munching extremely salty snacks and over-caffeinating!
QARIN AND I ARE IN A TUG-OF-WAR OVER OUR POWERS. THIS FIGHT COULD COST ONE OF US OUR LIVES.

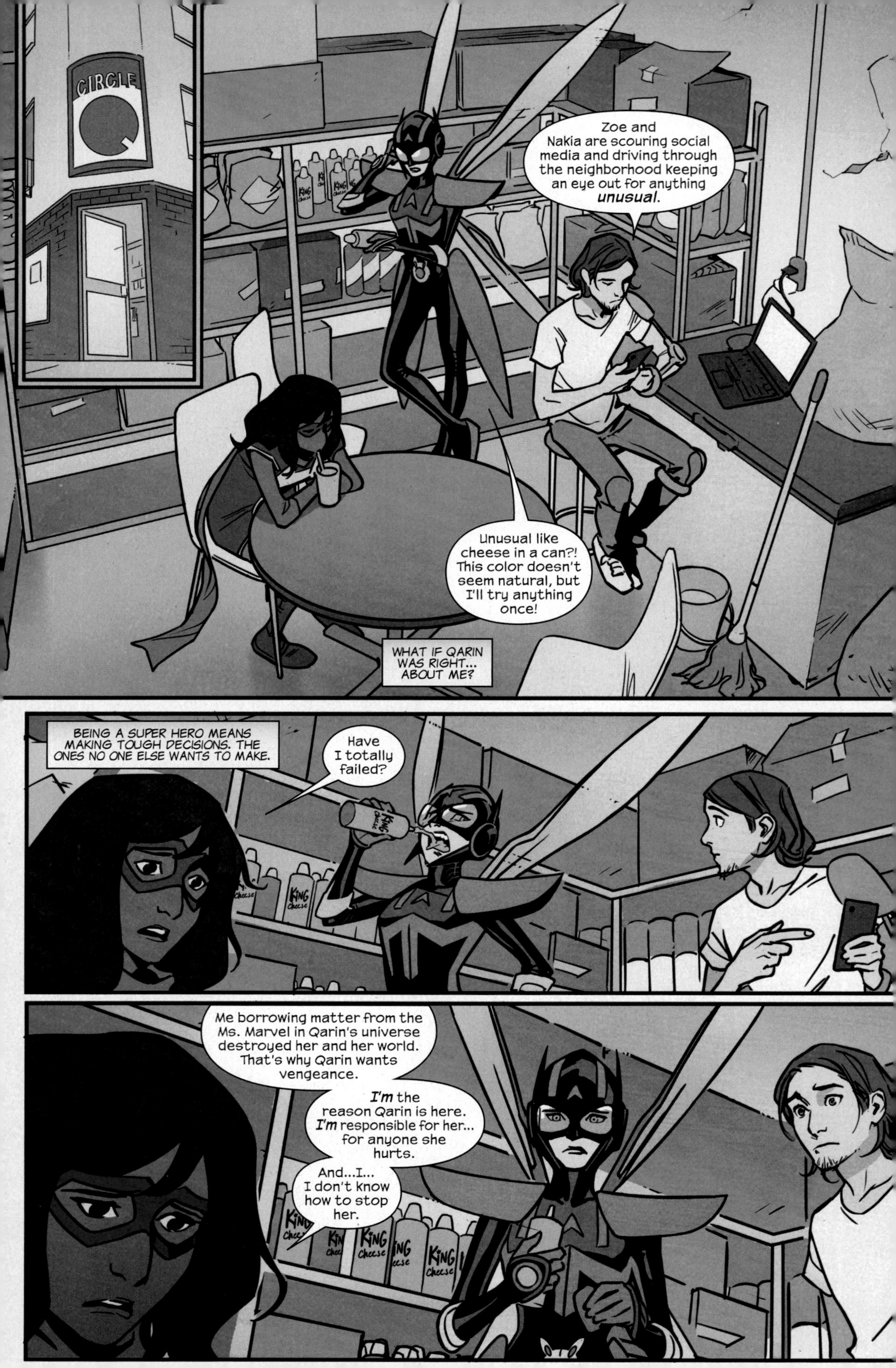
CIRCLE Q
Zoe and Nakia are scouring social media and driving through the neighborhood keeping an eye out for anything *unusual*.
Unusual like cheese in a can?! This color doesn't seem natural, but I'll try anything once!
WHAT IF QARIN WAS RIGHT... ABOUT ME?
BEING A SUPER HERO MEANS MAKING TOUGH DECISIONS. THE ONES NO ONE ELSE WANTS TO MAKE.
Have I totally failed?
Me borrowing matter from the Ms. Marvel in Qarin's universe destroyed her and her world. That's why Qarin wants vengeance.
I'm the reason Qarin is here. *I'm* responsible for her... for anyone she hurts.
And...I... I don't know how to stop her.

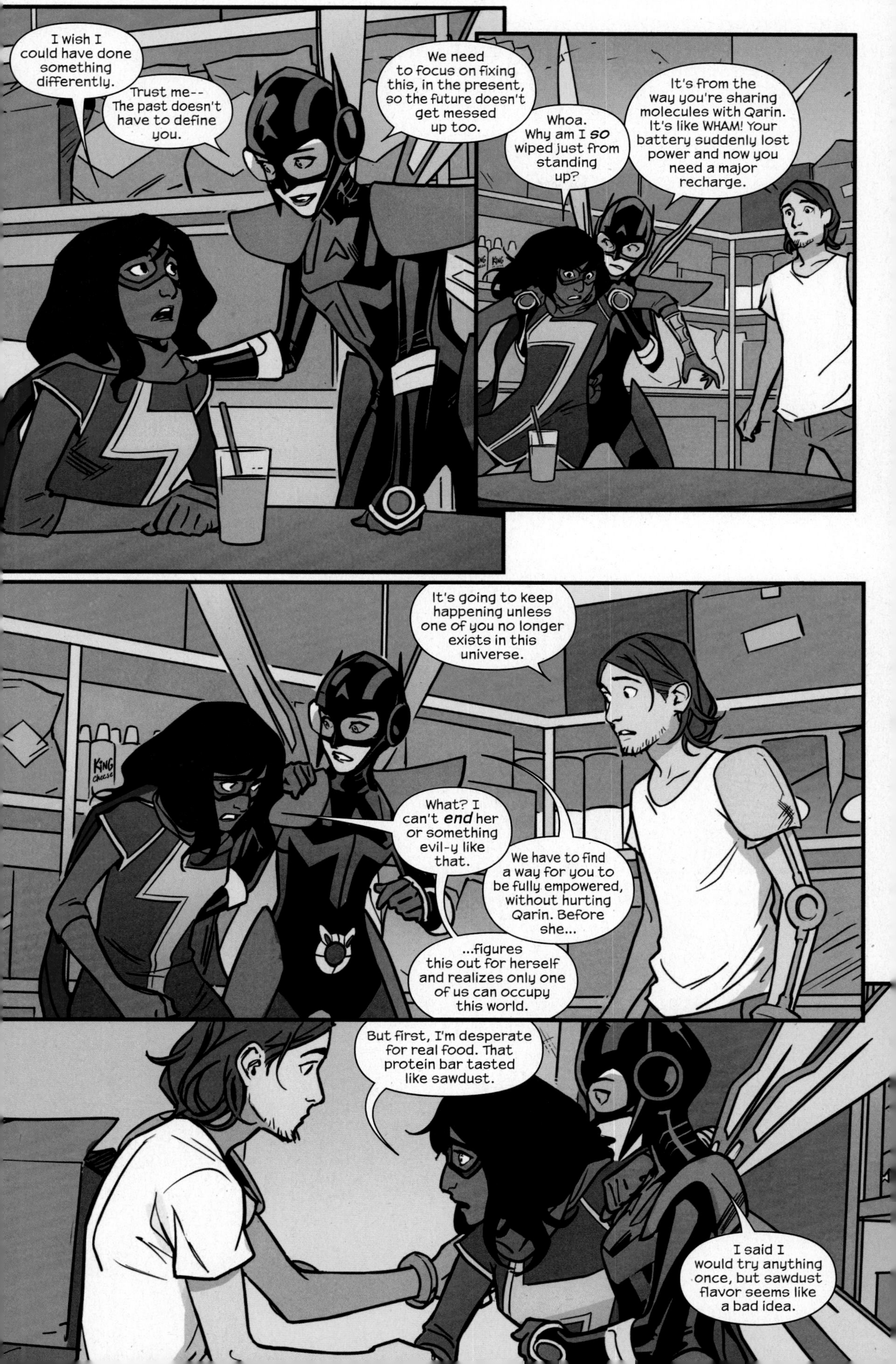
I wish I could have done something differently.
Trust me-- The past doesn't have to define you.
We need to focus on fixing this, in the present, so the future doesn't get messed up too.
Whoa. Why am I *SO* wiped just from standing up?
It's from the way you're sharing molecules with Qarin. It's like WHAM! Your battery suddenly lost power and now you need a major recharge.
KING
It's going to keep happening unless one of you no longer exists in this universe.
KING Cheese
What? I can't *end* her or something evil-y like that.
We have to find a way for you to be fully empowered, without hurting Qarin. Before she...
...figures this out for herself and realizes only one of us can occupy this world.
But first, I'm desperate for real food. That protein bar tasted like sawdust.
I said I would try anything once, but sawdust flavor seems like a bad idea.

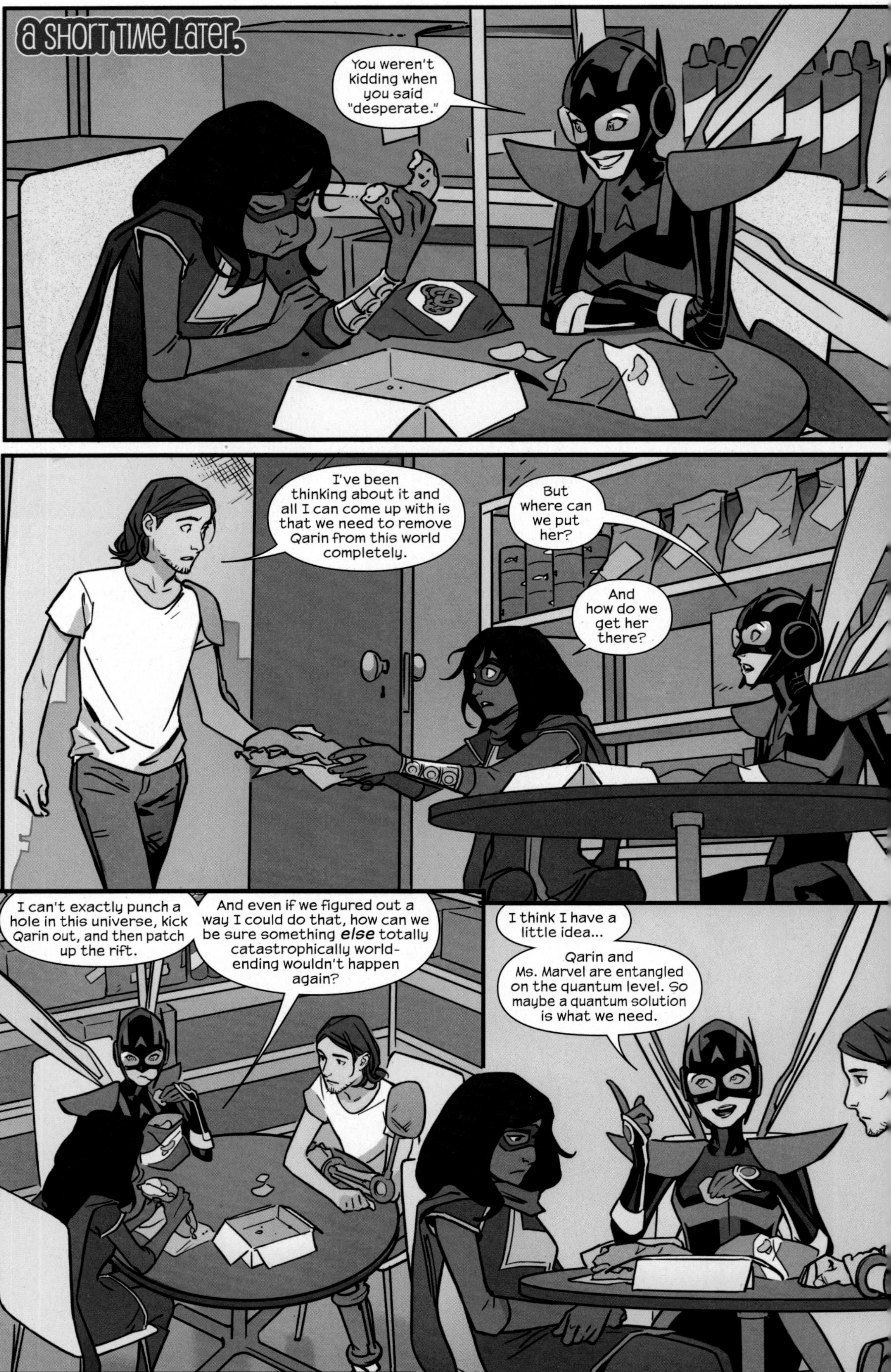
A SHORT TIME LATER.
You weren't kidding when you said "desperate."
I've been thinking about it and all I can come up with is that we need to remove Qarin from this world completely.
But where can we put her?
And how do we get her there?
I can't exactly punch a hole in this universe, kick Qarin out, and then patch up the rift.
And even if we figured out a way I could do that, how can we be sure something *else* totally catastrophically world-ending wouldn't happen again?
I think I have a little idea...
Qarin and Ms. Marvel are entangled on the quantum level. So maybe a quantum solution is what we need.

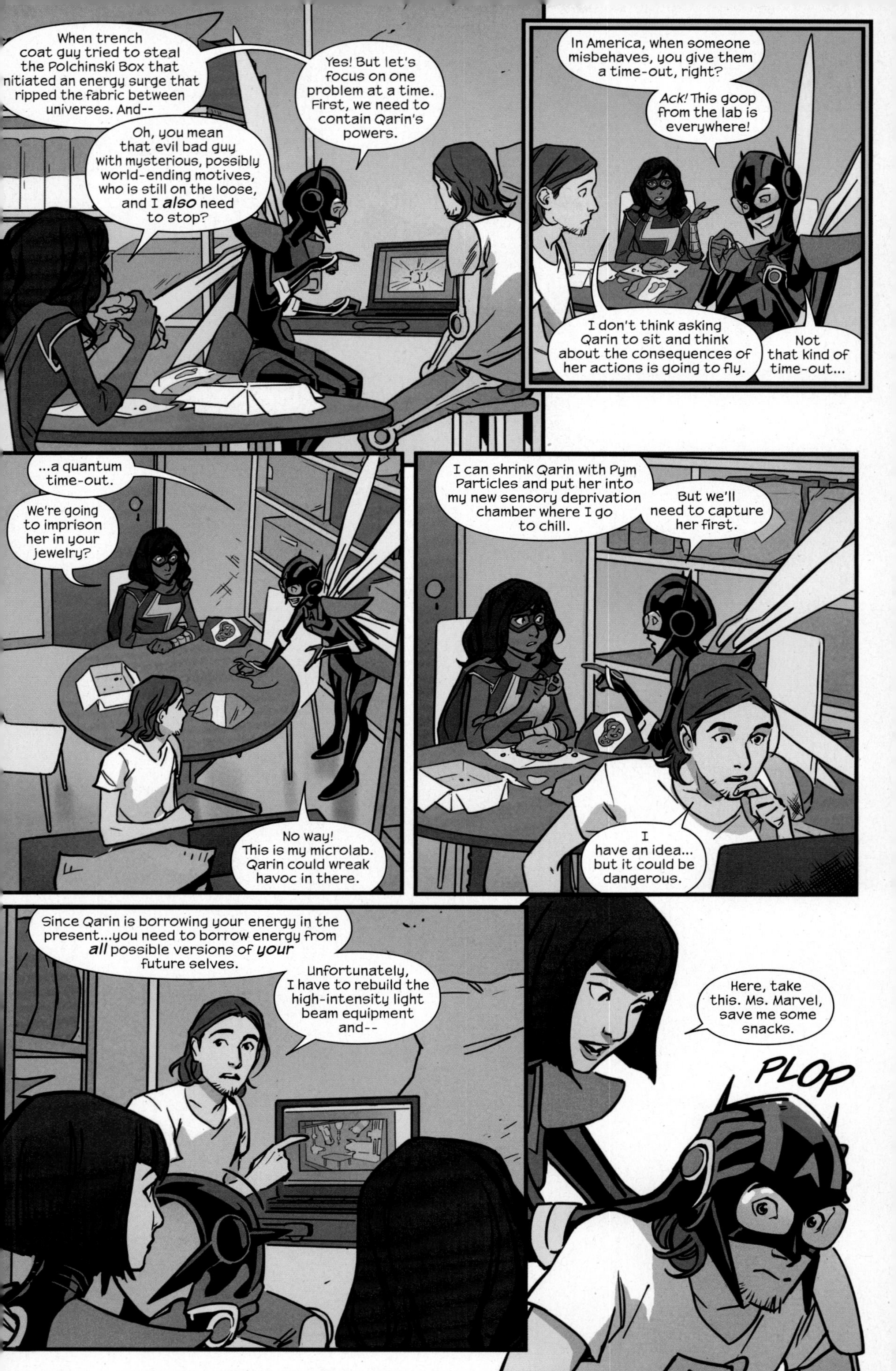
When trench coat guy tried to steal the Polchinski Box that nitiated an energy surge that ripped the fabric between universes. And--
Yes! But let's focus on one problem at a time. First, we need to contain Qarin's powers.
Oh, you mean that evil bad guy with mysterious, possibly world-ending motives, who is still on the loose, and I *also* need to stop?
In America, when someone misbehaves, you give them a time-out, right?
Ack! This goop from the lab is everywhere!
I don't think asking Qarin to sit and think about the consequences of her actions is going to fly.
Not that kind of time-out...
...a quantum time-out.
We're going to imprison her in your jewelry?
No way! This is my microlab. Qarin could wreak havoc in there.
I can shrink Qarin with Pym Particles and put her into my new sensory deprivation chamber where I go to chill.
But we'll need to capture her first.
I have an idea... but it could be dangerous.
Since Qarin is borrowing your energy in the present...you need to borrow energy from *all* possible versions of *your* future selves.
Unfortunately, I have to rebuild the high-intensity light beam equipment and--
Here, take this. Ms. Marvel, save me some snacks.
PLOP

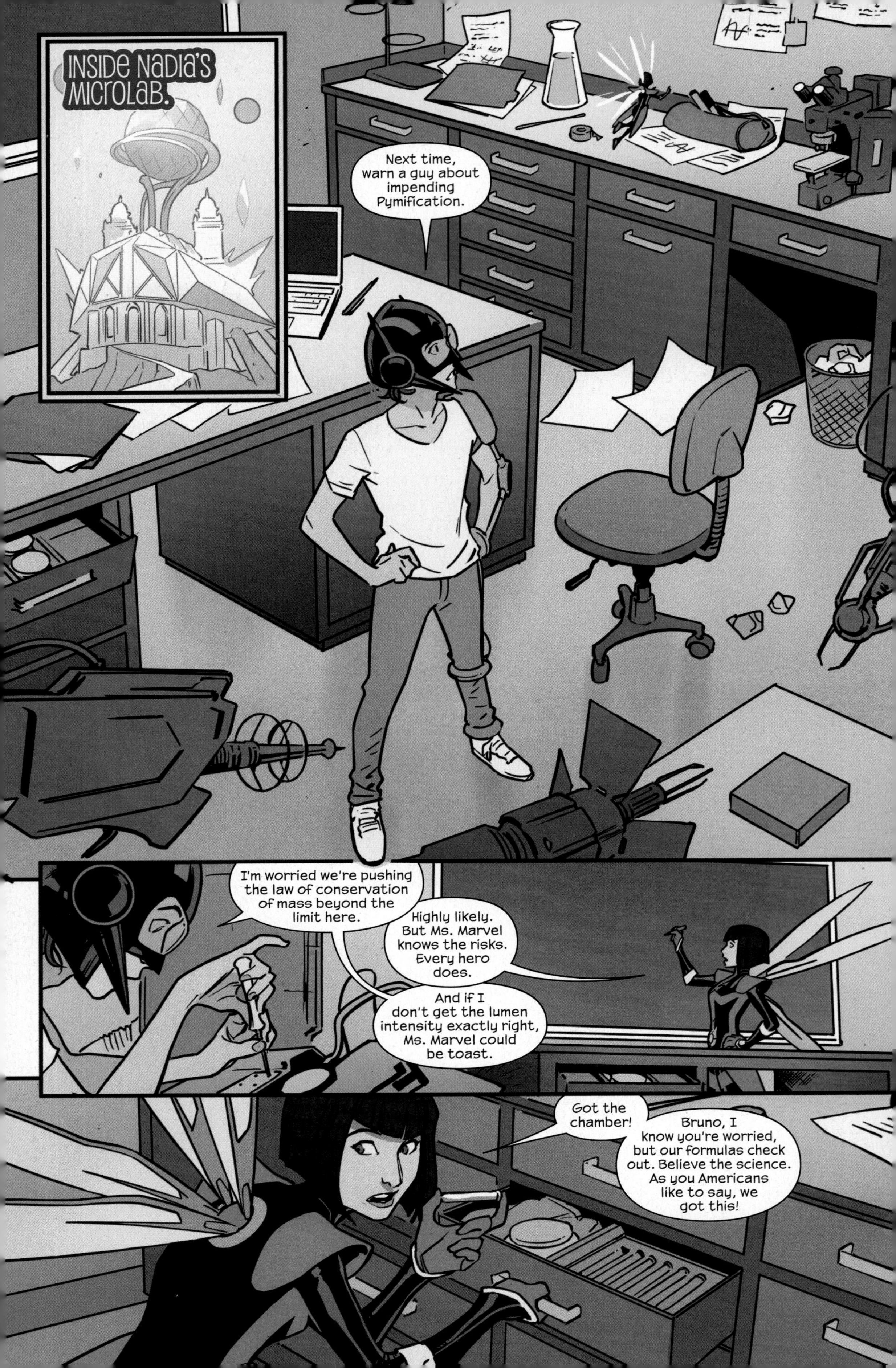
INSIDE NADIA'S MICROLAB.
Next time, warn a guy about impending Pymification.
I'm worried we're pushing the law of conservation of mass beyond the limit here.
Highly likely. But Ms. Marvel knows the risks. Every hero does.
And if I don't get the lumen intensity exactly right, Ms. Marvel could be toast.
Got the chamber!
Bruno, I know you're worried, but our formulas check out. Believe the science. As you Americans like to say, we got this!

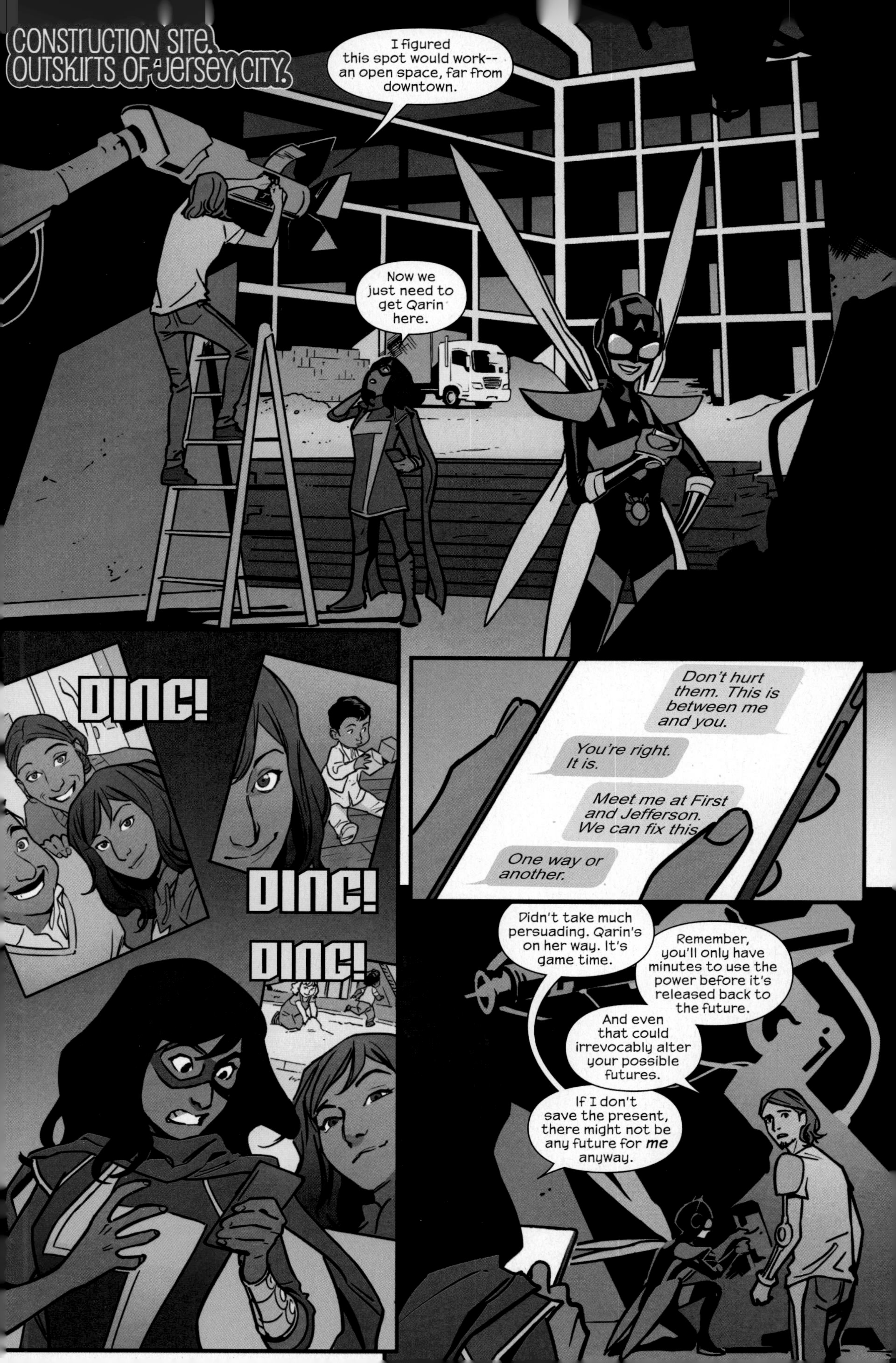
CONSTRUCTION SITE. OUTSKIRTS OF JERSEY CITY.
I figured this spot would work-- an open space, far from downtown.
Now we just need to get Qarin here.
DING!
DING!
DING!
Don't hurt them. This is between me and you.
You're right. It is.
Meet me at First and Jefferson. We can fix this.
One way or another.
Didn't take much persuading. Qarin's on her way. It's game time.
Remember, you'll only have minutes to use the power before it's released back to the future.
And even that could irrevocably alter your possible futures.
If I don't save the present, there might not be any future for *me* anyway.

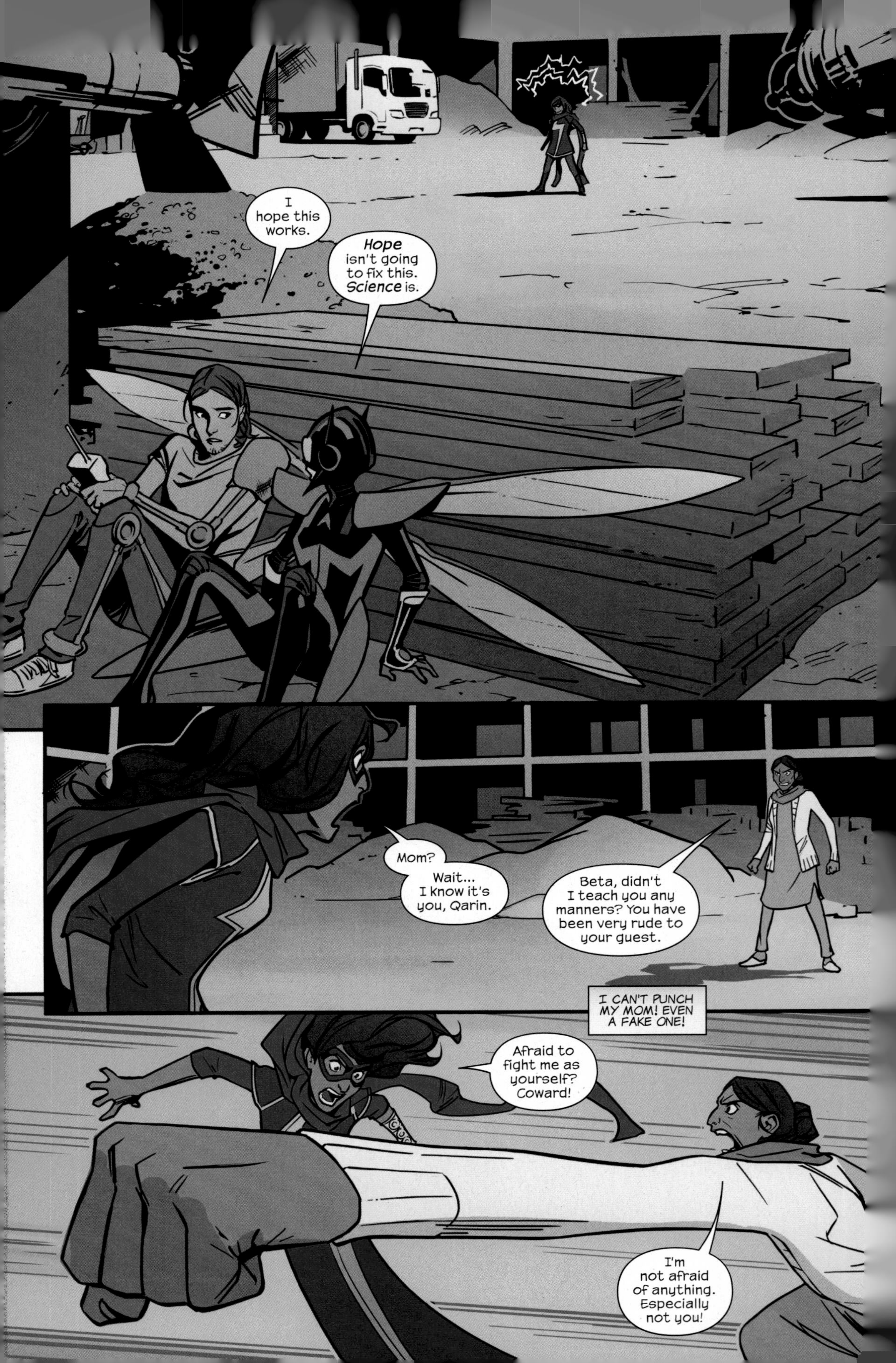
I hope this works.
Hope isn't going to fix this. *Science* is.
Mom? Wait... I know it's you, Qarin.
Beta, didn't I teach you any manners? You have been very rude to your guest.
I CAN'T PUNCH MY MOM! EVEN A FAKE ONE!
Afraid to fight me as yourself? Coward!
I'm not afraid of anything. Especially not you!

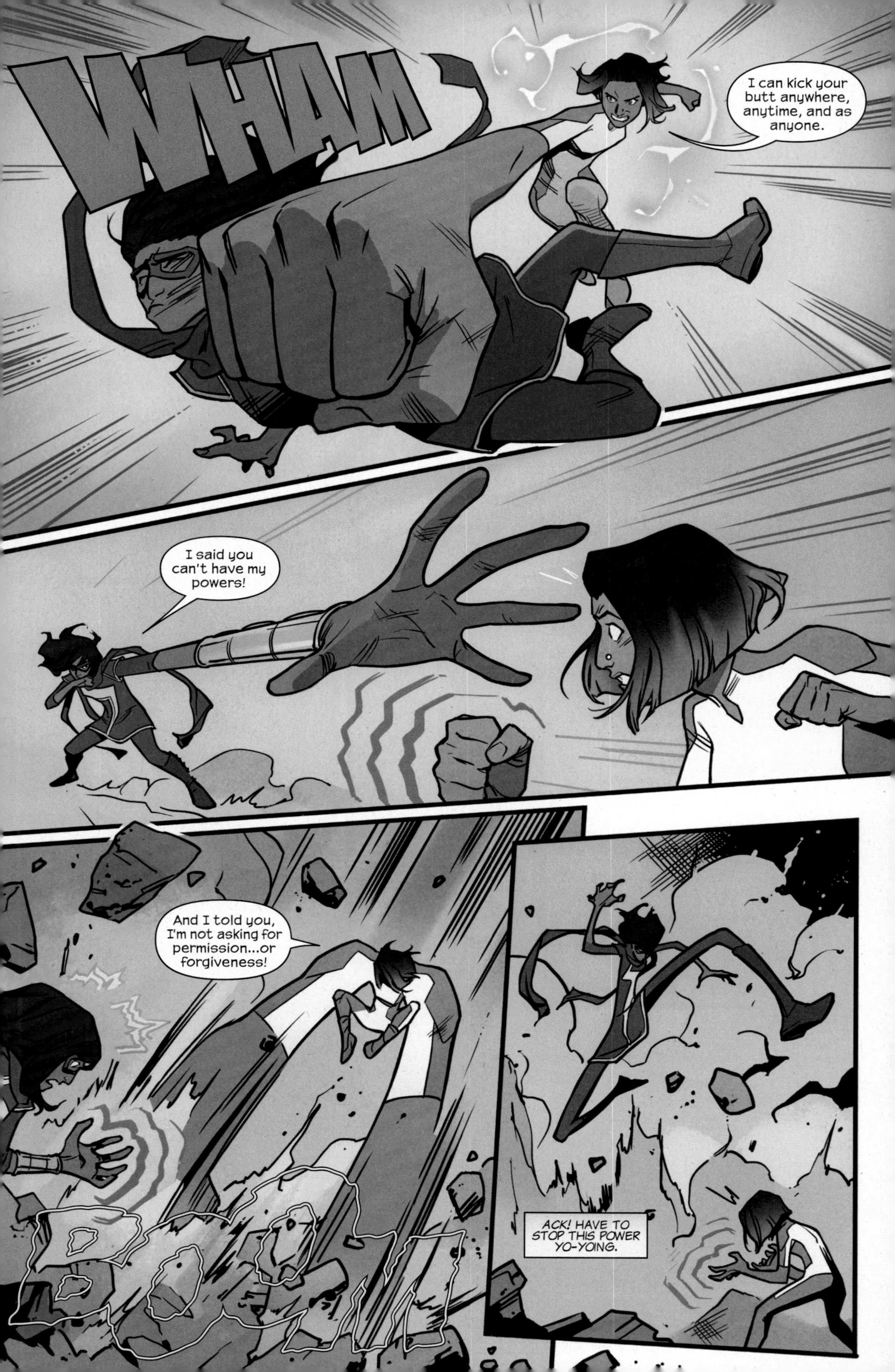
WHAM
I can kick your butt anywhere, anytime, and as anyone.
I said you can't have my powers!
And I told you, I'm not asking for permission...or forgiveness!
ACK! HAVE TO STOP THIS POWER YO-YOING.

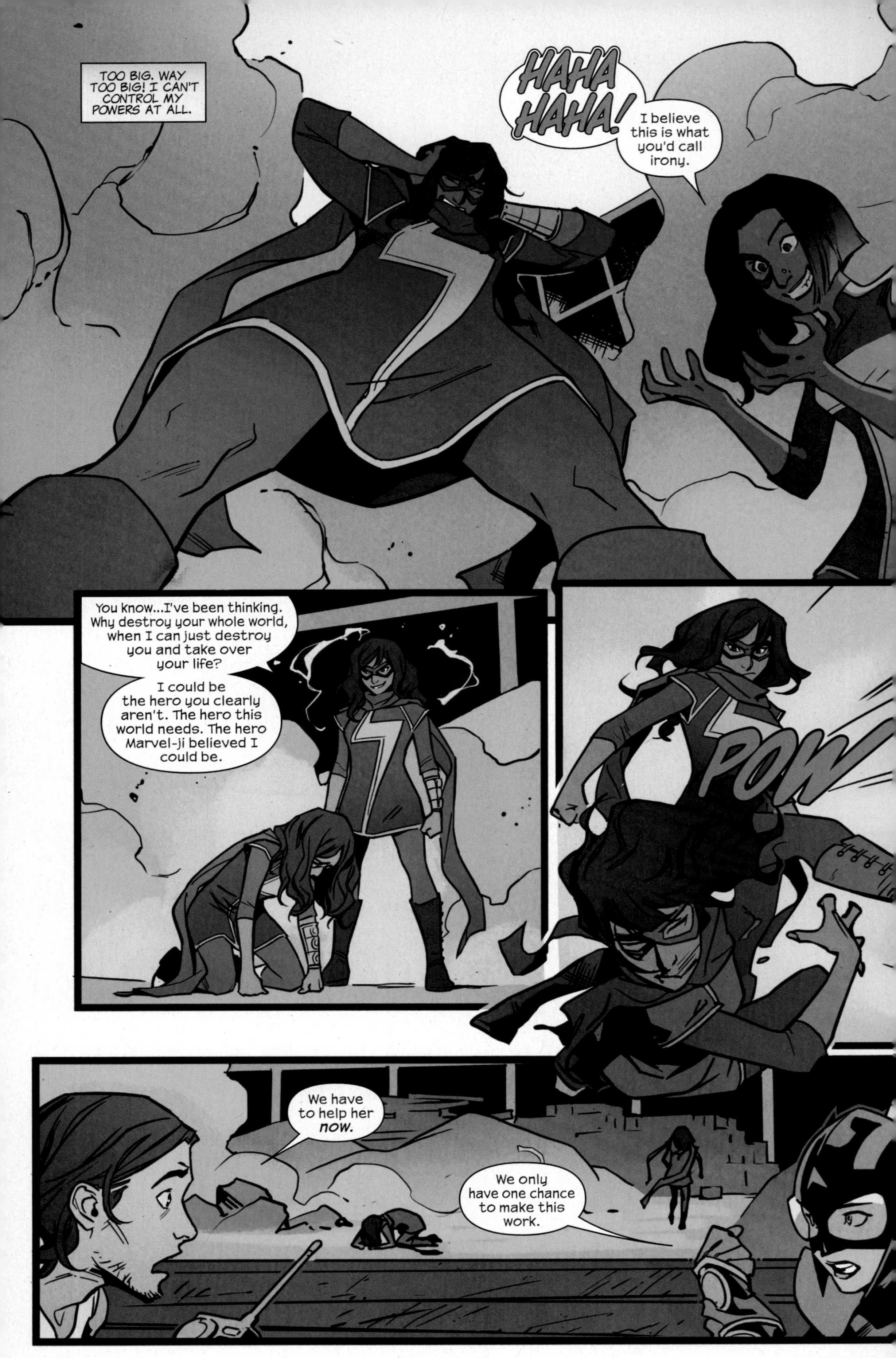
TOO BIG. WAY TOO BIG! I CAN'T CONTROL MY POWERS AT ALL.
HAHA HAHA!
I believe this is what you'd call irony.
You know...I've been thinking. Why destroy your whole world, when I can just destroy you and take over your life?
I could be the hero you clearly aren't. The hero this world needs. The hero Marvel-ji believed I could be.
POW
We have to help her *now.*
We only have one chance to make this work.

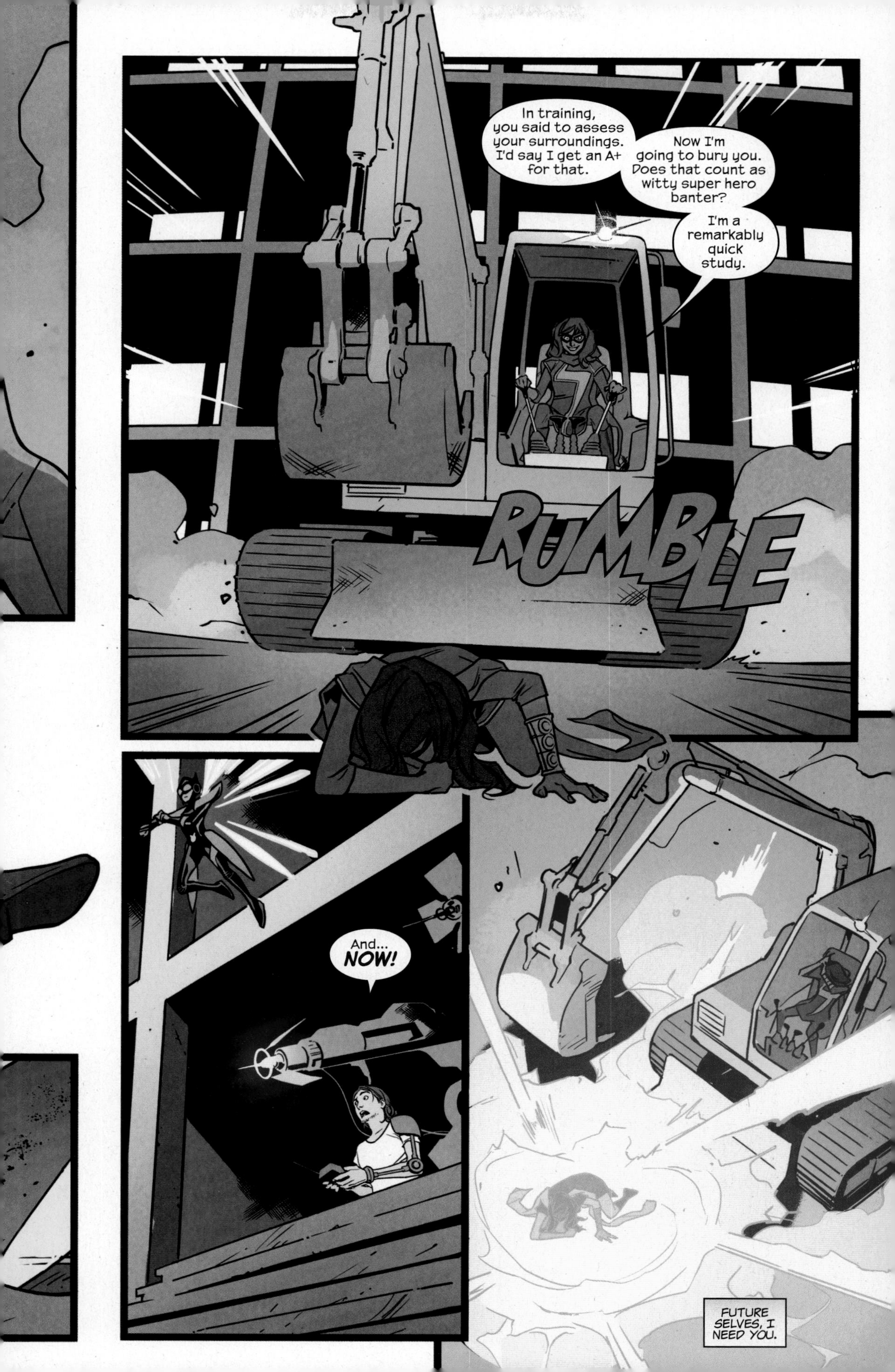
In training, you said to assess your surroundings. I'd say I get an A+ for that.
Now I'm going to bury you. Does that count as witty super hero banter?
I'm a remarkably quick study.
RUMBLE
And... NOW!
FUTURE SELVES, I NEED YOU.

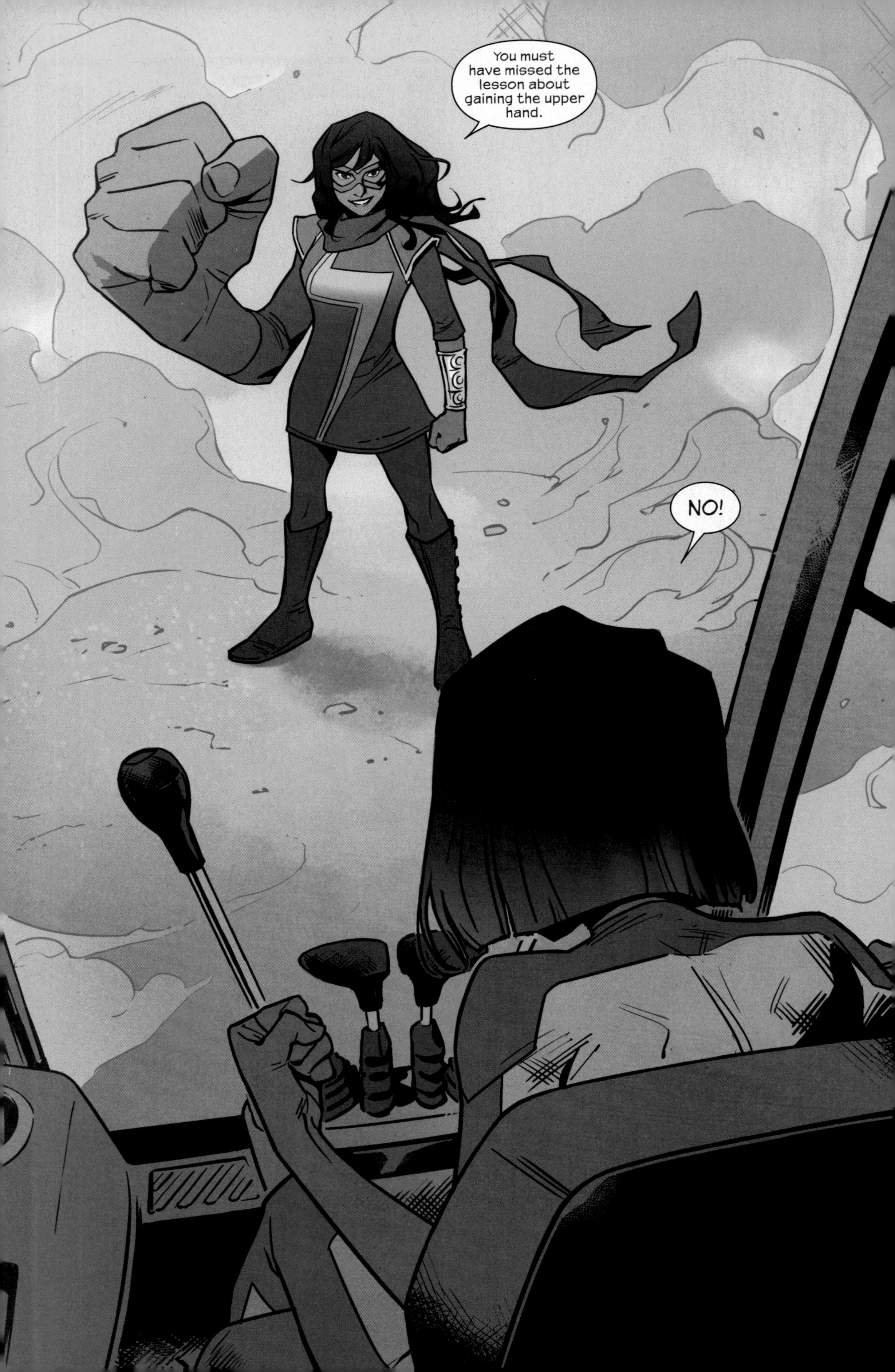
You must have missed the lesson about gaining the upper hand.
NO!

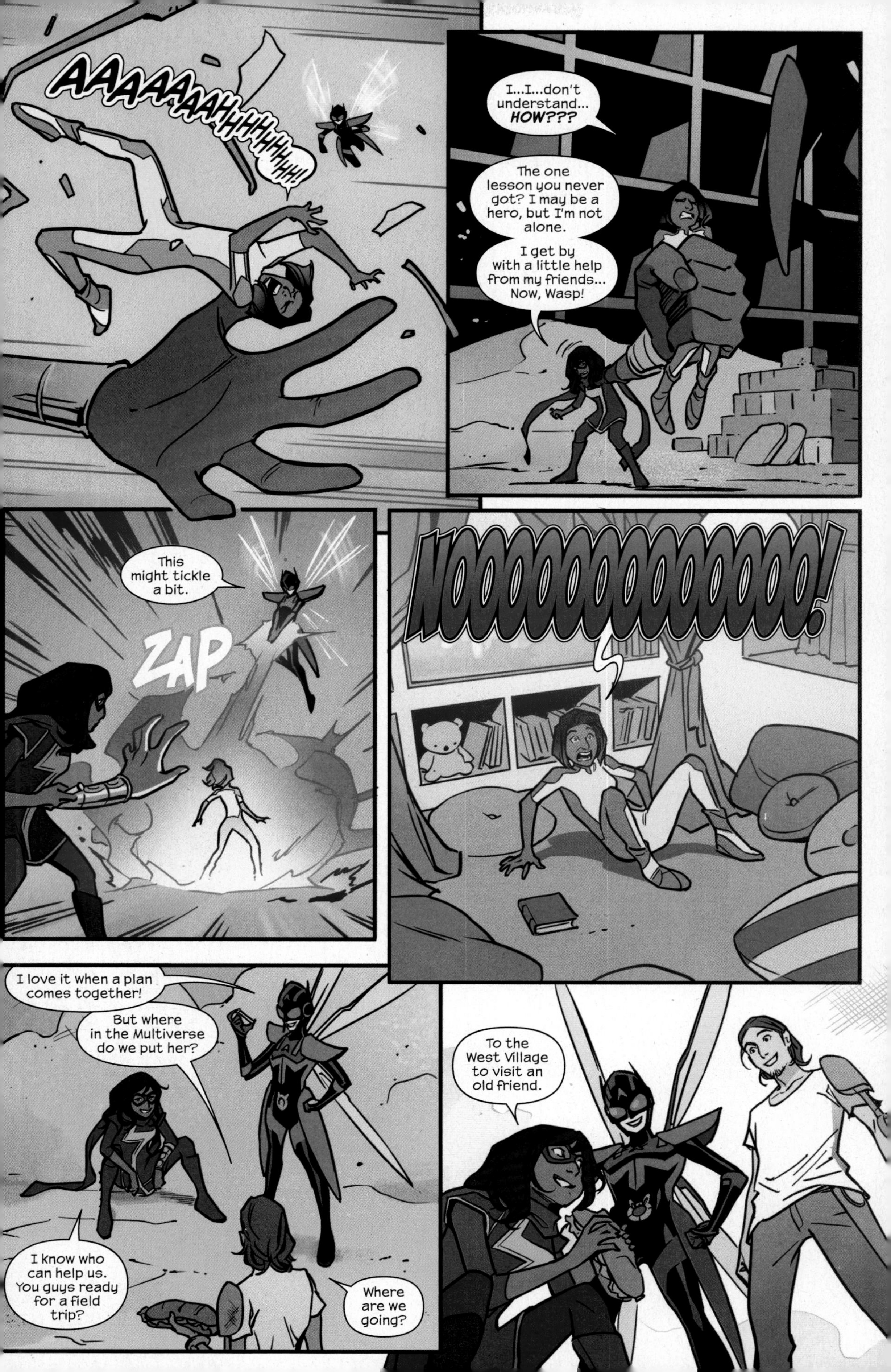
AAAAAAAHHHHHHH!
I...I...don't understand... HOW???
The one lesson you never got? I may be a hero, but I'm not alone.
I get by with a little help from my friends... Now, Wasp!
This might tickle a bit.
ZAP
NOOOOOOOOOOOOOO!
I love it when a plan comes together!
But where in the Multiverse do we put her?
I know who can help us. You guys ready for a field trip?
Where are we going?
To the West Village to visit an old friend.

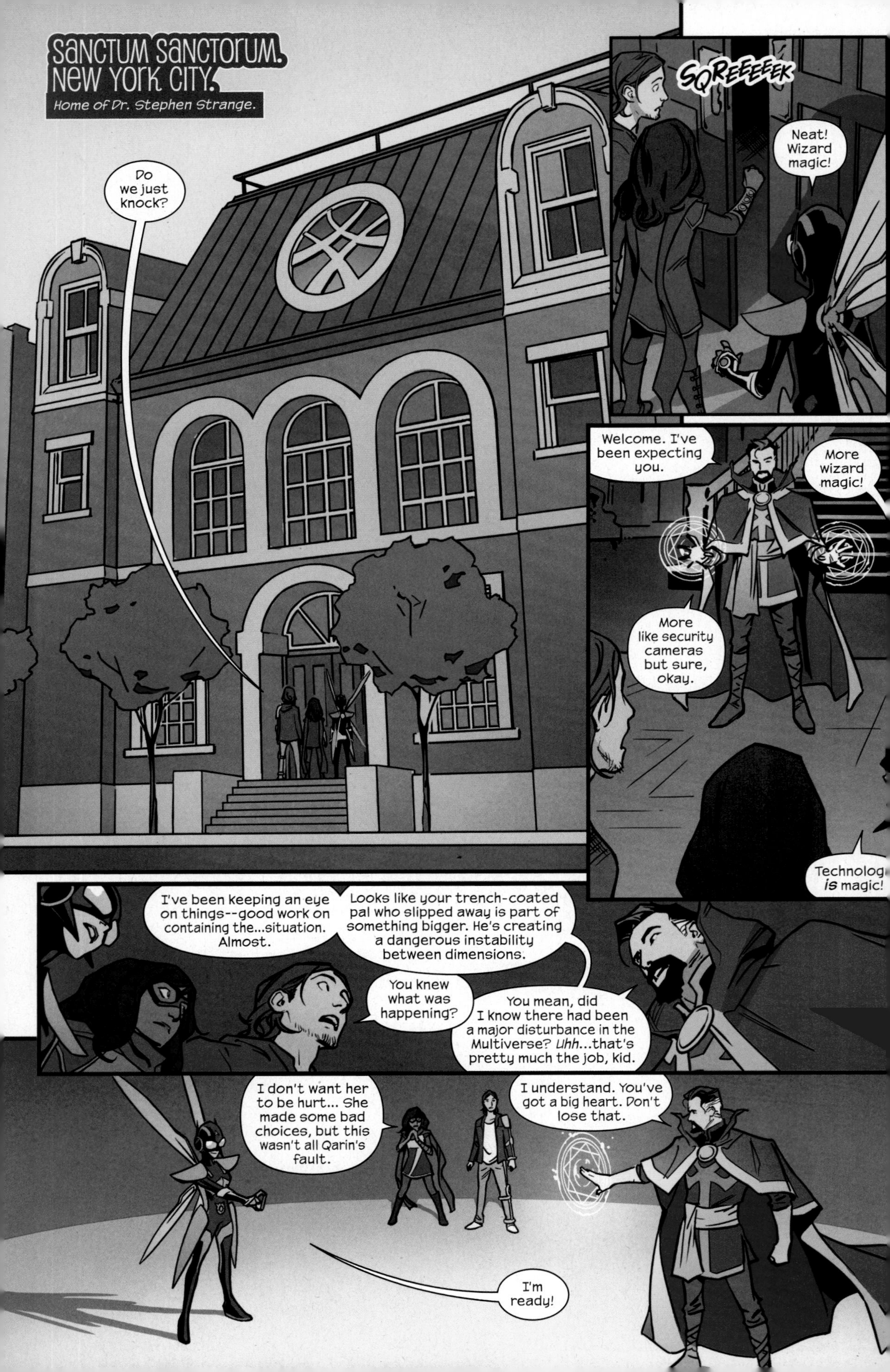
SANCTUM SANCTORUM. NEW YORK CITY.
Home of Dr. Stephen Strange.
Do we just knock?
SQREEEEEK
Neat! Wizard magic!
Welcome. I've been expecting you.
More wizard magic!
More like security cameras but sure, okay.
Technolog is magic!
I've been keeping an eye on things--good work on containing the...situation. Almost.
Looks like your trench-coated pal who slipped away is part of something bigger. He's creating a dangerous instability between dimensions.
You knew what was happening?
You mean, did I know there had been a major disturbance in the Multiverse? Uhh...that's pretty much the job, kid.
I don't want her to be hurt... She made some bad choices, but this wasn't all Qarin's fault.
I understand. You've got a big heart. Don't lose that.
I'm ready!

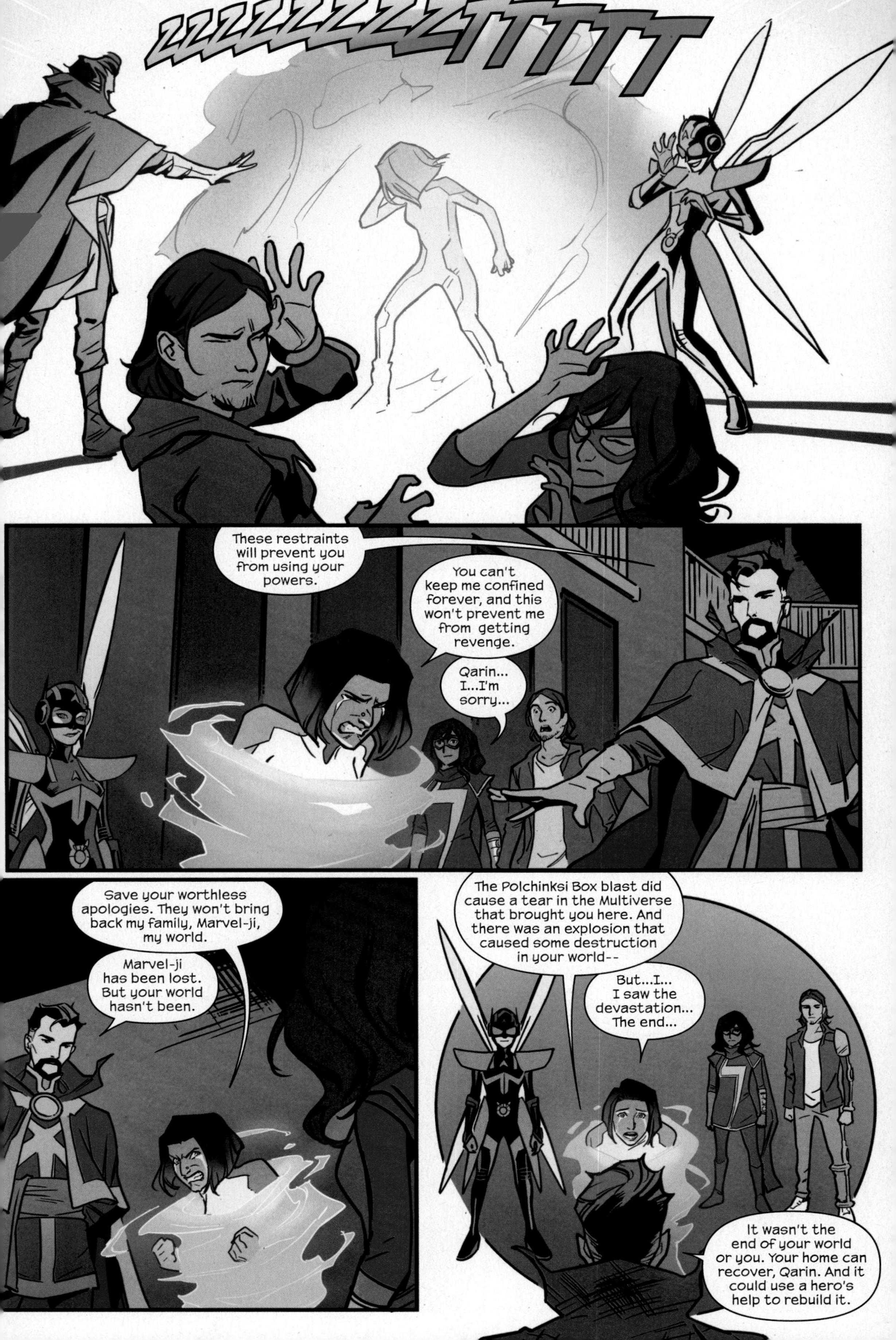
ZZZZZZZZTTTTTT
These restraints will prevent you from using your powers.
You can't keep me confined forever, and this won't prevent me from getting revenge.
Qarin... I...I'm sorry...
Save your worthless apologies. They won't bring back my family, Marvel-ji, my world.
Marvel-ji has been lost. But your world hasn't been.
The Polchinksi Box blast did cause a tear in the Multiverse that brought you here. And there was an explosion that caused some destruction in your world--
But...I... I saw the devastation... The end...
It wasn't the end of your world or you. Your home can recover, Qarin. And it could use a hero's help to rebuild it.

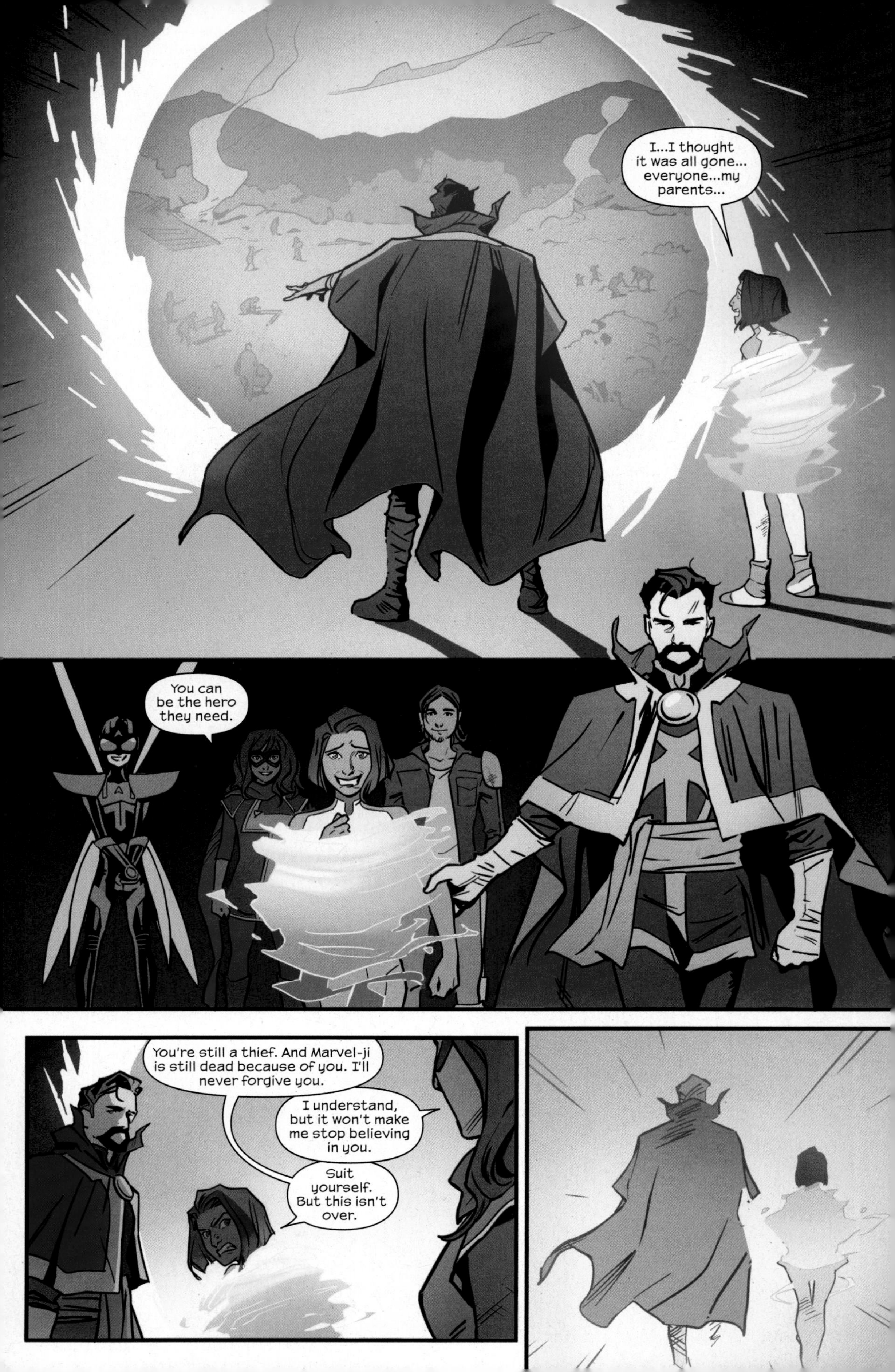
I...I thought it was all gone... everyone...my parents...
You can be the hero they need.
You're still a thief. And Marvel-ji is still dead because of you. I'll never forgive you.
I understand, but it won't make me stop believing in you.
Suit yourself. But this isn't over.

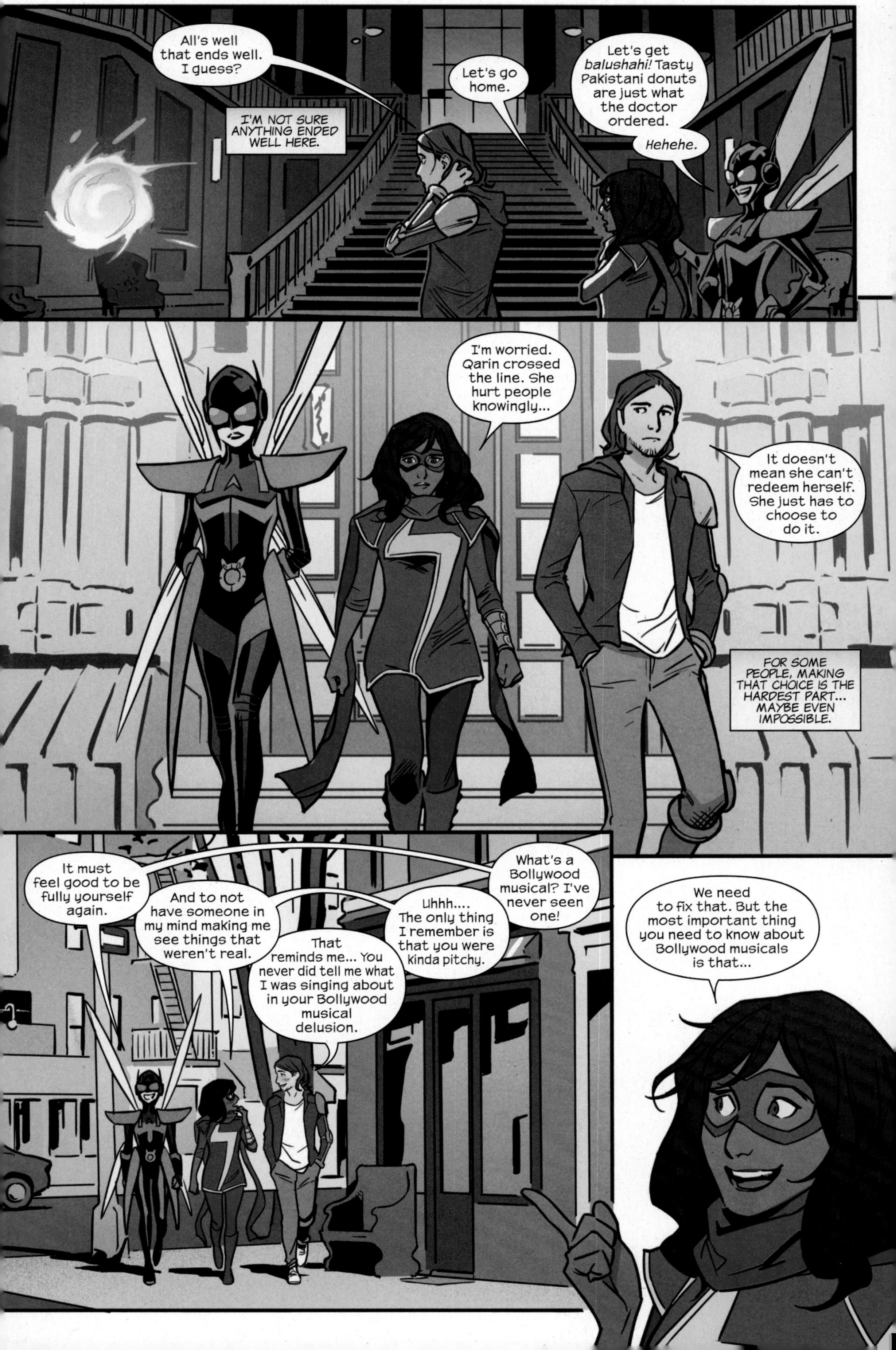
All's well that ends well. I guess?
I'M NOT SURE ANYTHING ENDED WELL HERE.
Let's go home.
Let's get *balushahi!* Tasty Pakistani donuts are just what the doctor ordered.
Hehehe.
I'm worried. Qarin crossed the line. She hurt people knowingly...
It doesn't mean she can't redeem herself. She just has to choose to do it.
FOR SOME PEOPLE, MAKING THAT CHOICE IS THE HARDEST PART... MAYBE EVEN IMPOSSIBLE.
It must feel good to be fully yourself again.
And to not have someone in my mind making me see things that weren't real.
That reminds me... You never did tell me what I was singing about in your Bollywood musical delusion.
Uhhh.... The only thing I remember is that you were kinda pitchy.
What's a Bollywood musical? I've never seen one!
We need to fix that. But the most important thing you need to know about Bollywood musicals is that...

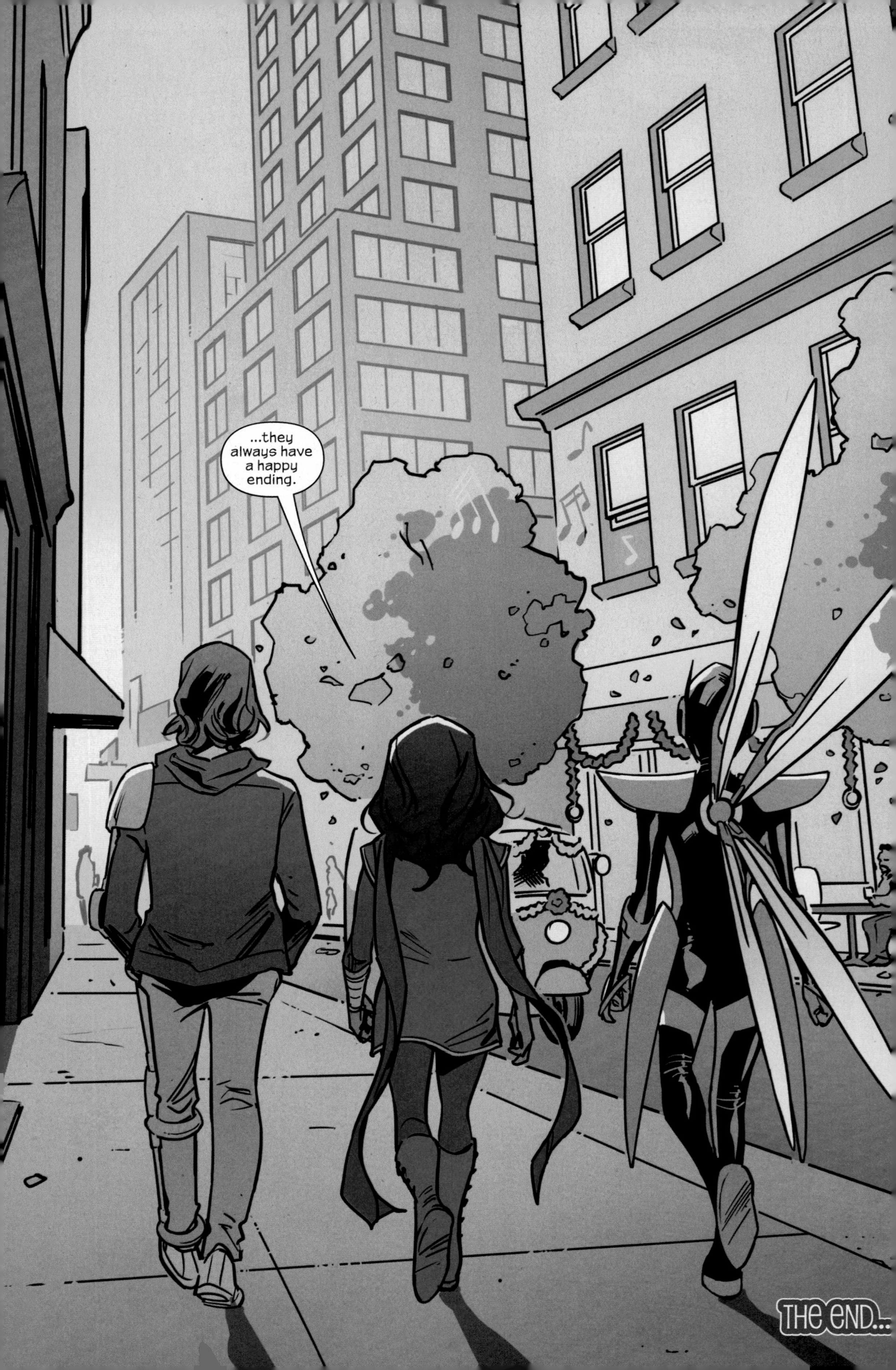
...they always have a happy ending.
THE END...

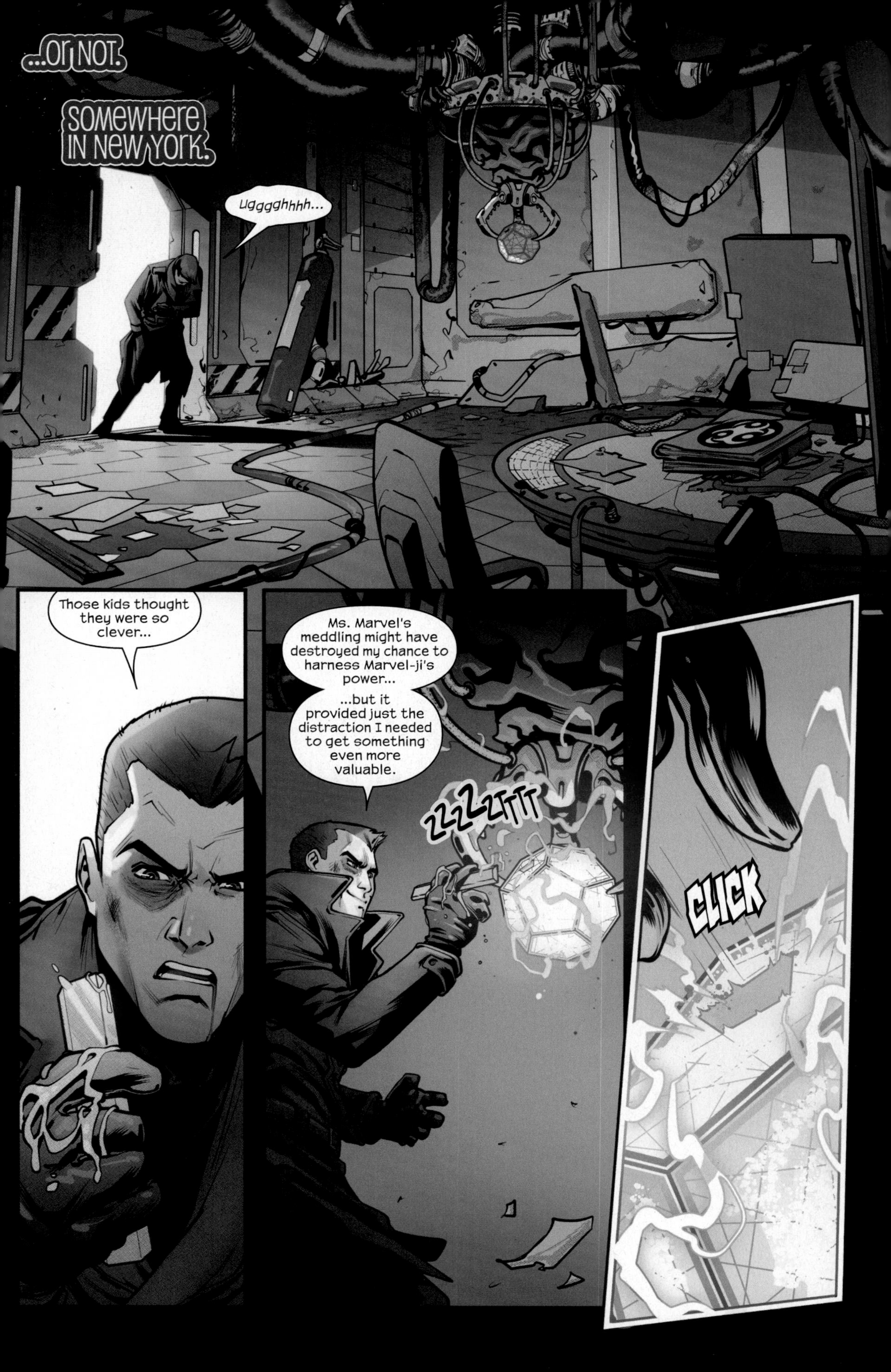

...Or Not.
Somewhere in New York.
Ugggghhhh...
Those kids thought they were so clever...
Ms. Marvel's meddling might have destroyed my chance to harness Marvel-ji's power...
...but it provided just the distraction I needed to get something even more valuable.
ZZZZZTTTT
CLICK

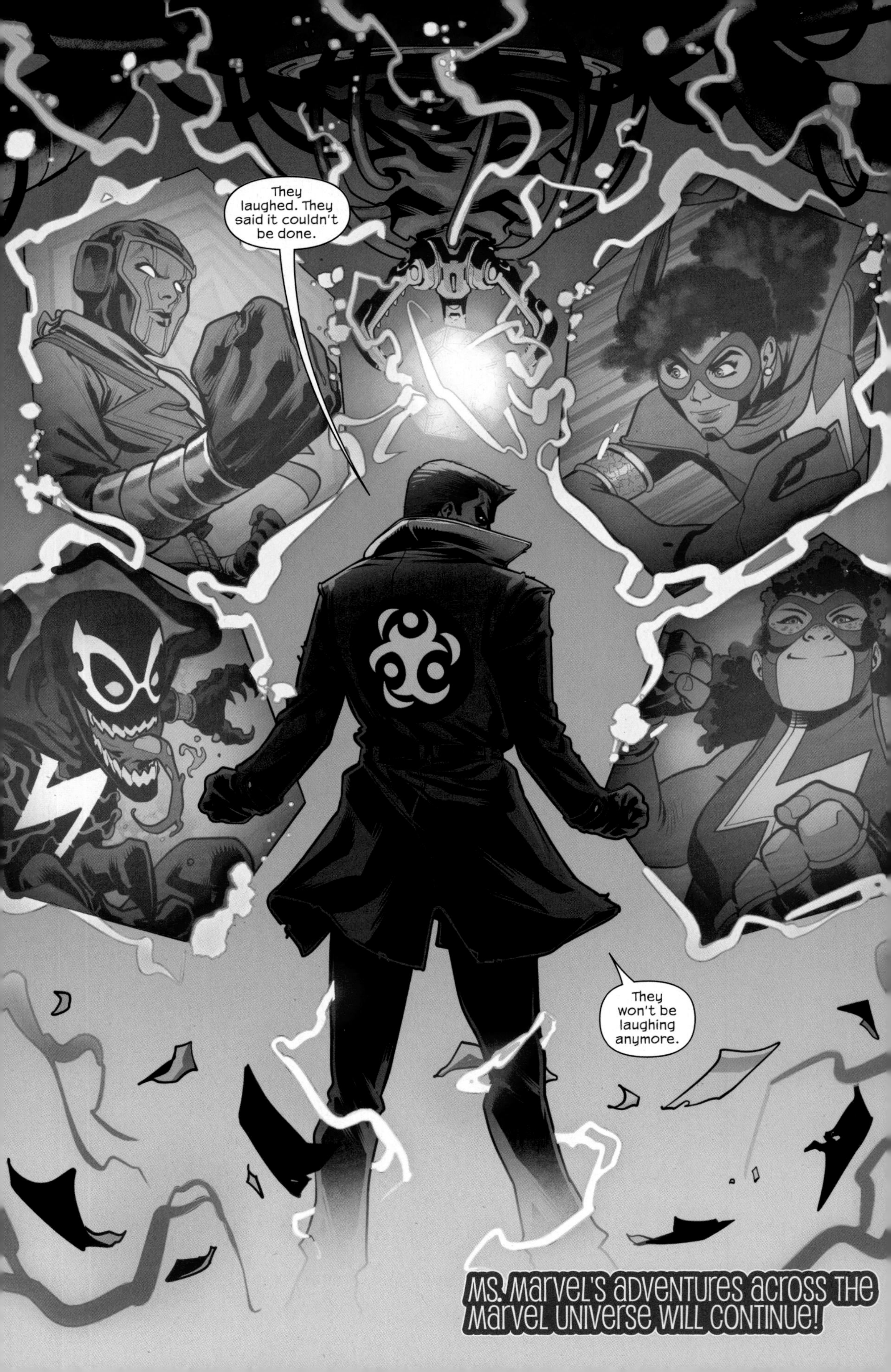
They laughed. They said it couldn't be done.
They won't be laughing anymore.
MS. MARVEL'S ADVENTURES ACROSS THE MARVEL UNIVERSE WILL CONTINUE!

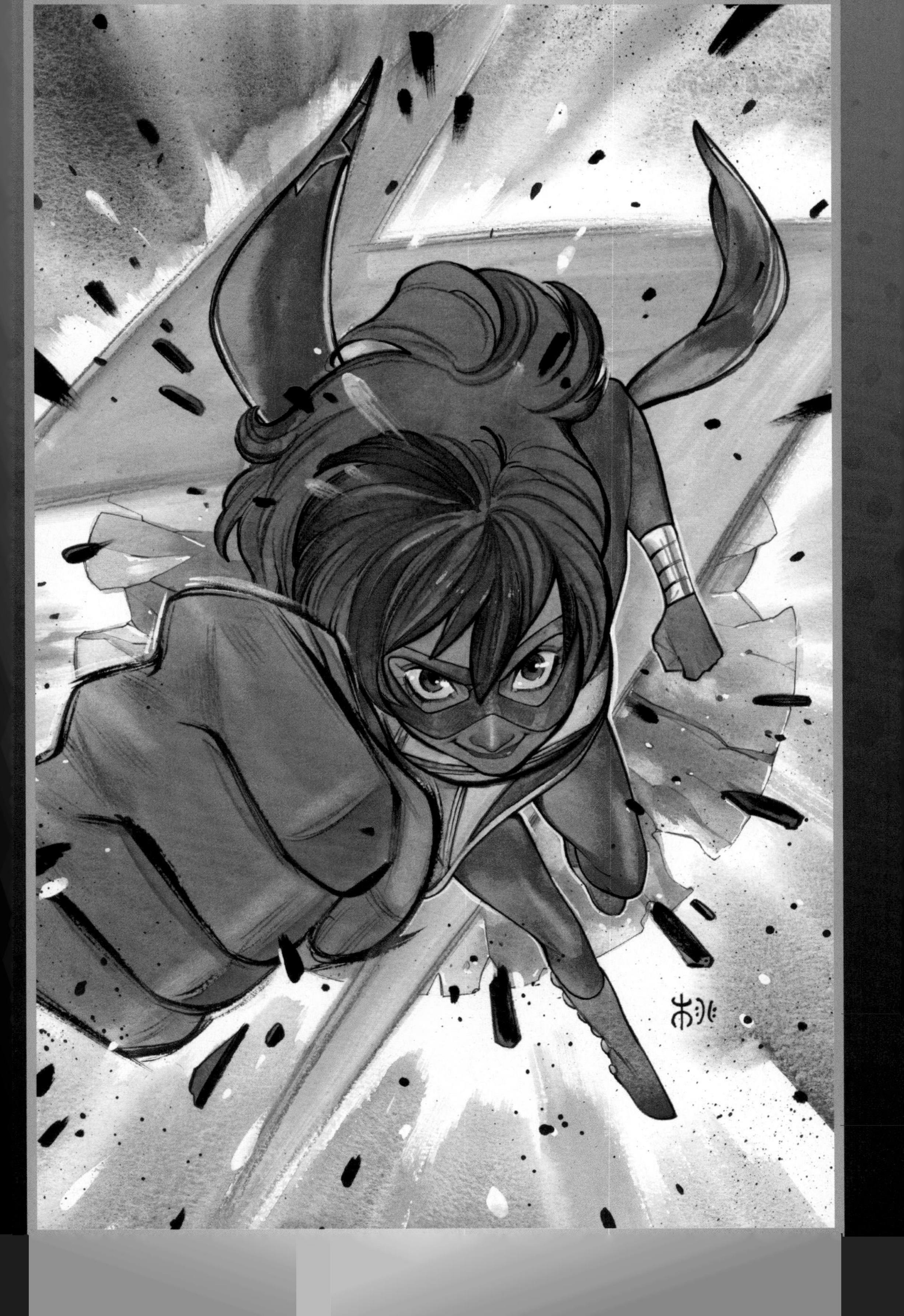

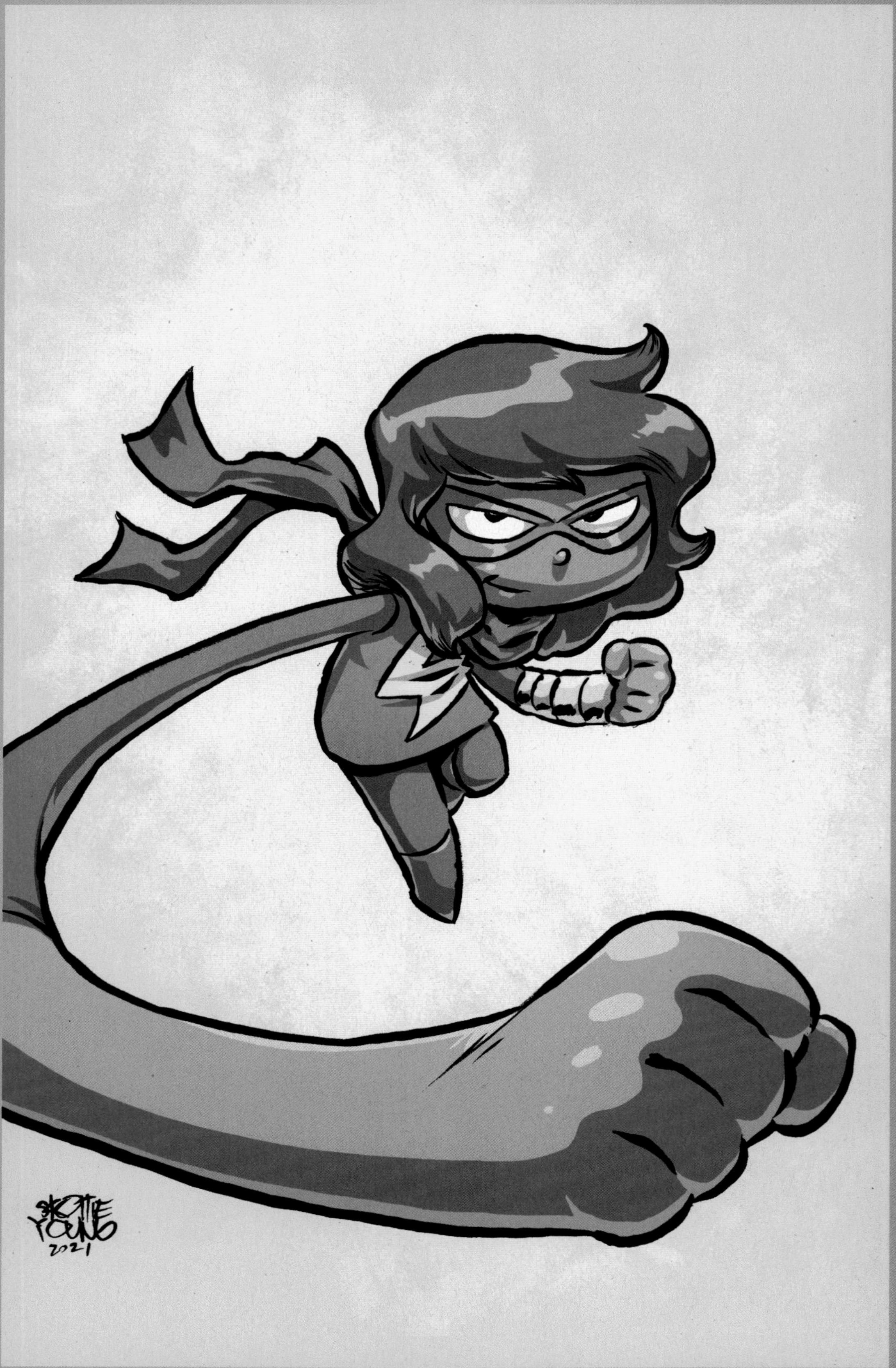
SKOTTIE YOUNG 2021

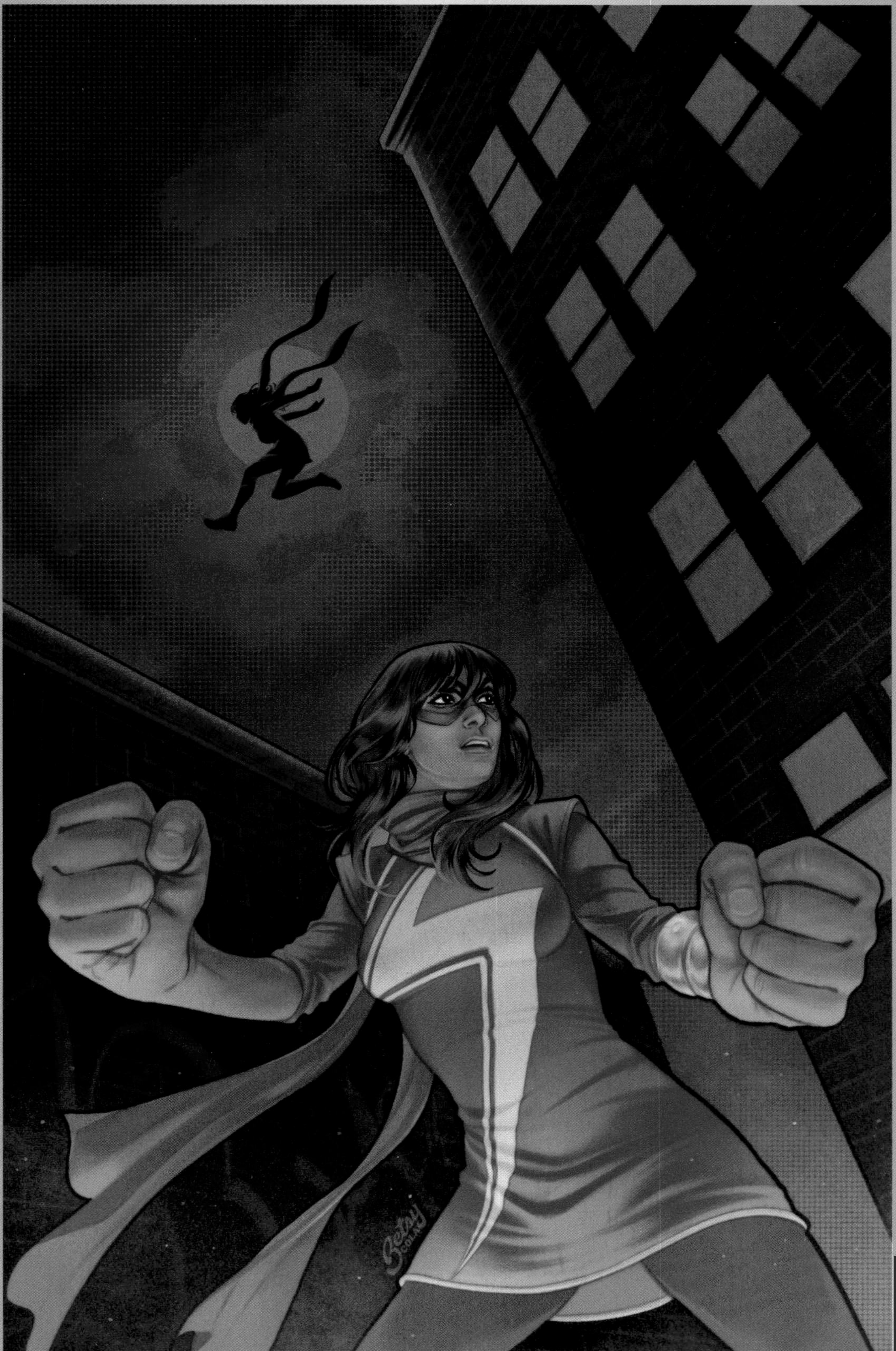

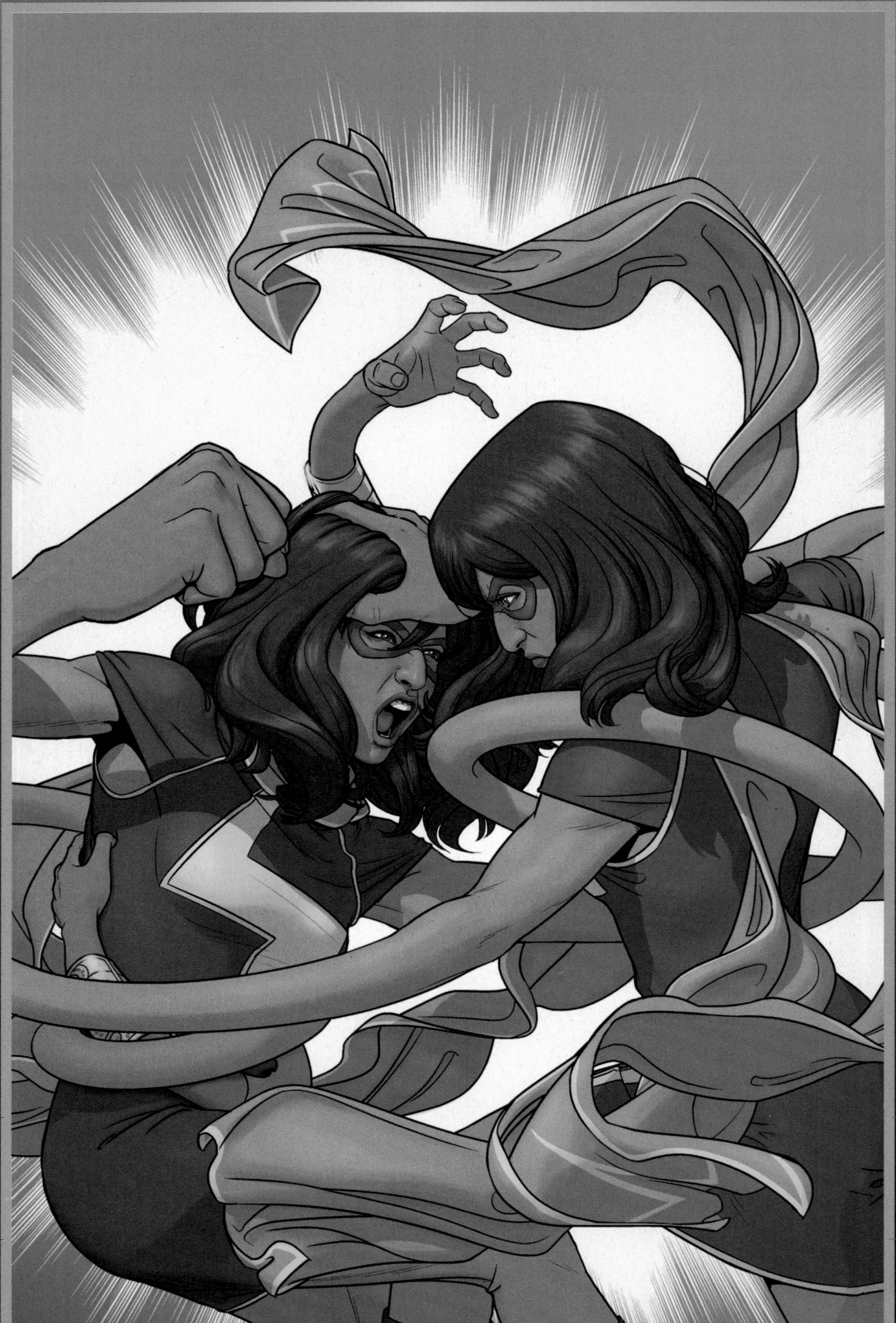

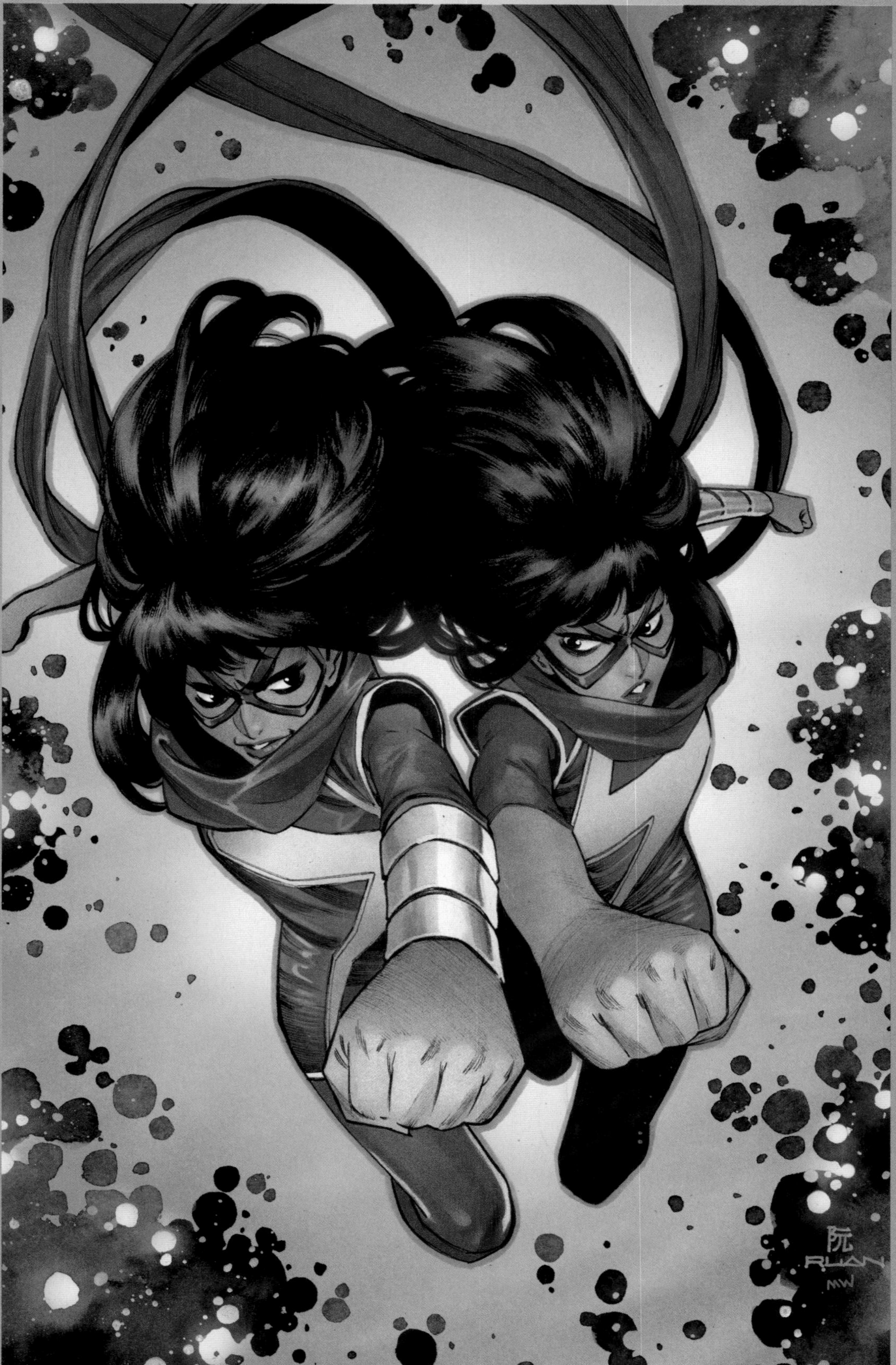
阮
RUAN
MW

DIKE RUAN & MATTHEW WILSON

#4 VARIANT

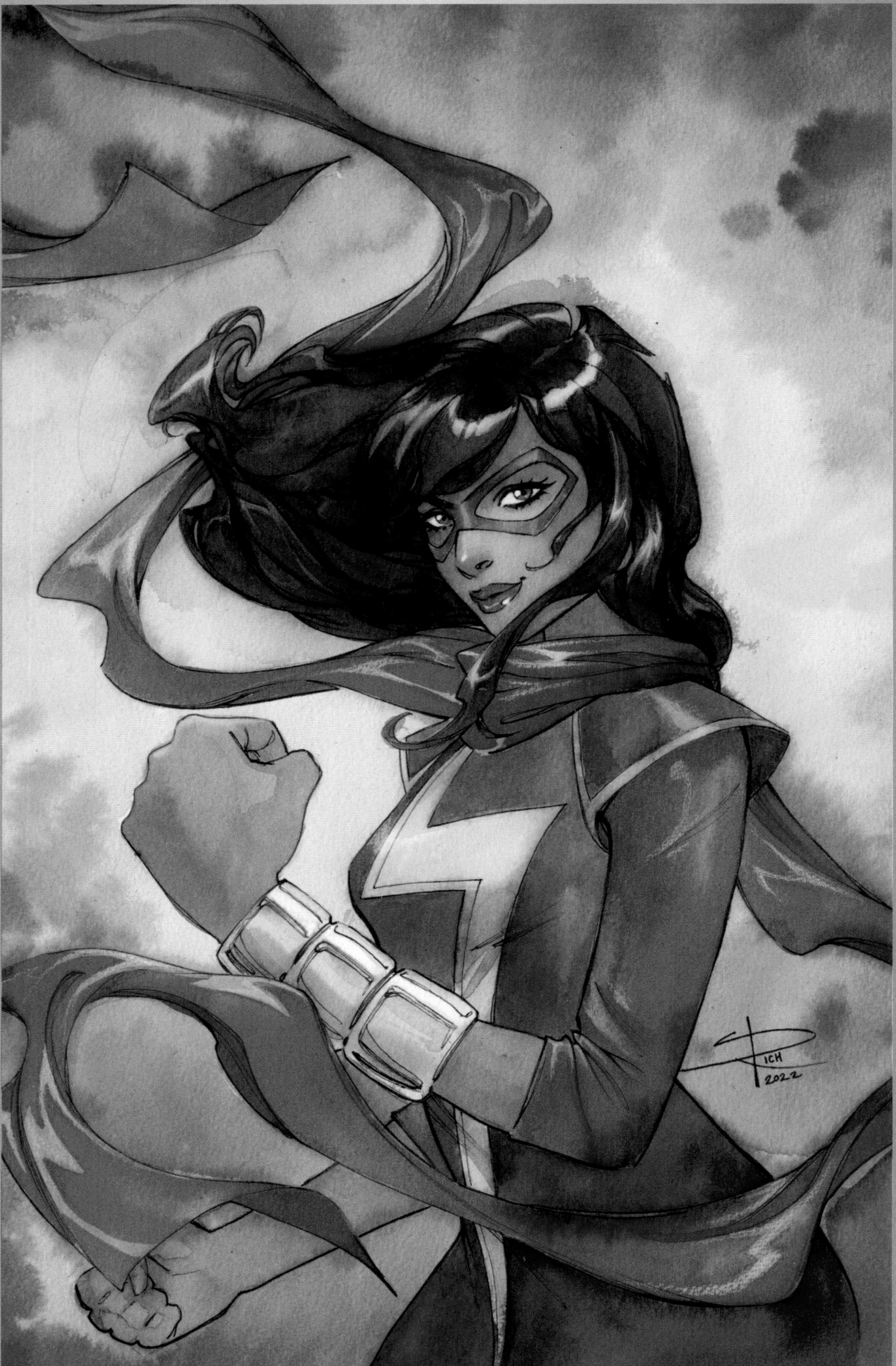
RICH
2022

SABINE RICH
#5 VARIANT